# SIDE BY SIDE

Children's Literature Association Series

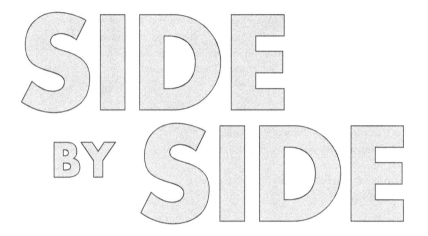

# SIDE BY SIDE

## US Empire, Puerto Rico, and the Roots of American Youth Literature and Culture

**MARILISA JIMÉNEZ GARCÍA**

University Press of Mississippi / Jackson

The University Press of Mississippi is the scholarly publishing agency of
the Mississippi Institutions of Higher Learning: Alcorn State University,
Delta State University, Jackson State University, Mississippi State University,
Mississippi University for Women, Mississippi Valley State University,
University of Mississippi, and University of Southern Mississippi.

www.upress.state.ms.us

The University Press of Mississippi is a member
of the Association of University Presses.

First printing 2021
∞

Library of Congress Cataloging-in-Publication Data

Names: Jiménez García, Marilisa, author.
Title: Side by side: US empire, Puerto Rico, and the roots of American
    youth literature and culture / Marilisa Jiménez García.
Other titles: Childrens Literature Association series.
Description: Jackson: University Press of Mississippi, 2021. | Series:
    Childrens Literature Association series | Includes bibliographical
    references and index.
Identifiers: LCCN 2020047936 (print) | LCCN 2020047937 (ebook) | ISBN
    978-1-4968-3247-4 (hardback) | ISBN 978-1-4968-3248-1 (trade paperback) | ISBN
    978-1-4968-3249-8 (epub) | ISBN 978-1-4968-3250-4 (epub) | ISBN 978-1-4968-3251-1
    (pdf) | ISBN 978-1-4968-3252-8 (pdf)
Subjects: LCSH: Childrens literature, Latin AmericanHistory and
    criticism. | Imperialism in literature.
Classification: LCC PQ7421.J57 2021  (print) | LCC PQ7421 (ebook) | DDC
    860.9/9282098dc23
LC record available at https://lccn.loc.gov/2020047936
LC ebook record available at https://lccn.loc.gov/2020047937

British Library Cataloging-in-Publication Data available

*To Mami and Papi,*
*who always said I was going to write a book.*

*Para Bayamon, Cataño y Vega Alta y todos los niñxs Boricuas del mundo,*
*especialmente mis hijxs en el futuro. Para todos los Nuyomiamiricans.*

# CONTENTS

# FOREWORD

I finally saw myself in books in 1972, and my life was never the same after that. It must have been sometime in the spring of that year. I went to work as always that morning at P.S. 25, The Bilingual School in the Bronx, an experimental public school for the newly emerging field of bilingual education. As usual, I first went to the staff mailboxes in the main office to pick up my mail, including what appeared to be a glossy newspaper that Muriel Pagán, our assistant principal, had left in the mailboxes of every staff member.

What immediately struck my eye was the name of the newspaper: *Interracial Books for Children* (Council on Interracial Books for Children, 1972). It was one I had never heard of before, but it would soon become a staple for me. The title of the main article really got my attention: "100 Children's Books About Puerto Ricans: A Study in Racism, Sexism, and Colonialism." Granted, the headline was not good news about the nature of the books. At least, I reasoned, it showed that I was visible, as were my people, even if only in, for the most part, negative ways. But it was the number of books that really shocked me. *One hundred books?* I had spent my entire life in New York City and had never read even *one* book about, by, or for Puerto Ricans. Yet all the books named in the article were in English, the language I learned when I began school as a six-year old in Brooklyn. Where had these books been all my life?

I devoured that issue of *Interracial Books for Children*. It spoke to me in a way that few articles had before then because it seemed to fill a need I had without even knowing it. Of course, I knew some Puerto Rican *stories* that my parents and other family members had told me and my sister, but I can probably be forgiven for thinking that only Americans (read "White people"), never Puerto Ricans, wrote *real* books. Fortunately, I was disabused of this idea when I studied for a master's degree in Spanish and Hispanic literature right after college. In that program, I was introduced to beautiful and powerful stories, plays, and poetry written in Spanish, but none by a Puerto Rican, much less by a Puerto Rican raised in New York. And children's books in English by and about Puerto Ricans? Never.

I was recently reminded of the soul-numbing impact of never seeing one's own people in books when I picked up Carlos Bulosan's semiautobiographical novel about the Filipinx American experience. Written in 1946, the book chronicles the plight of Filipinx migrant workers in the United States before World War II, including graphic scenes of racism and exploitation in the fields and factories of California and the Pacific Northwest. A recently released edition of the book (2019) begins with a new foreword by Elaine Castillo that asks the poignant question:

> Do you remember how old you were when you first read a book that had a character who looked and lived like you in it? Maybe the first book you read was like that, and every book after it since, and you've never had to wonder about finding someone like yourself or the people who made you in books—you've always been right there, at the center, unquestioned (Castillo 2019, ix)

The force of Castillo's question hit me to the core of my being. *Yes, I remember!*, I felt like shouting. I don't recall the exact year, but I know that I had graduated from college and was already teaching. When I began teaching at The Bilingual School, I had read a few children's books about Latinx people but none about people like me and my family. It took another several years before I read a book that deeply spoke to me as a member of the Puerto Rican diaspora. It was Jesús Colón's *A Puerto Rican in New York and Other Stories*, originally published in 1961. Those stories described people who could be my family members and neighbors, people who looked and sounded like me and my family.

As a child I had been an avid reader and writer, but I had never found a story or character I could imagine in my own home or neighborhood. I loved *Heidi* and *Little Women*, and I could relate to the main characters on some level: I was a member of a loving and close family, I was a female, and I loved to read and write. But something was missing. Castillo's foreword describes what it was: feeling both invisible and mute. I do not want other children to feel inconsequential the way so many do when they open a book.

Castillo's question also reminded me why, after having read that first issue of *Interracial Books for Children* so many years earlier, I had decided that Puerto Rican children's literature would be one of my major areas of research (see the ten-year update of that first CIBC issue, Nieto 1982). It was a lonely field at first. I didn't know many people who focused on this area of study, about which I found little research. That explains why I was thrilled many years later to meet Marilisa Jiménez García at the 2012 Puerto Rican Studies

Association conference, where she was awarded the organization's dissertation award. To say that I was immensely proud of this young woman whom I had never even met is an understatement. And now, to see *Side by Side*—this beautiful book, the result of the hard work to which she has dedicated her professional life—serves as confirmation that the future of Puerto Rican and Latinx children's literature is in good hands. She and other committed and talented children's book authors and researchers have taken up the mantle and shaped the field in a way I could not have predicted back in 1972.

In this book, Jiménez García has greatly expanded the base of what has come to define our field. Not only does she do an outstanding job of highlighting excellent Latinx children's literature, but she also introduces readers to many of the authors who are now writing the books that our children— and *all* children—have available. In addition, and just as important, she provides us with a critical perspective on the major themes and issues that need to be part of an understanding of Latinx children's literature, issues including colonialism, inequality, racism, and power.

In the pages that follow, Jiménez García makes a notable contribution to the study of Latinx children's books. She has made a space for children like me who once felt that only white people wrote books, a space for teachers like me who had a hard time finding books to which her students could relate, and a space for lonely researchers like me who yearned for colleagues with the same burning questions as she had. In the final analysis, she has made a space for all of us who care about children, good literature, and honest conversations about equity and social justice.

Sonia Nieto, Professor Emerita

College of Education

University of Massachusetts, Amherst

**REFERENCES**

Bulosan, C. *America Is in the Heart*. New York: Penguin Books, 1946 (revised edition, 2019).

Castillo, E. Foreword in C. Bulosan, *America Is in the Heart*. New York: Penguin Books, 2019.

Colón, J. *A Puerto Rican in New York and Other Sketches*. New York: International Publishers, 1961 (second edition, 1961).

Council on Interracial Books for Children. "100 Children's Books about Puerto Ricans: A Study in Racism, Sexism, and Colonialism." Vol. 4–5 (1–2). New York: Author, 1972.

Nieto, Sonia. "Children's Literature on Puerto Rican Themes. Part l: The Messages of Fiction; Part ll: Non-Fiction." *Bulletin of the Council on Interracial Books for Children* 14 (l–2), 1983.

# ACKNOWLEDGMENTS

This book would not have been possible without the love and support of my family: my father, Carlos, my mother, Carmen, and my sister, Losmin. My grandparents, Abuelo Daniel and Abuela Basilisa, and Abuelo Ramon and Abuela Maria Luisa, I see throughout all the pages of this book. My precious uncles and aunts, Tio David and Tio Ramon, some who started this journey with me and didn't see it end, especially Tio Daniel, Titi Laura, and Titi Nidia. My Tias Matilde and Luisa Jimenez supported me and gave me the living history of this project all the way up the hills in their house in Vega Alta. My family gave me a living, breathing faith in Jesus which has led me through everything, even the impossible. I want to acknowledge all the teachers in my family including my sisters, Dafne and Ana.

My mentors who held me up and believed in me when no one else did: Kenneth Kidd, Anastasia Ulanowicz, Tace Hedrick, Stephanie Evans, Carmen Martinez-Roldan, and Sonia Nieto. My friends and peers who inspire me: Reanae McNeal, Jennifer Hinojosa, Leonela Medina, Imani Nuñez, Melissa Garay, Jillian Baez, Natalie Havlin, Lara Saguisag, Ricardo Gabriel, Ebony Elizabeth Thomas, Tracey Flores, Sarah Park Dahlen, Edi Campbell, Sujei Lugo, Breanna McDaniel, Edwin Mayorga, Alia Jones, Llana Barber, and Sonia Alejandra Rodriguez.

My colleagues at the Center for Puerto Rican Studies and Hunter College: Edwin Melendez, Harry Franqui-Rivera, Consuelo Martinez Reyes, Patricia Silver, Carlos Vargas-Ramos, and Luis Reyes. Xavier Totti, Pedro Juan Hernandez, Arlene Torres, and Michael Dowdy. New York University colleagues and the greater CUNY family who spoke life: Arlene Davila, David Kirkland, Carrie Hintz, William Orchard, Kandice Chuh, and Marcos Gonzalez.

My colleagues at Lehigh, but especially: Elizabeth Dolan, Suzanne Edwards, Stephanie Watts, and Edward Whitley.

My students at Lehigh and Hunter College, who are way smarter than their teacher ever was and help me think through the pages of this book: Kevelis Matthew-Alvarado, Ruben Rosas, Gabi Montes, Felicia Galvez, Sam Sorensen, Paige Pagan, Kristen Mejia, Karen Valerio, Yasmin Cortes, Alex

Gonzalez, Anacelis Martinez, Alissa Flores, Cynthia Estremerra, Justin Mc-
Carthy, and Berto Sicard.

I am indebted to the wonderful writers and artists, some of whom I count
as friends, for taking time to read my work and teach me about their histories
and love of Latinx children's literature: Meg Medina, Eric Velasquez, Nicholasa Mohr, Georgina Lázaro, Tere Marichal, Wanda de Jesus, and Ada Haiman.
Scholars and writers whose work and lives left me forever impressed: Traci
Sorrell, Leah Henderson, Debbie Reese, and Michelle Martin. The space and
support of the Highlights Foundation, especially Alison Green Myers and
George Brown. The wonderful space and support of Teaching for Change,
especially the brilliant Deborah Menkart, Rosalie Reyes, and Faye Colon.

My beautiful, intelligent attack cats, Mr. Cat and Liebchen, typed many
words on keyboards across states and years. And my beloved dog, GiGi, was
often by my legs during the early writing process.

Huge gratitude to the National Council of Teachers of English Cultivating New Voices of Scholars of Color Program (especially Juan Guerra and
Marianna Souto-Manning and mentors such as Violet Harris, Leigh Patel,
and Jessica Martell) and the Center for Puerto Rican Studies for providing
intellectual support and training ground that sustained the growth of this
work into a book. At Centro, Helvetia Martell, Pedro Juan Hernandez, and
Yosenex Orengo helped me think through a ton of boxes. I received invaluable support from the New York Public Library, Schwartzman Building,
Allen Room residency, as well as coordinator Melanie Locay (Carrie Hintz,
recommended, thank you). Thank you to the librarians at the Inter-American
University of Puerto Rico, University of Puerto Rico, Princeton University,
Library of Congress Young Readers Center, and University of Florida, which
provided countless resources, especially Rita Smith at UF in the very early
days when I first typed "Puerto Rican" into the search catalog at the Baldwin
Library of Historical Children's Literature. Thank you to my chair, Dawn
Keetley, who provided advice and support regarding timeline of the manu-
script. Lehigh also supported my research trips to Puerto Rico through the
Franz Fellowship. Selah.

# SIDE BY SIDE

# SIDE BY SIDE

## At the Intersections of Youth Culture, Literature, and Latinx Studies

In the opening of the Academy Award-winning *Spider-Man: Into the Spider-Verse* (2018), Miles Morales sings his favorite song and packs his belongings into a suitcase with a small Puerto Rican flag clipped at the bottom. The first half-African American and half-Puerto Rican Spider-Man is only a recent example of how Puerto Rican narratives of empire, resistance, and belonging play out in American youth culture. Morales's character also exemplifies a North American tendency to manage Puerto Ricanness, and ambiguity over mixed racial heritage, as universal. It turns out that in a movie centering the only Black and Boricua Spider-Man, "Anyone can wear the mask. Anyone can be Spider-Man." I use the phrase "side by side" to refer to the dynamics of the US and Puerto Rico colonial relationship as one that is functionally dysfunctional, inherently close, and awkwardly ambiguous. The proximity and seeming partnership between the colonized and the colonizer—as is the case with the US and Puerto Rican flags swaying in every major government building in Puerto Rico—is manifested in the irony of being so prominently displayed yet so overwhelmingly ignored. Representations of closeness and universality in youth literature and culture are often a guise for colonial violence and tie to deeply embedded, interrelated notions in US culture about race, literacy, embodiment, language, and, ultimately, citizenship.

In July 2019, over a million Puerto Ricans gathered in San Juan's streets and beyond to protest the Ricardo Rossello administration, ultimately calling for the resignation of the governor. Within a week, federal agents arrested key administration members, including Education Secretary Julia Keleher and Health Secretary Ángela Ávila-Marrero. Some speculated Governor Rossello's own arrest within hours. Yet, what unfolded was perhaps the most important political three weeks in la nación de vaivén's history. For years, Puerto Ricans organized against government austerity measures and whole-sale privatization after Hurricanes Maria and Irma and the government's fall into bankruptcy in 2015, which resulted in a US congressionally appointed Financial Oversight and Management Board (PROMESA). The federal arrests and a leaked chat among Governor Rossello and his cabinet, published by the Centro de Periodismo Independiente—revealing a culture of corruption and mockery of Puerto Rico's most vulnerable, including feminists, the LGBTQ community, and even Hurricane Maria's dead—sparked twelve days of creative protests by older and new generations of Puerto Ricans on everything from motorbikes, horses, and jet skis. Even children joined in the call: "Ricky Renuncia." Among the dance-offs, social media takeovers, and beating of pots and pans, as a youth literature and culture researcher, one particular protest got my attention: when protesters decided to read "bedtime stories" to the Puerto Rican Constitution. Those in attendance or following the protests via television or social media could predict that Puerto Rico's Police combat squad, la Fuerza del Choque, would begin dispersing tear gas around 11 p.m. each night. Near the end of those three fever-pitched weeks, the police said protestors constitutional rights expired after 11 p.m. since "La Constitution Duerme/the Constitution sleeps." Inventive protesters—from La Clara, a feminist organization, and children's authors such as Laura Rexach Olivencia—organized a read-aloud protest where attendees symbolically and literally read to the Puerto Rican Constitution (1952) stories including the text of the Constitution and children's books such as Olivencia's *Por Ahi Viene El Huracán* (2017), which centers on the lives of schoolchildren before, during, and after Hurricane Maria. Youth literature and culture, and children's literacy activities, have a longstanding history at the frontlines of Puerto Rican politics and protests—a literary and cultural history *Side by Side* unearths, centers, and questions. *Side by Side* is simultaneously about Puerto Rico's history of youth literature and culture as much as it is about the history of what came to be known as American (US) youth literature and culture.

Throughout the twentieth century and into the twenty-first, American youth culture and literature grew up with Puerto Rico. The contemporary US tradition of youth literature and media, along with how young people, as authors, narrate their part in social struggle, is inseparable from Puerto Rican thought and writing. Youth literature, media, and youth-led movements have played a prominent role in portraying the political and cultural relationship between the US and Puerto Rico, from the US acquisition to Puerto Rican writer's pleas for a place in US letters and culture. During the early colonial encounter, children's books were among the first kinds of literature produced by US writers introducing the new colony, its people, and the US's role as a twentieth century colonial power to the American public. Subsequently, youth literature and media was an important tool of Puerto Rican cultural and educational elite institutions and Puerto Rican revolutionary thought for negotiating US assimilation and upholding a strong Latin American, Caribbean national stance. For example, elite leaders in Puerto Rico, including Manual Fernandez Juncos, intervene on US colonial schooling policies concerning English-language school readers yet taper down the anti-imperialist ideas of Eugenio Maria de Hostos and Ramon Emeterio Betances, both philosophers and organizers for liberation. Into the forming of the Commonwealth, or ELA (Estado Libre Asociado), picture books, textbooks, and poetry anthologies function as the building blocks of the commonwealth ideology, continuing into the 2000s with the resurgence of the current Puerto Rican picture book which authors such as Georgina Lázaro seek to break from any official island pedagogy. *Side by Side* peels back the neutrality, and benign celebration, in which scholars have often considered the tradition of Puerto Rican children's literature, specifically its relationship to Puerto Rican and US governments. I analyze the nuances among generations of writers, particularly how women writers and educators ascribed to different ideas about the future and potential of Puerto Rican transnationalism as opposed to the male dominant tradition of "insularismo" (Pedreira 1934). Such women writers for youth, such as Ángeles Pastor, a Boricua educator credited with writing several children's and practitioner textbooks, whose works form part of K-12 traditions, as opposed to reading lists for doctoral exams, are often left out of even feminist academic traditions in Puerto Rico and the US. A theme that persists throughout this book is how those Puerto Rican writers traditionally left out of definitions of the nation (Afro-Boricuas, women, and young people) center a network of intellectual mothers and fathers and knowledge systems rooted in networks of literacy and community-based education and public spaces. Indeed, *Side by Side* speaks to a movement back to community-based education and public projects of critical literacy especially in times of extreme austerity and economic and environmental crisis. It also underlines that battles over Ethnic Studies, as well as pedagogies for radical liberation, are always over young people's reading lists and curriculum. Studying Ethnic Studies movements in higher education without taking into account foundations and connections in K-12 fails to account for how such movements might grow sustainable futures.

Puerto Rican youth literature and culture is a transnational project, joining the Puerto Rican archipelago to the diaspora in a time continuum which has become even more evident in the aftermath of Hurricanes Irma and Maria. Perhaps, more than any other kind of literature, youth literature and culture allows us to see how the "Diaspora Strikes Back" in a sometimes seamless conversation with its land of origin (Flores 2009). This transnational project ranges from resisting cultural nationalism, dependent on rigid cultural iconography, to the cultivating critical literacy and self-education to radical liberation evident in the work of Pura Belpré, Nicholasa Mohr, Eric Velasquez, Edgardo Miranda-Rodriguez, and Sonia Manzano. Writers in the diaspora have used youth literature and media as a repository for historical memory, as a foundation for a literary legacy, and as a plea for a rightful place in US history and culture. During the rise of the commonwealth in Puerto Rico, under government censorship, Boricua women educators, through youth literature and culture, narrate how it is possible to engage in strategies of radical liberation without even mentioning the word "patria." In contemporary Puerto Rico, the diaspora has become a symbol of hope and renewal for defending Puerto Rican youth's access to stories and literature in public venues. The role of Puerto Rican youth and youth literature also intersects directly with past and current movements including the work of the Council on Interracial Books for Children and We Need Diverse Books, movements which tie directly to the call for Ethnic Studies in K-12 and higher education. Puerto Rican writers have interrupted and transformed US youthscapes, revising tropes and traditions as a means of expressing the Puerto Rican condition. Moreover, contemporary Puerto Rican youth literature and culture, in the context of the growing body of Latinx literature for youth, has become a space for critiquing the ELA's doctrine of cultural nationalism, particularly by women writers, in terms of causing lasting social and political change, and imagining new, interactive ways forward for political and social progress such as stories that contemplate the unexpected and unanswerable by Georgina Lázaro or the super-heroine mythology created by Edgardo Miranda-Rodriquez.

In *Side by Side*, I use the term "youth literature and culture" to extend to those works written for younger audiences. At the same time, I also engage this term as more inclusive of texts and media created by and centered on young people, such as hip hop, youth-run newspapers, performance, and comics as alternative texts and counter-stories. Beyond terms such as "popular culture," my aim is to highlight how much of what we know as pop culture exists in unexplored, interrelated notions of race, youth, childhood, and the nation. This term also encompasses youth as both objects and participants in the creation of texts and media; it allows for a more comprehensive and intersectional analysis of texts falling out of the purview of what is often studied as Latinx literature and literature for youth. The materials and analysis I present call for a reconsideration of how Latinxs, as marginalized communities in the US, reinterpret and reimagine what constitutes a text and challenge us to do the same. Moreover, bringing together my interests in Ethnic Studies and Latinxs Studies, I find that contemplating how youth and childhood is encoded or functions as a symbol helped me bring together disparate areas important to Latinx and Black women's writing and history in the US and Caribbean more than focusing solely on discourses of race and/or feminism. Indeed, although we know that theorists such as Gloria Anzaldua and bell hooks wrote for young people, suggesting the social intervention for racial and social justice through youth literature, rarely is cultural and academic capital assigned, even in discourses of feminism, including Third World Women and Black feminism, to librarians, K-12 teachers, and writers for youth, female or male.

My privileging of the term "youth literature and culture" is also a deliberate decision to signal how the term "children's literature" has so often been coded as white, Anglo-British, and white US in academic discourse. Children's Literature Studies in English, as became known through associations such as the Children's Literature Association, and their subsequent meetings and publications, made a conscious choice in the 1970s, during the height of Ethnic Studies movements, to steer away from "ethnic" literature which they deemed "faddish" (Jiménez Garcia 2017). Even as education and library science scholars in the 1980s, among them Rudine Sims Bishop, Violet Harris, and Sonia Nieto, began introducing research on the role of race in children's literature and multicultural analysis with metaphors such as "windows, mirrors, and doors," conversations about the systematic lack of representation of people of color in books were mostly absent from critical discussions in the field. Michelle Martin, Katherine Capshaw Smith, and Phil Nel have introduced some fundamental research on race, particularly through African American children's literature into Children's Literature Studies. However, as Emer O'Sullivan has argued in her book *Comparative Children's Literature* (2005), the field mostly centers English-language texts, and internationalization of field has been difficult to develop. I argue that in a desire to legitimize children's literature in the academy, the field has functioned and organized itself in a sort of hyper-canonical and hyper-hegemonic way, centered on Victorian and American traditions about what it means to be young person, and so whiteness and anti-Blackness, in many ways, serve as organizing factors of what is known as Children's Literature Studies. In previous work, I argue that this lack of racial and ethnic diversity in scholarship has led to disparities in the field in terms of critical theory and public facing work (2017). My use of "youth literature and culture" is a move away from these kinds of exclusionary scholarly practices; it signals an understanding of literature for youth as a fluid, multi-textual, multiracial, multilingual space from the inception of the youth literature industry in this country.

The phrase "side by side" in the book's title and throughout the text also connotes a move away from monolithic literary and print culture histories of the US and England, on which traditional US literature scholarship, nomenclature, and print culture rests, toward a comparative, decolonial methodology for studying US literature and in conversation with the greater Americas. Actually, Lisa Sánchez-Gonzalez has said that scholars studying Latinx "children's literature *as literature*" must have "a strong command of comparative literary history" (16). Often comparative methodology in literature signals a space for comparison of Western and non-Western, comparative European traditions, and perhaps British and American literatures (Bernheimer et al 1995). Yet, the story unearthed in *Side by Side* disrupts longstanding traditions of "American" literature by approaching US literature as product of multiple-settler colonial projects in which English and whiteness became the dominant signifiers. In turn, ideas about the parameters of "American childhood" are destabilized. By centering Puerto Rico in a conversation about US colonialism, inviting comparisons from other US colonial projects such as in Hawaii, the Philippines, and Alaska, "side by side" calls attention to the erasure and silence possible even when subjects are placed in proximity and comparison. As a lens, "side by side" acknowledges the hard work of intertwining histories and stories, and placing images and figures in conversation and comparison, as an opportunity to hold them in tension rather than reconciling that tension. In a US context, this lens magnifies how Latinx colonial histories and narratives vis-a-vis Puerto Rico are often juxtaposed as a means of showing neighborly relations, even kinship, although such comparisons serve to further isolate, marginalize, and even invisiblize those histories and narratives. Hidden in plain sight.

Some examples of how I model this lens include my analysis in chapter one of how US authors imagined the proximity of Puerto Rican "brothers and cousins" yet clearly used race as a means of disqualifying them from citizenship. Or in chapter four when I describe how *Sesame Street* presents Maria, played by Sonia Manzano, as a friendly arbitrator of languages, mainly English and Spanish, though English always reigns supreme—yet looking closely one sees how *that* English has been shaped by its interactions with Spanish. Indeed, *Side by Side* functions as a lens of analysis for seeing the "breaks and silences," which allows me to see where transformations occur (Jiménez García 2017, 2019).

## THE (RE)VOLUTION OF LATINX LITERATURE FOR YOUTH: OR HOW SOCIAL MOVEMENTS CHANGED THE STUDY OF YOUTH LITERATURE

My early research journey shaped the methodological and comparative lens I demonstrate in *Side by Side*. During my Master's and Bachelor's degree years, I studied nineteenth-century Transatlantic culture, fascinated by the ways US and British literature diverged in terms of the kinds of cultural values that young people were expected to learn through literature. However, in my doctoral program, as I began planning a research agenda in American children's literature, I noticed key omissions that guided my research into Latinx Studies, Third World liberation movements, women of color feminisms, and youth literature more broadly:

1) How often writers and youth of color were left out of the concept of America in terms of the books often associated with a tradition of American children's and young adult literature.

2) How the imaginative landscape of youth literature and children's literature scholarship was populated by predominately white protagonists, therefore youth of color were rarely seen as active agents in stories.

3) How the population on the pages of American children's literature, even in the realm of fantastical worlds, differed greatly from the lived experiences of US youth (even compared to other youth media, such as television shows including *Sesame Street*).

4) How the absence of youth and writers of color influenced how scholars spoke about and theorized youth and youth literature and culture.

5) How American children's and young adult literature tended to further the US as a nation of immigrants rather than a settler colony. Into the twentieth century, how did US authors describe the country's relationship to its colonies? Clearly, youth literature covering enslavement and the removal of Indigenous nations as in tandem with a colonial project was present, though in problematic ways, as Indigenous and African American scholars have pointed out (Reese 2017). Yet, somehow, US colonial practices are often couched as a thing of the past instead of a continuing project, and not just as neocolonial or postcolonial, but colonial. How do you explain the role of colonies to young people learning about the US as a great democracy? Latinx Studies/Ethnic Studies perspectives would ask us to consider US policies such as the Monroe Doctrine and the history of US interventions in Latin America and the Caribbean. What about the acquisition of lands and people beyond US Southern Reconstruction? What of the Spanish American

War, and the Philippines, Guam, the Virgin Islands, and Puerto Rico? What of Hawaii and Alaska, even Florida? How are these Americans treated in children's and young adult texts?

When I began graduate studies, Latinx literature for youth seemed impossible to locate as literature, dually marginalized in literary and Latinx Studies. The forerunners of research in Latinx literature for youth (which was sometimes coded as bilingual literature or books for English-language learners) such as Sonia Nieto, Oralia Garcia Cortes (founder of the Pura Belpré Medal), Lillian Lopez and even Pura Belpré organized in the areas of library science and education research. This negotiating of disciplinary spaces by Latina women, and women of color more broadly, speaks to the history of youth literature scholarship and the place of children's literature in the academy in the US, Latin America, and the Caribbean. Puerto Rican picture book author Georgina Lázaro has said that a barrier in developing children's literature as a medium in Latin America and the Caribbean is the notion that such texts exist solely for conveying national didactic standards (Lázaro 2017). Certainly, published texts and readers for young people flourished in Puerto Rico in the 1920s, when texts for youth were tied to national projects of schooling Puerto Rican students in a kind of cultural citizenry under US rule (Jimenez 1935; de Piñeiro 1935; del Moral 91). The picture book, in particular, a form central to my analysis in chapter one, evolved as the preferred medium for visually modeling for youth what normative behaviors, songs, and poems a young Boricua should rehearse at home, in the community, and in school. The picture book, however, transformed into a feminist project by the 1930s, championed by what I call "autora-cátedras," women writers deeply invested in creating a Puerto Rican tradition of readers and textbooks. Writers include Ángeles Pastor, Flor Piñeiro de Rivera, and Isabel Freire de Matos in the 1930–1960s. The picture book, as opposed to chapter books, middle grade, and young adult novels, remains the genre of choice in Puerto Rico, a legacy I analyze in chapters one and five as a remnant of the autora-cátedras' legacy yet also a contemporary site for what writers such as Georgina Lázaro and illustrator Antonio Martorell seek to transform beyond didacticism. More recently, the University of Puerto Rico began teaching children's and young adult literature in their English department which combines specialities in linguistics and comparative literatures (UPR Rio Piedras, Literatura caribeña infantil y de adolescentes, English department).

The categorization of youth literature as didactic in Puerto Rico, and in Latin American and Caribbean cultures, mirrors the kinds of stigma which Beverly Lyon Clark sought to refute in her seminal study, *Kiddie Lit: The*

*Cultural Construction of Children's Literature in America* (1998). Clark's book helped carve a path for children's literature in the humanities by elevating children's literature into the realm of literary criticism. Clark writes, "We value childhood. But we also dismiss it" (1). Clark's foundational text tracks how scholars undermined children's texts and young readers—who formed an important part of the readership of texts central to the formation of US literature such as *Uncle Tom's Cabin*—in such seminal works as Jane Tomkins's *Sensational Designs*. Yet, even in Clark's move to redeem children's literature from the realm of "juvenility," I underline the hegemonic nature of how children's literature has been reframed as valuable for literary critics. For example, part of what Clark laments in *Kiddie Lit* is how "[i]n the realm of children's literature, trade publishers happily turn to children's books to bolster their revenues, yet contemporary critics have been slow to take children's literature seriously and treat it canonically" (2). Clark cites "academic evasion and condescension" as a stigma for children's writers, and cites gender bias in the construction of a male canon marginalizing white women who often wrote for young people. However, in her appeal to the canon, Clark neglects to acknowledge the racial and ethnic biases which permeate such a canon; for example, writers of color—many women—have been the target of similar kinds of academic evasion and condescension whether they wrote for an adult audience or not. In elevating youth literature to literary criticism, how have scholars favored prominent white male and female authors, who carry some cultural capital in English literary circles, such as Lewis Carroll, Nathaniel Hawthorne, Harriet Beecher Stowe, and Louisa May Alcott? How has whiteness and anti-Blackness been an organizing factor for the literary study of youth literature?

Literature for youth is also more prominent in public conversations about racial diversity than books for adults. For example, Elizabeth Acevedo's recent win for National Book Award for Young People's Literature for *The Poet X* (2018) was received by scholars such as Vanessa K. Valdes as a win for AfroLatinx representation in the larger literary canon.[1] Additionally, scholars such as Sarah Schwebel have underlined the importance of children's literature scholarship engaging the public (2013). Yet, discussions on public humanities should encompass how the humanities, as an institution, has historically positioned itself as existing apart from the public and how such a public is imagined in terms of race, class, and gender. For example, as I have emphasized, the formation of Children's Literature Studies in the humanities during the 1980s contained a desire to steer away from arguments in Ethnic Studies movements (Jiménez Garcia 2017). It is notable that during a time when the canon was under scrutiny by literary scholars for its privileging of the white male gaze in the 1970s into the 1980s—a moment which intersects with the work of the Council on Interracial Books for Children and pleas such as those by Walter Dean Myers and Nancy Larrick against "the all-white world of children's literature"—raising the academic prestige of children's literature in literary scholarship meant choosing to exclude ethnic literature (Annette Wanamaker, Francelia Butler Lecture 2016). Although librarianship is valued in terms of book prizing, the divisions between youth literature in the humanities and youth literature in library and education have as much to do with the intersections of race and gender as academic discipline—perhaps more than some might like to admit.

Because Ethnic Studies was excluded from the formation of children's literature in the humanities, works by and for people of color were mostly left out of youth literature scholarship. The mantle of studying writers and youth of color, however, fell to education and library science scholars who often dealt directly with racial and ethnic disparities in communities, schooling, literacy education, and practice. Yet, the place of youth literature in Latinx literary studies also presents a rough terrain. Lisa Sánchez-Gonzalez writes in her introductory essay to *The Stories I Read to the Children* (2012), "Literature for Latino children and young adults is sometimes deemed less important than other literary forms, or less sophisticated" (16). Sánchez-Gonzalez notes that, although "North American ethnic studies may appreciate the educational or entertainment value" of Latinx youth literature, these texts designation as "bilingual or multicultural children's books (especially folktales)" marks them as "the domain of the anthropologist, the education specialist, or the child psychologist" (16). Here, Sanchez-Gonzalez also hints at the danger of valuing such texts as ethnographic and even as helping solve social problems—something quite relevant to our current conversations on racial diversity in children's literature. Our want for racial diversity is not exempt from our want for artful literature that values the intellect of young people; such qualities should not be mutually exclusive.

Sánchez-Gonzalez and Ann Gonzalez (2010) both underline how children's literature has fallen out of the periphery of Latin American and Latinx literary scholarship. The lack of critical assessment of writers of color, coupled with the marginalization of youth literature and culture in English and comparative literature departments, exemplifies the complexity of highlighting this area of study. A need exists for scholarly interventions through comparative methodologies, and underlines a need for uncovering layers of structural racism in multiple locations. Books and media for youth take precedence in debates about educational equity and representation, however, the relationship of these texts to the larger body of Latinx writing and artistry is rarely analyzed. As with the Anglo canon and writers for youth, scholars should engage with how Latinx women shape literature for youth as an aesthetic for reframing racial, social, and political oppression and community goals for organizing. Yet, Puerto Rican male authors have also written for and imagined young people as part of political movements, for example, as I show in my analysis of Eugenio Maria de Hostos and Eric Velasquez. *Side by Side* highlights how Latinx authors and artists model, and at times embody, a literary, cultural aesthetic for community engagement.

Since 2012, sparked by the killing of Trayvon Martin, the Black Lives Matter social movement, and the We Need Diverse Books movement in the literary world, energized by the passing and legacy of Walter Dean Myers, the way scholars and readerships talk about books for young people has changed. I mark these two social movements as necessary public, intellectual interventions into the way US popular culture reflects its history with structural racism and white supremacy, and the lingering lack of representation of its Black and Brown population in so-called mainstream literature, media, and culture. I think it is important to see these social movements as intellectual and a form of public pedagogy placing pressure on institutions such as the literary industry, including prizing and publishing and the professoriate, lest we think without these public conversations, the academy would have come, on its own, to its current place in terms of elevating the work of writers and scholars of color. Arguably, Robin Bernstein's book, *Racial Innocence* (2011) helped bring a Critical Race lens to the humanities community studying childhood, youth, and literature for young people, though she never uses the phrase "Critical Race Theory." I say "arguably" because Bernstein was not the first humanities scholar in childhood studies who analyzed children's literature as an institution upholding white supremacy, although Bernstein perhaps never uses that term. Donnarae MacCanns's *White Supremacy in Children's Literature* (1998) provided a critique of the racial formation of children's literature as an "interlocking system [of institutional gatekeeping including] authoring, publishing, and marketing" (xviii). MacCanns's argument is about the persistence of the postbellum "slavocrasy" ideology, or the ideology that sustained slavery as a financial and cultural institution in the US—an ideology which she credits as "in many respects a cultural winner" for its ability to continue teaching racial hierarchies rooted in slavery long after its abolishment. McCann writes, "Cultural and social historians have a useful tool in the record created by children's books. The simple, transparent images contrived for the young are often an unselfconscious distillation of a national consensus or a national debate." During its release in the late 1990s, however, perhaps scholars had more faith in a progressive narrative of multiculturalism. Through the 2010s, with the demise of post-racialism and beginning of the Trump era, faith for the tenets of multiculturalism seems absent.

In the era of Trayvon Martin, Bernstein connected notions of race, innocence, and performance, perhaps highlighting more for scholars how readings of racialized bodies affect the lived experiences of youth more so than MacCanns. Bernstein traced the history of how conceptions of race and innocence worked together in nineteenth-century culture, and how, through popular, influential texts such as Beecher Stowe's *Uncle Tom's Cabin*, innocence was coded as white, while Blackness was coded as insensate and inhuman. Bernstein argues that these ideas about the absence of Black pain, feeling, and innocence was a form of rationalizing the exclusion of Black Americans from participation in childhood, humanity, and, subsequently, US citizenship. Before Bernstein, conversations about structural racism in youth literature in the humanities were usually regulated to discussions about ethnic literature, the postcolonial "other," and international and global literatures. My study of US imperialism through Puerto Rico emphasizes the need to examine the differences among settler colonial projects throughout the world. Varied racial paradigms, histories of enslavement, resistance, and literacies come together in a study of nation and empire-building, particularly in the Caribbean and the Americas (Valdes 2018; Gonzalez 2000). Again, there has been a hesitancy to view the US as an empire, preferring an immigrant paradigm in locating difference rather than a settler colonial model regarding past and present land acquisition, occupation, removal, and continuous displacement of Indigenous populations. Particularly in the case of Latinxs, the dominant discourse lingers on issues of immigration and the border rather than seeing the Latinx presence in the US as a "harvest of empire" (Gonzalez 2000).

Bernstein gave scholars in the humanities, intersecting with childhood, an entry point into structural racism; since then, works have followed such as Phil Nel's *Was the Cat in the Hat Black?* (2017). Nel more specifically names institutional racism and its effect on the children's literature industry and academy: "Racism endures because racism is structural; it's embedded in the culture, and in its institutions. One of the places that racism hides—and one of the best places to oppose it—is books for young people" (1). Nel points out the persistence or racist ideologies in youth literature as kind of hidden in plain sight, particularly in the organization of the book publishing industry. He writes, "[W]hite people who hold nearly all positions of power in children's publishing, and who write the vast majority of children's books—are much less likely to see structural racism" (4). However, in order to have a frank conversation about how race has shaped the world(s) of youth literature and culture, we need to turn our attention to the pipeline of institutions which participate in the distribution and advancement of these texts. We must look at how academic institutions, including syllabus creation, schools of education and library science, literature departments, and libraries, function to uphold a status quo. As professors of literature, we would be naive to believe we hold objective positions that have somehow been imagined as race neutral. The literary history of youth literature in the US was certainly not imagined as race neutral, especially when examining how spaces such as children's libraries developed and the study of children's literature for the humanities avoided incorporating ethnic literatures (Jimenez 2017). Also, in terms of calls to "decolonize" youth literature and the academy, we need to make sure we are not simply depending on decolonization as a metaphor (Tuck and Yang 2012). The cultural work of movements such as Third World feminism and Black Lives Matter has emphasized the consequences of systems of oppression for Black and Brown bodies; these movements call for us to go beyond the metaphorical and empathetic, and imagine taking steps to enact a society which centers marginalized knowledge and communities. Such a society indeed calls for a displacement of white supremacy.

*Side by Side* demonstrates the need to intertwine theory and literary histories in order to reflect the kinds of coalition-building and interrelationships that existed and persisted, for example, between the African American and Puerto Rican communities in the US that undergird these groups' aesthetics today. The work of multiple generations of scholars and writers of color, through activism, writing, archiving, embodiment, and storytelling, represents the roots of youth literature in the US. It is my argument that figures such as Pura Belpré, Arturo Schomburg, and Augusta Baker may have been marginalized in our understanding of the foundations of youth literature in the US, but they are not marginal. Actually, the contributions of such figures to the formation of youth literature and culture mean that—at its core—the world of youth literature was imagined as an intergenerational and interdisciplinary space of text and performance. However, to a certain extent, the research and recovery work I have done in preparation for this book testifies to the lack of interdisciplinary and intersectional coalition-building that exists in the historiography and study of youth literature and culture, particularly in the ways these writers and artists, and youth literature, have been studied in the academy. For these reasons, I prioritize, cite, and centralize the intellectual, aesthetic, and cultural work of writers and scholars of color.

The We Need Diverse Books and Own Voices movements, led by writers and scholars of color in the youth literature industry, helped pull back the curtain of mystery which sometimes shrouded book publishing in terms of how race and ethnicity shapes the field including publishing, critical reviews, prizing, library orders, author visits, and panels. The University of Wisconsin-Madison's Cooperative Children's Book Center's statistics on racial representation in books often guide public conversations on diversity statistics, particularly when considering "books by" and "books about" people of color. Latinxs represent 2.5 of all books published. Since 2012, some pivotal moments have occurred in Latinx literature for youth which have caused the Latinx literary world to turn their attention to writing for young people. An important barrier was broken when Mexican American author Matt De la Peña won the 2016 Newbery Medal for the picture book *Last Stop on Market Street*. The Newbery Medal, as the prize for the best "American children's literature," has been a predominantly Anglo enterprise since its inception in the 1920s. To date, wins for authors of color have been in the single digits. De La Peña was the first Latinx author in Newbery history, simultaneously highlighting the invisibility and importance of Latinx voices in youth literature. In 2019, Meg Medina broke another Newbery barrier as the first Latina to win and the first person of Caribbean descent. Again, Elizabeth Acevedo's National Book Award and then top honors in young adult literature and Latinx literature, with the Printz and Belpré medals, respectively, center the AfroLatinx experience as the face of Latinxs in the US. The reclaiming of the AfroLatinx roots of Latinx youth literature in the US is something I cover extensively in chapter two.

*Side by Side* lingers on the intersectional lives of Latinxs, particularly since a portion of the writers and stories I center work out of Afro-Boricua phenomenology and aesthetics. Actually, Afro-Boricua aesthetics are central to the lifeblood of what has become popularly known as Latinx literature for youth. The story of Puerto Rican youth literature in the US and in Puerto Rico resists the idea of Puerto Rico, and Latinxs use of mestizaje as a means of explaining race in media, book industry and beyond, as a racial democracy. The history of colonization in the Caribbean and Americas means that the African diaspora and the Indigenous populations of these lands were subjugated by the Spanish through colonial violence, slavery, and displacement. Complex histories of immigration from regions such as the Middle East, Asia, and Europe mean that Latinxs could represent a multitude of cultures and languages, and certainly races. Alma Flor Ada and F. Isabel Campoy beautifully portray the racial, national, and ethnic diversity of Latinxs in the picture book *Yes! We are Latinos* (2013), yet it is certainly the case that most Latinx literature for youth is predominately about and by light-skinned Latinxs, a topic seldom analyzed. Illustrator and writer Eric Velasquez has said, for example, that AfroLatinxs are among the most underrepresented in youth literature (2018, Bank Street). Velasquez's work in youth literature—along with the scholarship of Juan Flores and Miriam Jiménez-Roman, and the term "AfroLatinx"—aids in resisting the silence around Blackness and anti-Blackness in Latinx communities. Despite the wide acceptance in Latin American and Caribbean cultures of mestizaje or mixed-race ancestry, a white/Black racial paradigm still guides how Blackness and anti-Blackness have been manifest in representations of the nation, or more specifically, who gets left out. Indeed, the concept of mestizaje itself contributes to the erasure of Black Latinxs—the preference for a mixed, "bronze race," as Vasconuelos theorized in his famous "La Raza Cósmica/The Cosmic Race" (1925), which has somehow evolved past racial distinction problematically preferring blanqueamiento/whitening as progress. Scholars have also analyzed the whitewashing of Latinx identity in mainstream media, casting white passing Latinxs as the norm while also hinting at Latinxs conforming to an ideal of the white, middle-class in a narrative of upward mobility (Davila 2001).

Returning to Miles Morales, the first African American and Latinx Spider-Man, I remind audiences that the face of Latinx literature for youth has been an AfroLatinx one for the last twenty-years on the Pura Belpré Medal. Yet, the legacy of Pura Belpré, like Arturo Schomburg, is a complex one. Belpré's embodiment as a Black Puerto Rican woman has contributed to the historical erasure surrounding her portrait. Indeed, the face of Latinxs in literature, since the founding of the Belpré Medal in 1996, has been predominately light-skinned in terms of the stories published and rewarded by the medal, until Elizabeth Acevedo's 2019 Belpré win for *The Poet X* (2018). However, the epistemological and cultural roots of Latinx literature for youth are deeply rooted in the AfroLatinx experience, something I delve into much more in chapters two and three.

## US EMPIRE THROUGH A LATINX LENS

In his essay "Nuestra America/Our America" (1891), Cuban intellectual and leader José Martí referred to the United States as "our formidable neighbor," a colonizing force ready to "visit" upon the continent and the Antilles. Images of bloodshed, previous colonization, and abuses by the Spanish empire haunt Martí's prose, but the nefarious "octopus," "seven-leagued monster," predatory "tiger," and threat to the soul of "Nuestra America" is the US. The image of a tiger and an octopus provide a snapshot of an expansive, encroaching empire who, by the end of the nineteenth century, had excelled to the top of the political hierarchy in the Western hemisphere. Martí's use of "America" emphasizes the "two continents" of North and South as one—a concept which, even today, challenges key issues in American, Latinx, and Latin American Studies. As J. Hector St. John de Creveocoeur once asked, "What is an American?" (1782). Los Tigers del Norte, of Norteño music fame, might respond, "Somos más Americanos que el hijo del Anglo-Saxon / We are more American than the son of the Anglo-Saxon." Martí tempers his extension of neighborly unity with a warning:

> Therefore the urgent duty of our America is to show herself as she is, one in soul and intent, rapidly overcoming the crushing weight of her past and stained only by the fertile blood shed by hands that do battle against ruins and by veins that were punctured by our former masters. The disdain of the formidable neighbor who does not know her is our America's greatest danger, and it is urgent—for the day of the visit is near—that her neighbor comes to know her, and quickly, so that he will not disdain her.

The culprit of such disdain, Martí writes, would come through "ignorance" of America's great qualities, honor, and ability to fend for itself. Ignorance would lead the US to "covet" America, which he describes as a woman in need of defense from an unwanted suitor, indeed perpetrator, "[b]ut when he knows her, he will remove his hands from her in respect" (Stavans 288). The lady, Latin America, in Martí's imagination, must prove herself dignified by uniting with her fellow nations in cause and intellect in order to fend off an unsolicited relationship, and impending domination. The predatory image, including the image of the tiger and the (seemingly welcomed though unwanted) suitor, returns as a metaphor for colonialism in Pura Belpré's folklore. Among generations, the themes of demonstrating dignity through education—even educating the colonizer—national unity, and self-determination, all practiced within close proximity of such a colonizer, prevails in children's texts by Latinx diasporas, albeit at times problematically. Within Latinx diasporas, the values and themes of elite Latin American leaders must also be negotiated in close proximity to race, class, and gender inequities in Latin American and Caribbean communities which continually affect incoming migrants or immigrants. Martí begins a transnational conversation about what a child of the Americas should encompass through his magazine *La Edad de Oro / The Golden Age* in 1889 in New York, perhaps the first Latinx text for young readers, "para los niños de América." Martí, who migrated to New York as a journalist in hopes of observing an ideal democracy, documented his observations of excess and inequity in essays such as "Coney Island." He left with a sense that the US—including the US academy's role in educating elite male leaders of Latin America—was on the brink of dispossessing Latin America and the Caribbean. Martí's prophetic essay is frequently forgotten in American Studies courses and the US canon. Latinx Studies, as a field, magnifies the US as a settler colony rather than a nation of immigrants, and the Latinx population in the US as a "harvest of empire" (Gonzalez 2000). How would our study of the US literature change if we approached the US as a conglomeration of competing settler colonial projects—on Indigenous land—through race, class, gender, and language?

The contemporary US academy, including its pipeline of K-12 curriculum which includes youth literature, tends to resist the notion of the US as an empire in ways which other colonial powers, such as England, France, and even Spain, make much more plain to young readers. It might be said that the US academy upholds a tradition of American exceptionalism, and the role of the US as benevolent conqueror by veiling literatures of nineteenth-to-twenty-first century colonialism, especially Indigenous and Latinx literatures where the issue of land occupation is particularly astute—both of these contingents continue fighting for visibility in English departments. Beyond literary studies, locating Puerto Rican youth literature and culture, as part of a collective story about what constitutes American youth and childhood, necessitates an examination of US education policy and how these policies have served to silence and erase Latinx stories and knowledge. As Jonathan Rosa and Nelson Flores have argued, a racio-socio-linguistic perspective helps scholars understand the ways in which conceptions of race and language "interplay" and justify discriminatory policies toward immigrant and/or youth of color (621). The deficient model has long been the standard of the US classroom in which normative whiteness was rewarded, and the interplay between race and language accounts for much of the historical erasure of Latinx youth and communities. Puerto Rican authors and cultural-producers must be located in a context in which Latinx ways of writing and knowing have been categorized as nonexistent, impoverished, and to some extent, criminal and/or contraband. The US may not have a national standardized curriculum, but the silences around Indigenous and Latinx texts in the US classroom into higher education underlines an unofficial sanctioning of whose histories are represented and why, particularly in parts of the continental US where physical and linguistic borders collide such as the Southwest and Puerto Rico.

In 2010, while I was doctoral student at the University of Florida, Arizona passed its controversial HB 2281 law banning Mexican American Studies. This legislation was in conjunction with Arizona SB 1070, the "show me your papers law" that allowed law enforcement to racially profile individuals who so-called "looked undocumented." The ban on Mexican American Studies, which was also referred to as the ban on Ethnic Studies, included youth literature by Mexican American authors, such as Matt De la Peña's *Mexican White Boy* (2008) and Sandra Cisneros's coming-of-age novel *House on Mango Street* (1984). Scholars of US empire should note the MAS case since a curriculum centering Latinx texts and culture, was singled out and legally banned for instilling "anti-American sentiment." Indeed, according to award-winning, Latinx author Meg Medina, Latinx young readers often express concerns that their stories and experiences will be categorized as un-American or at odds with American values.[2] As Laura Alamillo, Larissa M. Mercado-López, and Cristina Herrera write in *Voices of Resistance: Interdisciplinary Approaches to Chican@ Children's Literature* (2018), the ban provided an opportunity for educators to reflect on how educational practices and policies have criminalized Latinx and Indigenous ways of knowing for generations, usually through racially coded practices concerning language proficiency and acquisition. The ban calls for a reconsideration of a history of curricular policies that specifically "invisibilize" Latinx youth and texts (ix). In 2017, the judge's decision in the MAS case ruled the ban racist for denying a particular group access to curriculum which improved school performance. This ruling was celebrated by social justice educators as setting a precedent for courses at the K-12 level. The MAS case underlines how texts associated with the role of the US in settler colonialism and land seizure have been designated as anti-American for young readers; Indigenous and Latinx texts, especially those centering Chicano and Puerto Rican histories positioning the US as a border-crosser, represent an unsettling reality about the myth of the US as a nation of immigrants.

The US-Puerto Rico relationship, and the place of Puerto Ricans in US culture, complicates all of the markers of US history and national culture which adults might prefer to simplify for young readers, such as language, geographical boundaries, and racial status. Puerto Rico and its continual status as a US colony is absent from US history lessons even in histories celebrating US expansionism. In her introduction to *Cultures of United States Imperialism* (1993), Amy Kaplan emphasizes the absence of the US in postcolonial studies, something she says "curiously reproduces American exceptionalism from without. The United States is either absorbed into a general notion of "the West," represented by Europe, or it stands for a monolithic West" (17). Kaplan writes that scholars should treat empire into the twentieth century and beyond "as an expansionist continuum," noting how US historians detach doctrines such as Manifest Destiny and expansionism from colonial paradigms (17). However, Kaplan also locates US colonial projects as continental which aids in the erasure of non-continental land acquisition such as Alaska, Hawaii, the Philippines, Guam, the Virgin Islands, and Puerto Rico. In 2017, such erasure contributed to the disparities apparent in US media coverage and federal humanitarian aid for Hurricane Harvey in Texas versus Hurricane Maria in Puerto Rico and the US Virgin Islands. Focusing on the continental US as the main site for a study in American empire also erases the past and present political, educational, and legal policies governing twenty-first century US colonialism, such as the Jones Act which restricts ships and supplies from other countries beyond the US docking in Puerto Rico, something US journalists struggled to explain during Hurricane Maria. As the MAS case demonstrates, battles in K-12 through higher education often hinge on young people's reading materials. In marginalized communities, youth literature and texts function as counterstories essential for building a sense of collective memory and history (Delgado 1989). Similarly, as Ann Gonzalez, Clare Bradford, and MacCanns have argued, children's and young adult literature plays a prominent role in sustaining colonialism, empire-building, and modes of white supremacy. The texts I examine in chapter one, created by US and Puerto Rican cultural-producers, span from 1899 to 1965 and portray Puerto Rico's shift from Spanish to US colony and from military occupation to industrious commonwealth and the creation of the Estado Libre Asociado (ELA). Puerto Rico appears on the American children's bookshelf as early as the US invasion and children's texts serve as a means of explaining US policy in non-continental expansion in the Caribbean. US authors portray a rich island ripe for exploration and US intervention, however, struggle when conveying information about "our new [mixed-race] American brothers."

A study of Puerto Rican youth literature is also a study of how the US publishing industry shapes and counts what gets seen as "Latinx," therefore my work here intersects with how mainstream publishing struggles to see and integrate this diverse community in literature. Also, what was viewed as "Latinx" and "children's literature" coincides with issues of equity for women of color in the 1970s such as Nicholasa Mohr, who has posited that her first work, *Nilda* (1973), was not written for children yet was published as children's literature. Mohr is also one of the only Latinx writers to have stayed in print for over forty years, mostly due to how her works were institutionalized in US curriculum and libraries. In a consumerist society, issues of commodification take precedence. Indeed, our current conversations about diversity on our bookshelves and in our classrooms have more to do with commodification than we may like to admit. I am not talking about how childhoods and childhood experiences have become a market, but rather about how youth and creators of color are esteemed and valued in terms of access to cultural and market capital. This is a system that makes diversity a viable market while still excluding creators and scholars of color. The representation of people of color on the children's bookshelf, both in terms of quality and circulation, has always been a central concern to communities of color. On one hand, as Sarah Park Dahlen refers to it, the "autonomy" of such representation coincides with authors of color creating content. On the other hand, community authorship may not safeguard against issues such as sexism and racism. Additionally, youth literature and culture, as a market, relates to issues of commodification, belonging, and citizenship, especially in the case of Latinxs (Dávila; Báez). As Latinx Studies scholar Arlene Dávila has analyzed in *Latino Spin: Public Image and the Whitewashing of Race* (2008) and *Latinos, Inc.: The Marketing and Making of a People* (2012), dominant US society views Latinxs as consumers and Latinx bodies as commodities, which may heighten the visibility of Latinxs while ignoring political struggles and lack of political representation. This is something to think about as Latinx content continues to get more visibility on the children's bookshelf, and specifically which voices have been coded as Latinx. "Own voices" authorship in Latinx communities, I suggest, connects with how Latinx audiences have been categorized as readers and consumers, an area that requires more research. Media Studies scholar Jillian Báez writes about the tendency toward extremes in her study of Latinx media, *In Search of Belonging* (2018), in which she asks scholars to

> avoid[] a populist approach or celebratory stance toward audiences and instead complicate[] the passive-versus-active debate. Latina audiences are viewed as neither passive dupes nor all-powerful agents, but instead as subjects who engage with media in sometimes troublesome ways that can be consumerist, assimilationist, heterosexist, racist, or classist, all in the struggle for recognition, and hence citizenship. (5)

The struggle for visibility in youth literature, and the right to tell our stories, connects with complicated notions of belonging, disenfranchisement, and citizenship. The Latinx experience also teaches us that citizenship is something one can experience even symbolically, as our Dreamers will tell you. The balance between consumerist notions of what it means to be seen and valued in the US and in youth literature presents particular challenges for decolonizing work, once again, understanding that decolonization is more than just a metaphor (Tuck and Yang, 2).

In terms of markets, belonging, and visibility, the Pura Belpré Medal served to ensure Latinx books circulated more widely, and stayed in print, yet the medal committees rarely embrace Indigenous and African heritage in what it rewards as Latinx (Jiménez García, 114–15). Anti-Blackness is very much a reality in Latinx communities. As Afro-Boricua illustrator Eric Velasquez has stated, "AfroLatinxs are some of the most erased in all of children's literature." This makes Elizabeth Acevedo's recent National Book Award win all the more significant: a brilliant AfroLatina composing stories centering AfroLatinx lives on a (trans)national stage. Acevedo's winning of the 2019 Belpré Medal, another first for an AfroLatinx, also highlights the importance of visibility for AfroLatinxs in our top prize for Latinxs children's and young adult literature. Velasquez's recent pictorial work in *Schomburg: The Man Who Built a Library* (2018), written by Carole Boston Weatherford, places into the hands of young readers the legacy of Arturo Schomburg, a man who helped shape epistemologies of library services and scholarly research on Africana, and who worked alongside Pura Belpré during the formative years of library and archive services and storytelling for young people of color. Yet, because of what so often gets memorialized as Latinx, Schomburg's position as a member of both Black and Latinx communities get erased.

The term "Latinx,"[3] like "Latina/o" and "Latin@," which scholars have revised for further gender inclusivity, helps with bringing together the various nationalities represented in the US. As a field, Latinx Studies acknowledges the tension and complications present even in its act of naming—from the more nationalist discourses of Chicano and Boricua (Puerto Rican) Studies in the late 1960s to the more transnational position of Latinx Studies today. However, Afro and Indigenous Latinx ways of knowing and being, along with the various racial, gender, and class struggles of these communities in the US, Latin America, Central America, and the Caribbean, are often ignored for the sake of the so-called mainstream. We see a single story about Latinxs as light-skinned Spanish speakers, and it is important as scholars that we don't homogenize and also tell a single story in our research. Scholars in children's literature seeking to conduct research on works with Latinx content should also research the various histories of migration, colonialism, and US intervention and land seizure that make Latinxs part of the US population. Similarly, bridging together fields and accomplishing "crossover" scholarship, as Michelle Martin has called it (97), means respecting histories of scholarship by scholars of color. Writing about Latinx content without engaging the liberatory epistemologies in which Latinx Studies was born and has continued to grow—by student demand—presents a hollow analysis to readers and scholars. Also, if you are Latinx, you can be Asian, Arabic, Jewish, Black, or

Indigenous—this diversity has become even more important as our stories come to voice in the twenty-first century. Moreover, we have departed from what epistemologies were meant to accomplish when we feel comfortable naming a children's literature prize after an AfroLatina even as AfroLatinxs and other members of our diverse Latinx community still struggle for visibility in children's literature texts and scholarship.

Latinx writing asks us to reconsider what gets counted as a text and what gets studied as texts, and how Latinxs literally revise the scripts handed to them by US culture. More scholarly attention on music, theatre, and television as texts is needed in Latinx literature and culture, especially when the publishing industry and the canon has so often silenced the voices of communities of color in the US. For this reason, among many others, I turn to *Sesame Street* and children's television mid-book. Sonia Manzano continues a tradition of Puerto Ricans writers and artists cultivating literacy practices in relationship to the literary world with a critical eye. *Sesame Street* continues to play a critical role in representing the multilingual lives of Latinx and other communities of color. Each articulation of Puerto Rican youth literature, through the generations, struggles with the question of a young person's right and ownership of language, such as Manuel Fernandez Juncos translation of English readers and Pure Belpré's defense of a child's right to maintain, even cling to, Spanish. The language border is traced on the imagination through the violence and exchange of the colonial encounter, and in turn, how colonialism lingers and continues to dispossess and disempower long after wars are fought, such as through gentrification and climate change. The conversation on a decolonized imagination, and a decolonized youth literature, is also a conversation about language, and the question of which languages are rewarded and esteemed. Does the world of youth literature do more than represent a monolingual world with subtitles? In US discourses, a multilingual imagination is often not allowed to wander free when loyalty to US English is frequently seen as undergirding a unified political ideology. Puerto Rican artistic and literary culture, as Juan Flores and Eugene Mohr emphasize, is distinguished by its defiantly bilingual nature, particularly in the post-civil rights era. The Nuyorican movement of the 1970s, led by poets such as Sandra Maria Esteves, Miguel Piñero, and Pedro Pietri, was characterized by radical experiments with language sometimes called code-switching—the interchanging of languages without translation. Puerto Rican discourse, as Flores writes in *From Bomba to Hip Hop* (2000), is characterized by its "porousness" and its "breaking of the authority of monolingual discourse"—a discourse representing a serious challenge to a monolingual children's literary world (Flores, 58). Ofelia Garcia introduced the term "translanguaging" as a means of highlighting the artful decision-making and precision that account for bilingual thought and expression (Garcia, 1). For Flores, language is an issue linked to identity and memory. The bilingual aspects of diaspora art and literature, Flores asserts, frame Puerto Rican memories in a "dual vision . . . a communication where languages bifurcate and recombine . . . Puerto Rican memories are mixed code memories, lodged at the points where English breaks Spanish and Spanish breaks English" (52). *Sesame Street*, among many things, provides one of the few examples in youth culture where English is presented as bending and adapting in a multilingual universe.

## STORIES ACROSS THE GENERATIONS OF PUERTO RICAN WRITERS

*Side by Side* is the first extensive study of Puerto Rican writers for youth from Puerto Rico and the diaspora through the twentieth century and into the twenty-first century. My work opens up a more robust conversation about these writers and artists by centering the epistemologies they offer and elevating their works which, in the case of Puerto Rican textbooks, are often left out of literary conversations. In particular, *Side by Side* unearths how Puerto Rican women writers created stories for young people which resisted status quo narratives during each of Puerto Rico's re-imaginings into the current discussion on rebuilding Puerto Rico after Hurricane Maria's natural and man-made disasters. I am also the first to look at how contemporary Puerto Rican authors on the archipelago have used literature to respond to the economic decline since the 1990s which resulted in the dismantling of Puerto Rican publishing and distribution beyond Puerto Rico. The book is organized around a timeline of events from US colonization into the twenty-first century economic crisis and rebuilding after Hurricanes Maria and Irma.

Chapter one, "Indescribable Beings: Reframing Empire and Priming the Public in Illustrated Youth Texts," establishes children's books as a prominent, visual medium used by US and Puerto Rican writers, both those in the diaspora and the island, throughout the history of the US-Puerto Rico relationship. Indeed, children's literature has been a vehicle in representing the Puerto Rican experience to US audiences, such as the playful book *My Dog is Lost* (1960), written by Ezra Jack Keats before *Snowy Day* (1962) and featuring a similar story of a little Puerto Rican boy and his adventures on the streets of New York. Using Keats's story as an example of the Puerto Rican child's complicated yet prominent place in the American imagination, I contextualize how the 1898 acquisition of Puerto Rico during the Spanish-American

War sparked a US literary tradition. This tradition spans material based on accounts by anthropologists, newspaper reporters, and children's writers who fed the American public's curiosity about the non-incorporated territory and its inhabitants. Later, with the arrival of hundreds of thousands of Puerto Ricans into the US metropolis, primers and texts feature the struggle of Puerto Rican youth with schooling and police in problematic ways. Citing passages from volumes such as *Greater America Our Latest Insular Possessions* (1899), I argue that a proliferation of US-produced children's books signals two periods of Puerto Rico's history perhaps of greatest importance, for matters of US capital and investments, to US readers: the 1898 acquisition, as well as the 1948 Operation Bootstrap in which millions of federal funds were used to, among other things, industrialize Puerto Rico. I place these volumes, and the overwhelming sense of creating a historical account for this new colony in this tradition, in conversation with the project of Puerto Rican writers, beginning with cultural theorists of the late 1920s such as Belpré, who also used children's literature as a platform in which to develop a historical and literary tradition for displaced Puerto Rican migrants.

This chapter ultimately positions the development of both island and diaspora literature and culture as a counter-canon disputing colonial US writing on the island's lack of history and culture, though the two diverge in terms of the classism and anti-Blackness of several island texts and island pedagogy. In this context, I examine the development of island textbooks, such as those by Ángeles Pastor in the 1940s–1950s and Isabel Freire de Matos of the 1960s–1980s, and the evolution of the Puerto Rican picture book.

Chapter two, "From the Ground Up: Pura Belpré, Arturo Schomburg, and Afro-Boricua Pedagogies of Literacy and Resistance," focuses on the education and role of Black librarians during the founding and professionalization of children's literature and librarianship at the New York Public Library. This chapter seeks to uncover the Afro-Boricua epistemologies, working from Puerto Rico into the diaspora, which helped found archival and library services for people of color in at the New York Public Library from the 1920s to the 1940s. It interweaves the stories of Arturo Schomburg and Pura Belpré during the moments in which they participated in a Harlem Renaissance at a key moment for Latinx, African American, and AfroLatinx communities. I also connect Belpré and Schomburg to the contemporary work of illustrator Eric Velasquez in *Schomburg: The Man Who Built a Library*. I argue that both Belpré and Schomburg participated in a decolonial renaissance which encouraged youth of color, through the African diaspora principle of Sankofa, to seek out and recover their histories through alternative means outside of established schooling. Belpré and Schomburg both work out of an

Afro-Boricua tradition of community education and critical literacy which maintains educational institutions at a distance while still benefiting from them. A key idea here is the notion of a "renaissance" of Puerto Rican culture occurring during the 1920–1940s period of New York migration and the place of children's literature and storytelling in this "renaissance." I also consider passages from Belpré's published and unpublished folklore collections, among them *The Tiger and the Rabbit* (1944) and *Once in Puerto Rico* (1973), in order to argue that Belpré sought to create another historical account for Puerto Rican children, opposed to the US-produced accounts, in which she continually presented children with ways of resisting US colonialism by invoking notions of the "trickster" and "passive resistance." Moreover, this chapter centers Belpré's Afro-Boricua aesthetics and practices for how they shaped her work, and how to a certain extent, they have been left out of her portrait in an effort to read her as what the publishing industry counts as Latinx.

Chapter three, "Nicholasa Mohr Writes Back," looks at Nicholasa Mohr as a voice for those children of the Puerto Rican diaspora, born and raised in New York, who felt increasingly out of touch with the island of old described in Belpré's folklore. I also see Mohr as representing children who felt absent from the world of children's literature, perhaps due to the abundance of either island folklore or Anglo children's narratives available. Mohr underlines children's literature as of utmost importance in terms of searching for representation in an imagined literary landscape. Here, I argue that Mohr, through my readings of her works *Nilda* (1973) and *El Bronx Remembered* (1975), takes issue with established Puerto Rican and Anglo iconography circulating in children's literature by the 1970s. Mohr resists the desire of Puerto Rican authors to forever imagine the island as the homeland, creating the first Puerto Rican diaspora child protagonist in literary history, Nilda, a character who literally plants her feet in US soil in her own "secret garden." Mohr, I propose, critiques Puerto Rican folkloric iconography such as the "jíbaro" and Anglo "Golden Age" classics such as Frances Hodgson Burnett's *The Secret Garden* (1910), remaking them into traditions that demonstrate the Puerto Rican child's place as an "adopted" heir of the United States. Indeed, this chapter engages with the metaphor of adoption and the orphan as a means of expressing sentiments of national belonging and citizenship which intersect with arguments in childhood studies such as those by Robin Bernstein and Carol Singley.

Chapter four, "The Letter of the Day is Ñ," presents the case of *Sesame Street* and its frank, cutting-edge performance of bilingual culture on children's television for over forty years, mainly through its creation of the lovable, instructional, Spanglish speaker "Maria," conceived by show producers as a representation of urban Puerto Ricans. I turn to *Sesame Street* and children's television at this moment in the study to think through some of the limitations of children's literature, particularly when it comes to expressing bilingual culture, as opposed to television, a performance-based media. For example, during the 1970–1980s-era heyday of "Maria" on the show, how is children's television able to produce such a prominent portrayal of Latino culture when children's literature is virtually void of such characters? I argue that as bilingualism becomes a prominent marker for identity within US Latino communities, and as public programs like Head Start champion the cause of teaching basic, preschool reading, writing, and numbers to urban African American and Latino children, particularly Puerto Rican migrant children, children's television, as a kind of televised musical theatre, relies on the use of performance to reach what are perceived as low-income, illiterate children. I engage the theories of Walter Benjamin, Homi Bhabha, and John Beverly to think about how performances on *Sesame Street* challenge our notion of what children's literature is, particularly when we are not able to use literature in order to introduce children to literary forms and genres. I also analyze skits on *Sesame Street* such as "What Happens Next," "Captain Vegetable Rhymes," and "Big Bird Visits a Casita" for how they portray power relationships between Spanish and English. "Maria," played and cocreated by Sonia Manzano, reflects producers desire to reach what was particularly seen as an "at-risk" group during the 1970–1980s. Through my analysis of Manzano's performance, I follow the many roles played by "Maria." From *West Side Story* heroine to bilingual muse to mime, "Maria" reveals the important connection the show draws between language as a performance and performance itself as a language. I also consider how Manzano challenges stereotypical portrayals of Latinx culture which links to contemporary Puerto Rican authors questioning of so-called authentic culture.

Chapter five, "How to Survive the End of the World: Founding Fathers, Super-Heroines, and Writing and Storytelling When the Lights Go Out," contextualizes the contemporary era of literature and media in Puerto Rico and its diaspora, both those in the US and those returning to Puerto Rico. I analyze the group of writers in Puerto Rico to have written since the 1990s, from the era of economic decline into the current economic crisis and Hurricanes Irma and Maria. Authors such as Georgina Lázaro, Antonio Martorell, Tere Marichal, and Wanda de Jesus continue a trend of feminist transnationalism yet also create stories about surviving impending disasters, both man-made and natural. This chapter also analyzes the notion of "restoring power" and "rebuilding" Puerto Rico in the context of hurricane recovery and the projects to lift morale through cultural arts of Lin-Manuel Miranda with his performances of *Hamilton: An American Musical* (2015) and Edgardo Miranda-Rodriquez's *La Borinqueña* (2016). When the lights literally go out, Puerto Rican authors turn to Afro-Boricua literacy practices of storytelling theaters and cultivating community critical literacies, understanding that government institutions often fail to support communities of color. This chapter intertwines the histories of school closures and disaster capitalism in Puerto Rico with the contemporary work of Puerto Rican authors and how they have prepared young audiences to survive disasters, wrestle with instability, and unpredictability of living in a US colony.

Chapter One

# INDESCRIBABLE BEINGS

## Reframing the History of Empire and Priming the Public in Illustrated Youth Texts

I found Ezra Jack Keats's picture book, *My Dog Is Lost* (1960) at the Bank Street College Library while researching books about Puerto Rican children recommended for 1960s-era New York City classrooms (Jorgenson 1962). Michelle Martin writes that Keats's better-known text, *A Snowy Day* (1962), though sometimes criticized for tokenism, "gave black children the chance to see themselves and their experiences reflected positively in the literature they read" (xviii). Peter, as the first Black male protagonist made the focus of a mainstream picture book, impacted cultural norms in publishing, but before Peter, there was Juanito. And what about Juanito? How did racially ambiguous children fare in a literary landscape known for polarizing Black and white childhoods (Bernstein 2010)? What kinds of portrayals of Puerto Rico and Puerto Rican youth existed which may have made Keats's Juanito an intervention? Even earlier than Juanito, what representations of Puerto Ricans occupied the bookshelves Pura Belpré and Arturo Schomburg passed in the New York Public Library in the 1920s? How did the US public learn about Puerto Rico and its colonial subjects through children's texts?

Newly arrived from Puerto Rico, Keats's Juanito needs the help of his New York neighbors to find his lost "Puerto Rican" dog. By the 1960s, visual portrayals of Black and Brown youth resonated with white, middle-class stereotypes of inner-city violence. Puerto Rican youth in New York City were the subject of countless anthropological and psychological studies deeming them vagrants and problems (Nieto 2000). Keats's rendering of Juanito and Peter, to an extent, works out of racial, cultural, and social anxieties of how youth of color perform in the white imagination. In Juanito, Keats seemed to ponder the perplexities of being dually marginalized as a child of color with limited English proficiency, moreover, a colonial subject in a state of almost total dependence on his multiracial neighbors, including a white police officer.

Keats's Juanito is a reminder of how the publishing industry continues to fail youth of color in reflecting a rich landscape of possibilities beyond extremes, such as dropout and valedictorian. A protagonist of color, as opposed to an antagonist and/or victim character, is a stretch of the imagination rooted in colonial logics, particularly when such child characters reinforce notions of political and social dependence (Thomas 2018). This chapter offers a context of how characters like Juanito, idealized by white readers and writers, developed on the children's bookshelf, and how whiteness, to an extent, functions within and without the narratives Puerto Rican educators created for youth after the US invasion. The first part of this chapter examines illustrated primers and texts created after the US invasion of Puerto Rico, as sites for documenting and containing the embodied existence of mixed-race Puerto Rican youth, by white US writers. Picture books and illustrated textbooks serve as prominent sites for demonstrating US public anxiety about racial mixing and impurity of Puerto Rican bodies related to US citizenship. The second part of this chapter centers on how Puerto Rican writers and educators respond to US imperialism and schooling by creating varying traditions of school readers and texts for Puerto Rican students—from normative white "Dick and Jane" existences to feminist re-imaginings of Afro-Boricua and Taino strategies of resistance and survival. Ultimately, Puerto Rican literature for youth in Puerto Rico, as a remnant of the battles over Puerto Rican and US curriculum standards, provides a visual archive for tracing how different schools of writers imagine a kind of Puerto Rican cultural sovereignty. Images of childhood and children served the purpose of justifying colonial projects in Puerto Rico—from images of poor children needing US intervention to images of rosy-cheeked children upholding the notion of US progress and industry during Operation Bootstrap, the partnership between the US government and the first-elected governor of Puerto Rico Luis Muñoz-Marin to industrialize the island and export Puerto Rican labor in the late 1940s, and the beginnings of the Puerto Rican commonwealth or Estado Libre Asociado in 1952.

**PART I**

**Visual Dictionaries: Undermining Puerto Rican Citizenship through (Faux) Historical Primers, 1890–1960s**

Youth literature and culture testifies to the Puerto Rican experience perhaps more than any other kind of literature of the twentieth and twenty-first centuries. The story of Puerto Rico's position as a US colony and the diaspora's articulation of a distinct community apart from colonial influence begins on the children's bookshelf. "Juvenile novelists," as Jorge Duany calls them in his seminal study *The Puerto Rican Nation on the Move* (2002), created some of the first accounts and texts for the US public shortly after the US invasion. In the article "Their Islands and Our People: Writing about Puerto Rico, from 1898 to 1920 (1999), Felix V. Matos Rodriguez, cited by Duany, underlines this extensive documentary project by US authors, though he seems to find the presence of "children's and juvenile books" somewhat odd alongside the journalists, military historians, and anthropologists. One of the most read photographic books during this time was *Our Islands, Their People* (1898), which featured over 1,200 photos of "Porto Rico, Hawaii, and the Philippines," a book scholars of Puerto Rican Studies, including Matos-Rodriguez, Duany, and Lanny Thompson, have analyzed extensively. However, children's books, especially illustrated primers, played a similar role in documenting the first moments of US rule in Puerto Rico. Indeed, these books offer a curious look at how such "documentary" histories function as fiction since the illustrations and narratives are presented as eyewitness accounts when authors may have never visited Puerto Rico. Such books narrate the kind of logic used to justify US colonialism in Puerto Rico and undergirded the Supreme Court's Insular Cases in 1901 with regard to constitutional rights and citizenship extended to an "unincorporated territory" and whether US statehood should extend to a place inhabited by an "alien race"—laws still governing its status. Moreover, this tradition of readers provides a window into how white, US children were primed to understand their dominance of the US's latest colonial possessions even as authors used kinship language for relating to new Puerto Rican "brothers" (Singley 2011).

Children's texts about Puerto Rico illustrating the land and people at the turn of the twentieth century coincide with logics of foreignness and citizenship which still govern US imaginings. Scholar Natalie op de Beek analyzes in her book, *Suspended Animation* (2010), the role of picture books in portraying difference in the first two decades of the twentieth century. Op de Beek argues picture books played an integral interpretative role in how US readers negotiated racial, ethnic, and cultural difference regarding immigrants. Op de Beek calls this kind of literature "picture book ethnography" or picture books which served a purpose of introducing, naming, and describing the cultures and behaviors of immigrants to a white, normative audience. Yet, she demonstrates how US authors often portrayed racialized others as still living in distant, exotic lands. Picture book authors and illustrators managed difference through creating an imagined geographical segregation for white readers from immigrant and communities of color, even when those communities had a longstanding presence in US borders. Puerto Rico's treatment, as picture book ethnography, in illustrated primers reflects Supreme Court arguments on how the island should be treated with respect to the US, and its constitutional protections, in the Insular Cases of 1901—legal doctrine that still governs how Puerto Ricans fare in US policy. The Insular Cases were argued on precedents such as *Plessy v. Ferguson* (1896), which legally upheld "separate but equal" segregation. Cases such as *Downes v. Bidwell* argued Puerto Rico was "foreign in a domestic sense" for US enterprise: the land was designated as a non-incorporated territory, meaning its acquisition was not meant to lead to statehood. Actually, judges argued against extending US constitutional rights to a space which would remain inhabited by an "alien race." The illustrated primers, then, uphold Puerto Rico as a foreign land while struggling with the domestic nature of these newfound "alien" Americans. As op de Beek argues, the project of picture book ethnography normalized and "designated a white middle class dominant culture" by also erasing the existence of Black children from everyday life of the US up until the 1930s, although white children encountered "African and Caribbean children" in picture books (59).

Locating children of color in print for US readers also connects with Lara Saguisag's (2019) analysis of Progressive Era cartoons and comics strips, specifically how ideas about misbehaved children and "notions of race, ethnicity, gender, and class were used to sort and re-sort children into categories of 'future citizen' and 'noncitizen' (5). Similar ideas about the sorting and containing of children of color cross over into the pages of illustrated primers, underpinning US writers' managing of foreignness, racial nationalism, and benevolent conquest in the context of US non-continental expansionism. The erasure of Puerto Rican children from the US landscape corresponds to colonial and legal logic disqualifying these young people as children and, in turn, citizens, as Robin Bernstein underlines in *Racial Innocence*. Our contemporary discussions on the representation, and indeed existence of, children of color in youth literature has origins in the erasure and disqualification of children of color from full US citizenship. For Puerto Rican cultural-producers and educators, the argument becomes: how do we model white normative culture to young readers while still preserving Puerto Rican culture, as perceived by Puerto Rican elites at the time of US arrival? Interestingly, educators in Puerto Rico would differ over issues such as child agency and transnationalism according to genre and gender.

Children's literature was part of a larger colonial project to narrate the twentieth-century US empire as the benevolent conqueror of an archipelago void of history. Simultaneously, children's literature through the form of picture books and illustrated primers functioned as more than a process of ethnography, but as a visual dictionary that both documented and defined Puerto Rico and Puerto Ricans as unsuitable for citizenship on the same level as white US continental citizens. By adopting the mode of historical primer, these books posited an iconography and ideology suggesting to young white readers how to order a world they stood to inherit. This was a turn of the twentieth-century world of US conquest in which Puerto Ricans had clearly been rendered powerless and insensate through tropes carrying over from racial caricatures of the mid-nineteenth century. The mid-nineteenthcentury polarization between white and Black childhood which rendered white children as innocent and Black children as unfeeling pickannines, as Bernstein has analyzed, survives in these texts, thereby further complicating authorial attempts to narrate stories about mixed-race people. Scholar Lanny Thompson writes on the importance of visually documenting Puerto Rico and the other US colonies during the turn of the century: "Desde la llegada de los estadodounidenes a Puerto Rico en 1898, la fotographia fue un recurso para la descripción de la isla, vista como una 'nueva posesión' bastante desconocida / From the arrival of the Americans to Puerto Rico in 1898, photography was used as a recourse to describe the island as a new possession which was relatively unknown" (2007). Matos-Rodriguez refers to the post-1898 group of journalists, anthropologists, religious educators, and children's writers as "eyewitnesses of sorts" (34). Writers, such as the prolific and popular children's novelist Edward Stratemeyer, crafted these tales and picture books from the perspective of those on post-war frontlines, although Matos-Rodriguez specifies that children's writers may have had less "contact with the Island's reality" than others. In other words, these fictionalized accounts of the island, along with the tales of the early encounters between white Americans and Puerto Ricans contained therein, were presented as nonfiction and, to a certain extent, helped train young readers to accept the white gaze, even when performed, as definitive and factual.

These faux history books contain aspects one has come to expect from outsider depictions of the other: stereotypical, flat representations of Puerto Ricans, exoticism when concerning the island as a lush backdrop for US tourists and explorers, and greater emphasis placed on the land's natural resources as a capitalist enterprise, rather than on people. However, what is perhaps unexpected is how these books disrupt US mythologies of exceptionalism. That is, at the turn of the twentieth century, these books presented for a presumed US-based white, middle-class child readership guidance on how to act as part of a ruling class based on a hierarchy of race and how to inherit colonial possessions. Scholars have underlined the uses of children's literature in British culture as a means of depicting British exploits in South Asia, Africa, and the so-called British Caribbean (Bradford 2009, Bhadury 2013). Children's Literature and Childhood Studies scholarship is accustomed to discussing how authors depict young Britons as heirs of empire, yet what about white US children and young adults at the turn of the twentieth century? Certainly, it is a stance that is at odds with perhaps the kind of progressive narrative that came to rise after World War II and the Civil Rights Movement. Maccans (1998), Martin (2004), and Sanchez-Eppler (2005) each focus on white child readers learning racial hierarchies through plantation literature, abolitionist literature, or literature about US "frontier" politics and "Manifest Destiny" regarding Native American removal, such as the Laura Ingalls Wilder's *Little House* books. Little scholarly attention focuses on how white US children, after slavery and beyond the US South, were socialized to think about continental and non-continental expansion as capital, social, and political acquisition. Additionally, how were white children taught to consider and locate Indigenous and African diaspora peoples colonized outside the continental US? How were young readers presented with these racialized others in the twentieth century?

This historical moment, as Saguisag brilliantly argues, was also the era of progressive activism and social reform in the 1890s–1920s in the US, when the US acquired Cuba, the Philippines, Guam, and Puerto Rico as "spoils of war" in the 1898 Treaty of Paris (Saguisag 2019; PBS *Latino Americans*, 2013). As Saguisag writes, it was an era "defined by conflicts—between industrial and agrarian economies, workers and the wealthy, emancipation and white supremacy movements, immigration and nativism, the New Woman and the Cult of True Womanhood—and cartoonists used images of children to explore, dissect, and sometimes defuse these sociopolitical tensions" (1). Illustrated books and primers, too, were part of a visual campaign and guide for performing hierarchy and subjugation. Saguisag writes that comics "disseminated racist imagery including the figure of the pickaninny" and "introduced young readers to the notion that defining and performing American citizenship are thorny and turbulent projects" (11). In Puerto Rican Studies, a foundational debate concerns the second-class nature of Puerto Rican US citizenship, which scholars such as Pedro Malavet (2004) and Charles Venator-Santiago (2018) have analyzed extensively; children's texts offer a window into how this citizenship was imagined and performed early on in the US-Puerto Rico relationship. Picturing immigrants as children, and problem children at that, is complicated given that the Puerto Rican population became citizens through the Jones Act in 1917, though

Puerto Rico was maintained as a non-incorporated territory with limited constitutional protections. Some of the tales I analyze appeared as part of *The Youth Companion*, a popular, illustrated periodical for American youth, especially young men, published between 1827 and 1929, a periodical responsible for the first printing of the Pledge of Allegiance. *The Companion* has been analyzed by scholars as training US youth, particularly males, in a culture of consumerism sustaining capitalist enterprises, yet almost no attention is shown to how such consumerism goes beyond the desire for material and subsists on the human cost of Indigenous populations (Apol 2000; 2001). Such stories follow a similar pattern from British children's literature in portraying white children as explorers and hunters in US con-quered lands which posits islanders—as much as US authors call them cousins and brothers—as inhuman subjects.

**Cousins and Brothers: Kinship, Race, and Citizenship**

US subjugation of Puerto Rico, according to children's picture and illustrated books during this time, rested on the presupposition of a lack of history, the imagined subservience of the people—including an imagined lack of will for self-determination—and a racial hierarchy focusing on pure European heritage. Books affirm the message of vacant history and vacant subservient people. Joseph Seabury, who Matos-Rodriguez cites, writes in *Porto Rico: The Land of the Rich Port*, "Porto Rico has no prolonged or varied history, no exciting historical periods. For this reason, but little space is given to the annals of the past." Other books simply begin the history upon US arrival. *Greater America: Our Latest Insular Possessions* (1900), which contains chap-ters on Puerto Rico, the Philippines, and Hawaii, actually begins its history of Puerto Rico with an incident a few days before the official start of the Spanish-American War in which "[the US] navy threw a few shells into the grand old Castle of Morro . . . like callers leaving cards as an indication of a future visit" (2). In *Young Hunters in Porto Rico or the Search for the Lost Treasure (1900)*, writing under the pen name Captain Ralph Bonehill and adopting the stance of eyewitness, Edward Stratemeyer discusses the purpose of the book in introducing Puerto Rico to US readers:

The work was written primarily for the reader's amusement, yet I have endeavored within its pages to give a fair description of the Porto Rico of today, as it appears to the traveler from our States. This new island domain of ours is but little known to the majority of us, but when its picturesqueness, and its mild climate, becomes a matter of publicity, Porto Rico is bound to become a Mecca for thousands of American tourists, in search of health and pleasure. (iv)

Stratemeyer presents "this new island domain of ours" in the context of amusement. Puerto Rico is a blank canvas for adventurers and tourists, including US children. Young readers receive an invitation to regard Puerto Rico as their "domain" for future exploits. Matos-Rodriguez analyzes the literature produced by US writers, including children's literature dedicated to the Spanish-American War, as setting up a case for an ahistorical Puerto Rico and justifying US policy for occupation:

> Many of these writings accentuated the shortage of written histories of the island—a factually true statement—to create the sense of a lack of Puerto Rican culture and self-identity. An effective mechanism to convince audiences back in the US of the correctness of the colonial expansion into Puerto Rico was to show the lack of any real or deep sense of history or culture on the island. If Puerto Rico could be portrayed as a 'tabula rasa,' not only would the US intervention be seen as less intrusive, but also as less risky. Certainly an ahistorical country would be more susceptible to acculturation and change than a country with a deeply rooted sense of self and identity. (42)

The value assigned written histories in this account, and how such accounts affected our scholarship, is also a fiction in many ways. I say this because, in chapter two, I further examine the sort of myths of what was available when the North Americans arrived including the erasure of a limited Spanish publishing and schooling system. For example, Puerto Rican revolutionary and educator Eugenio Maria de Hostos had written two books for children by this time. As part of the Puerto Rican diaspora in the 1920s, Afro-Boricua author, librarian, and storyteller Pura Belpré would discuss a lack of printing presses and written stories during Spain's reign as proof of the resolve of Puerto Rican storytellers and folklorists to sustain a unique folklore ("Folklore of the Puerto Rican Child"). The development of public education and literacy, especially as preserved through Afro-Boricua epistemologies regarding history, oral, culture and performance, fell out of the purview of US writers, acting as faux historians interrogating the remnants of the Spanish empire. It is clear that the absence of written narratives in English perpetuated the myth of Puerto Ricans as ahistorical and, to some extent, devoid of sustained local cultures and knowledge. Puerto Rico's future was interpreted in consumerist terms by US writers whereas the Afro-Boricua literacies and epistemologies guiding many Puerto Rican cultural-producers during this era, such as Arturo Schomburg, taught that the future was recovered through reclaiming community histories.

The future of Puerto Rico, as imagined by US writers, was negotiated as separate from the role of those living in this new possession—an aesthetic which recurs in current iterations of Puerto Rico's value to the US after economic collapse and Hurricane Maria through the creation of infrastructures such as the Federal Oversight Board. An ahistorical Puerto Rico, an assumption gathered about the print cultures available on arrival, informs how US writers ascribe cultural capital to islanders, even those perceived as European elites, though even less for non-elites. US writers viewed islanders as remnants of an outdated, failed Spanish empire, an empire which, indeed, did little to invest in the cultural capital of its inhabitants through tangible institutions such as printing presses, schools, and libraries. The caricature-like portrayals of young Puerto Ricans—for example, children acting as obedient, clumsy translators and helping explorers find goods, such as "Inez" in *The Motor Girls in Water's Blue* (1915), who teaches the Motor girls the phrases "Quiero / I want" and "Cuanto / How much"—are plentiful in these volumes (88). However, the author of *Greater America* demonstrates how "the inhabitants" of this new dominion should be characterized through race and class:

> "[The islanders] number nearly a million, and of these about two-thirds are white. The others are every conceivable shade of brown, yellow, and black. Those of the people who boast a pure Spanish descent are not in large proportion, and form a separate class of extremely aristocratic tendencies. They are well educated, chivalrous and proud; distinguished for a love of good music.

Race and class hierarchies quickly turn into concerns about intellectual and cultural deficiencies, describing even affluent Puerto Ricans as simpletons: "Like all other dwellers in the warmer latitudes, the Porto Ricans are bitterly opposed to any work that is not absolutely necessary, and in a corresponding degree are constantly in pursuit of pleasure. Yet, either because they are easily entertained, or because of their chronic lack of energy, the popular amusements are exceedingly few and rather monotonous in essentials" (20–21). The simple, monotonous Puerto Rican, even as an aristocrat, is carved out as a stereotype lacking industry and resistance.

This US tradition of faux historical primers on Puerto Rico repeats a pattern, through portrait after portrait, of Puerto Ricans as people of color, and specifically Afrodescedientes, who are subservient, vacant, and hollow.

The concept of an unfeeling and will-less people is not so much expressed about feeling physical pain, though perhaps implied, but about US writers projecting onto the population a passive inability to defend and govern the land. Clearly, part of the US colonial project through the slavocracy in the continental US depended on the dehumanizing of the enslaved. Yet, as Bernstein analyzes, the concept of insensate people, even as children, justified the menial labor and brutal physical and psychological conditions of slavery. Black people, in nineteenth-century US culture, were excluded from the concept of childhood, and in turn, humanity and citizenship. Such racial ideologies were disproven by abolitionists, however, as Bernstein's framework of "racial innocence" demonstrates "when a racial argument is effectively countered or even disproved in adult culture, the argument often flows stealthily into children's culture or performances involving children's bodies. So located, the argument appears racially innocent. This appearance of innocence provides a cover under which otherwise discredited racial ideology survives and continues, covertly, to influence culture" (51). In Progressive-era conquest and colonization, illustrated primers on Puerto Rico provide a rare moment for US writers narrating stories about "nonblack children of color." The polarization of Black and white childhoods made it near impossible for US writers to imagine mixed-race childhood. So great was this imagined divide that Bernstein suggests it contributed to the "large[] disappear[ance]" of mixed-race peoples (43). How would US writers narrate a story to white young readers about a conquered territory in which the majority of the population is of African and Indigenous descent?

Mary Hazelton Wade's *Little Cousin* primer series provides an interesting case in rhetorics of benevolence, kinship, and racial subjugation in relationship to non-continental land seizure. As the title denotes, US children's authors writing on the conquest of Puerto Rico and other non-continental territories use kinship terms to describe relationship to the inhabitants, in particular the terms "brother" and "cousin," which distinguishes a close relation though varying in parentage. As Saguisag writes with regard to comic strips, images of childhood during this period resonate with specific fears about immigrants so that such imagery "articulates the fantasy of constraining the immigrant . . . and suspending him in a state of dependency and immaturity" (24). Indeed, in 1945, in an article titled, "Puerto Rico: The 49th State?," Belle Boone Beard described Puerto Rico as the United States "problem child" that had given "headaches" to congressional committees "whose business it is to listen to Puerto Rico's pleas for justice and help" (105). I mark how images of childhood and kinship function as a means of imagining a politically dependent relationship between the US and its colonial conquests. However, as with the politics of "side by side," the greater the perceived threat of uprising and overthrow, tied to deep-seated fears about a strong Black Caribbean population, the more kinship language shifts to denoting a closer relation.

From 1901 to 1920, the *Little Cousin* series narrates the exploits of the US in non-continental expansion and colonialism, featuring a child character and "cousin" from every region of the globe in a story meant to introduce the culture to US child readers. International regions in the series include Norway, Japan, and Africa, though in tandem with op de Beek's analysis in *Suspended Animation*, the books function as a way of distancing these children as far-off immigrants. In particular, Hazelton Wade carefully locates immigrants and those of African descent as existing in lands apart from the US, even as she alludes in *Our Little African Cousin* that the real home of "negro children" in the South is Africa. Occupied territories, however, such as Alaska, Hawaii, the Philippines, and Puerto Rico, present a challenge to Hazelton Wade as she struggles to justify the rationale for US intervention, especially in terms of proximity of lands and the future of the inhabitants. About Alaska, she writes, "Away up toward the frozen north lies the great peninsula, which the United States bought from the Russians, and thus became responsible for the native peoples from which the Russians had taken the land." Alaska is a business transaction, and although Russians "took the land," Americans only took responsibility for human subjects. About the Philippines, Hazelton Wade writes, "On the farther side of the great Pacific Ocean are the Philippine Islands. . . . Like most of the islands in the Pacific, the Philippines are inhabited by people belonging to the brown race, one of the great divisions of the family of mankind. And yet we shall call these various peoples of the brown race our cousins; for not only are they our kindred by the ties which unite all the races of men in this world; they have been adopted into the family of our own nation, the United States of America." The language of kinship and childhood veils racial degradation as Hazelton Wade describes the Filipino people as "wild and distrustful children," writing that "[t]hey have no faith in us; they do not wish to obey our laws. If we are in earnest in our wish to do them good, and not harm, we must learn to know them better, so that we may understand their needs. That is one reason why we are going to learn about our little Philippine cousin." The suggestion is that children learn how to simultaneously subdue and aid these outsiders.

Hazelton Wade presents the white reader-colonized peoples relationship as one between cousins, though I note a correlation exists among her use of kinship language, racial hierarchy, the proximity of land acquired to the US mainland, and how she imagines the subservience of the people. Her treatment of Puerto Rico and its people in relationship to the mainland demonstrates the dysfunctional closeness, born of colonial necessity, of what I refer to as "side by side" in this book—that is, proximity and friendship in youth literature and culture as a guise for colonial violence and rupture. Puerto Rico presents the challenge of being the closest acquired "possession" with a majority nonwhite population. Interestingly, *Our Little Philippine Cousin* (1902), *Our Little Mexican Cousin* (1905), and *Our Little Porto Rican Cousin* (1902) feature similar cover illustrations of Latinx children typical of the tropes available to the US public at the time—the so-called "Panama" hat, bare feet, vacant facial expression, and brown skin. These stereotypical tropes, common in newspaper articles about the Spanish-American War, evidence how these books stand in for historical documentation and ethnography, although authors may have never visited these lands. About Puerto Rico, Hazelton Wade writes: "The beautiful island of Porto Rico lies, as you will see by looking at the map, near that great open doorway to North America and the United States which we call the Gulf of Mexico. Very near it looks, does it not? So this little cousin with whom we are going to become acquainted today is our near neighbor as well." She encourages child readers to "think nothing of the distance between here and Porto Rico" compared to "our tiny Eskimo cousins who live near the icy pole, and our little African cousins south of the equator, as well as our Japanese cousins on the other side of the globe." José Martí, in "Nuestra America/Our America" (1891), wrote about the importance of Latin America making itself known to the "neighbor" to the North as a means of defense, understanding that the US was intent on controlling the hemisphere. Martí's use of "neighbor" drives from a fear of colonial domination in the Southern hemisphere, yet Hazelton's sentiments seem a guise for her fear of a reconquista. We see how the *Little Cousin* series traces the development of anxieties which eventually led to US policies such as the National Origins Act of 1924, undergirding ideals of white supremacy. As Clift Stratton writes in *Education for Empire: American Schools, Race, and the Path of Citizenship* (2016), migration from Latin American and the Caribbean was treated as a threat by white Americans to "control of the future race stock of the United States." For example, economist Robert Foerster submitted policy documents to Congress suggesting that a strong control over the Southern hemisphere was necessary if the US "desired to maintain a high average of ability, intelligence, and citizenship no simpler device is at hand than the nonadmission from this time forward of all dubious race elements" (qtd. in Stratton, 173). Ultimately, Stratton writes that it was as if white Americans feared the "impending colonization of the United States by allegedly inferior persons" (173). Perhaps, the fear of uprising and reconquista undergirds Hazelton Wade's invitations to white child readers to exercise dominion over Puerto Rico. She describes an entitlement to the land absent in other descriptions of territories: "We should expect to feel very much at home after we have arrived there, especially now that Porto Rico has become part of our own country."

*Our Little Cousin* series and *Greater America* underline a project to "introduce" lands, inhabitants, and cultures while also hinting at the inevitable violence of the colonial encounter. This texts contain suspicions of how subjugating mixed-race peoples may go awry during the transfer of power. Puerto Rican perspectives and knowledge systems remain safely marginal so as to define and manage islanders into a palatable image justifying US policy for US readers. Again, as the racial makeup of Puerto Rican inhabitants comes more clearly into view, metaphors of kinship and home collapse into images of blood ties and lineage. Indeed, Hazelton Wade dedicates much more space to the topic of race in this primer on Puerto Rico comparatively than her text on Hawaii, Alaska, and the Philippines:

> We shall find our Porto Rican cousins and neighbours, with their dark skins, black hair, and soft black eyes, somewhat different in appearance, indeed, from ourselves; and we shall not be able to understand what they say unless we have learned the Spanish language; for, as we know, the parents or forefathers of our Porto Rican cousins came from Spain to Porto Rico, just as the parents and forefathers of most of us who speak English came from England.

> However, these are slight differences; and the Spanish people, from whom our black-eyed Porto Rican cousin is descended, belong to the same branch of the great human family as we do, who are descended, most of us, from English people. That is, the Spanish people and their descendants, the Porto Ricans, belong to the white race. Manuel is thus a nearer relative than the little black cousin, who belongs to the negro race; or the little Japanese cousin, who belongs to the yellow or Mongolian race; or the little Indian cousin, who belongs to the red race; or the little Malayan cousin, who belongs to the brown race.

In her sketch of Puerto Rican "cousins and neighbors," I note Hazelton Wade's use of the phrase "family of human kind" in her description about the Philippine racial hierarchy as opposed to the phrase "the great human family," which she uses to describe how US readers should relate to Puerto Ricans through race. Perhaps, for white Americans, the anticipation of Puerto Ricans and US inhabitants interacting and potentially intermixing through settler colonialism seems much more inevitable given Puerto Rico's proximity to the US. This sense of inevitability heightens how the language of kinship now shifts to how US child readers should understand Puerto Ricans through white, European ancestry of Spain: "[A]s we do, who are descended, most of us, from English people. That is, the Spanish people and their descendants, the Porto Ricans, belong to the white race." She further distinguishes that "Porto Ricans" are "nearer relatives" than the "the little black cousin, who belongs to the negro race." Puerto Ricans, according to the description, are also separate from Asians, Indigenous, and the "brown race," terms she uses to describe the Philippine population. US children are encouraged to relate to those who claim white ancestry which would have meant those in the elite, disqualifying the majority of the population present when the US arrived. There is also an explicit erasure of the African diaspora and Indigenous ancestry in Puerto Rico, and a marker between what is seen as legitimately Puerto Rican, and in turn, legitimately "American," as excluding Indigenous and African descendants. The "family of human kind" excludes Black and non-Black people of color from bloodline kinship ties to the US. However, "the great human family" with its deliberate exclusion of Blackness and mixed-race peoples defines membership in the US family as demanding pure, white European heritage. Although books like *Greater America* contain sentiments about the possibility of citizenship, something they affirm the inhabitants desire, we see how US race-based ideology concerning conquest ultimately excluding a mixed-race people from being viewed as rightful heirs of the human family and as heirs of US humanity, citizenry, and ultimately, childhood.

### Race, Feeling, Self-Determination, and Suspicions of Revolt in the Caribbean

The preoccupation with racial ideologies and makeup—and the fear of Black bodies in the Caribbean—veil anxieties about the potential for community uprising and overthrow of the US. References to race in this US tradition of faux historical primers often coincide with descriptions about the possibility of government overthrow. Clearly, it benefits those justifying US policy in the Caribbean to depict the island and islanders as a racial mix associated with chaos and disease, a place in need of US intervention even into the 1940s around the time of Operation Bootstrap. We see this in books such as *White Boots* (1948), in which Helen Orr Watson, adopting the gaze of the main character, a pure-bred Boston Terrier lost in Puerto Rico, narrates images of Blackness alongside chaos and savagery: "Three-wheeled carts, piled-high with oranges and avocado pears . . . taxi cabs honked at them. They passed the open cafés where brown-skinned people sat at tables, while loud phonographs blared Puerto Rican music. . . . Crippled beggars help out their hands. . . . But the Negro paid no heed (20). *White Boots* underlines the lack of humanity ascribed Black Puerto Ricans and mixed-race peoples, considering a pure-bred dog is depicted as more human. However, the strong correlation between race and political instability in the US anti-Black imagination must be considered in any literature about the Antilles regarding the proximity of Cuba, Puerto Rico, Dominican Republic, and Haiti to the continental US. The Haitian Revolution's successful overthrow of slavery and empire by the population fomented suspicion in the Northern hemisphere about free Blacks, literacy, and education in regard to radical overthrow; I further explore these ideas in the next chapter on Afro-Boricua epistemologies and Pura Belpré and Arturo Schomburg. Anti-Blackness and fear of rebellion, for example, surface when the author of *Greater America* in 1899 issues a warning about the vast majority of the population of mixed-race peoples: "It must not be supposed, however, that the government of eight hundred thousand people, including nearly half a million of mixed Spanish and Indian blood, and three hundred thousand negroes, hardly one of whom can speak the English language, could be accomplished without political complications and civil disturbances." Fear of rebellion, revolutionary thinking, and Blackness, and the unlikelihood of establishing a white majority on the island, seem one and the same in this passage. Vanessa K. Valdes, in her book *Diasporic Blackness: The Life and Times of Arturo Alfonso Schomburg* (2017), discusses the difference between liberal and radical politics in the Caribbean and Puerto Rico in context of race and seeking independence from Spain. She writes, "Understanding the late-nineteenth-century Hispanic Caribbean in the aftermath of the Haitian Revolution and the island's struggles for freedom, both in terms of ending slavery as well as in terms of establishing independent nations" (28). Valdes reminds us that island politicians never advocated for complete independence; rather, separatism was an ideal of the exile community, such as those responsible for the 1868 Grito de Lares or Lares Revolt, including Ramon Emeterio Betances. In the Caribbean, separatism and revolt had been associated with Blackness and mixed-race peoples. *Porto Rico: Its History, Products, and Possibilities* (1898), by A. D. Hall, describes the struggle for Puerto Rican independence against Spain, as a kind of forewarning of possible rebellion if allowed to persevere, particularly through Black and Brown bodies:

As early as 1820, long before Cuba had made any attempt to throw off the Spanish yoke, the Porto Ricans made an effort to obtain their independence. After a short guerrilla war, this first rebellion was suppressed, as were also several other abortive attempts.

In 1868, the year of the great uprising in Cuba, the most formidable outbreak occurred in Porto Rico.

After two mouths of severe fighting the Spanish regulars were victorious, and the leader of the rebels, Dr. Ramon E. Betances, who has since resided most of the time in Paris, was captured, as was also J. J. Henna, afterward a New York physician. All the prisoners were sentenced to be shot, November 4, 1868.

On the very day preceding that date news came to the island that Queen Isabella had been deposed, and in consequence the political prisoners were released.

But they were afterward banished, and in their exile they have ever since been active in devising measures for the freedom of the island.

There is no reason whatever to think that there will be any discontent in the future under the liberal and beneficent government of the United States.

Hall suggests that the threat of uprising, led by the renowned Afro-Boricua intellectual and nationalist leader Betances, may have been eradicated before the US arrived. However, he also suggests that the success of containing "guerrillas" and "rebels" depends on beneficence and neighborly relations. However, Hall outlines a clear relationship among mixed-race peoples, warfare, and overthrow—all requiring containment, including solutions such as banishment and execution.

The challenge for US children's authors, then, becomes how to depict a population of mostly Black and mixed-race peoples, in close proximity to the already free Cuba, Dominican Republic, and Haiti, as docile to child readers in the states. What constructs of race would authors draw on in terms of rendering the character of these people? I argue that US authors relied on tropes and stereotypes from past African American characterizations, particularly notions of the insensate nature of Blacks, as a means of relegating race lines and substantiating white supremacy as crucial for future island relations. Along with presenting Puerto Ricans as ahistorical, which I emphasize as closely tied to notions of illiteracy and formal education, US authors presented Puerto Ricans as simple-minded and unresponsive in the face of invasion. Indeed, they were cast as simpletons willing to sing and dance at their political expense. The opening of *Greater America* depicts Puerto Rico, at the moment of acquisition, as a "insensate" and dead place:

> When the [US] flag was raised over San Juan, it overshadowed one house that, if insensate things could every awaken to feel emotion, would surely have groaned and crumbled. That was the White House that Juan Ponce de Leon built and lived in nearly four centuries ago: but the White House survived the American flag, although all that is left of the old conqueror himself is a handful of dust in a leaden casket that rests in the Dominican Church of San Juan. (Greater America 11)

I am particularly interested in how this symbolic passage about "dust" speaks to a larger narrative constructed by US authors about an absence of Puerto Rican self-determination and resistance. However, I mark the side-by-side images of benevolence and violence as a means by which US authors manage anxieties about, ironically, rebellion. Later on, the author writes that Puerto Rico was "acquired in the same way" as California, referencing a longer history of US continental conquest though without reference to the struggle for those Western territories by Indigenous and people of color. Puerto Rico, however, is "the largest in the number of people whose allegiance has been transferred from one country to our own," once again revealing a slippage about the anxiety of managing such a population, particularly in terms of allegiance to US government (5). The author implies that the symbol of conquest, the US flag, should indeed incite outrage from the disempowered, yet in this imagined arrival, there is no one to rise up to the challenge. The phrase "if insensate things could rise to feel emotion" also signals the Spanish Empire, and everything associated with it, as useless, ahistorical, and specifically, "insensate." The reference to death and dust contains an admission of the colonial violence enacted by conquest through empire. Yet, the author's perspective here as a so-called eyewitness veils the position of the US as the latest empire to claim the land and people. The implied child reader, empowered through the US colonial system, views the flag raising as an innocent act, though the remainder of the text celebrates possession and conquest yet always in tandem with beneficence: "With the sword in one hand, and the healing arts of civilization in the other, the United States moved upon the islands of the sea" (32). Black and Indigenous descendants were rendered as insensate and will-less for the sake of excluding entire populations from a claim to humanity, self-government, childhood, and citizenship. The author tells readers that "[t]he change in [political power] was made without the consent of the Porto Ricans, but there is reason to believe it was not against their wish" (6).

A key moment in *Greater America* occurs when the author imagines for child readers a scene of the first Fourth of July in Puerto Rico, notable since it also receives an illustration juxtaposing the narrative. US soldiers and journalism correspondents, according to the author, gather "laboring-class" islanders to perform for the festivities. The author employs the impassive pickannies trope in describing the inhabitants. The performers are joyful, "faithful" musicians who "perform their part" by singing for the group, in Spanish, at the expense of their self-determination. A young Porto Rican boy, as a kind of adorable fool, is described as coming into the circle at the insistence of the US group to perform "a Fourth of July yell." This image joins with this tradition's theme of kinship after conquest, but underlines how Puerto Rican children, and adults by extension as people of color, are imagined as excluded from US narratives of citizenship and freedom. Indeed, the child portrayed as performing US culture and patriotism renders him an actor and someone who might "play American" while still being excluded from the democracy. In this depiction, the Puerto Rican boy is also seen as suited to play the part of a Yankee rebel, though only in the staging of this scene: "We felt that we had to begin with the small boy. We had misgivings, for the Porto Rican small boy is very tame, so tame, indeed, that we doubted whether he could raise a good old-fashioned Fourth of July yell" (42). This portrait is an example of how US authors struggle to present Puerto Ricans as both objects of intervention and containment, in particular the author struggles to present the boy as both subservient and a potential danger. The boy is "very tame" yet as he plays the part of rebel and lets out a "yell," he proves his potential as a threat. Considering the hesitation of US authors about mixed-race peoples as untrusting and capable of US overthrow, this moment in *Greater America* seems to underscore an anxiety about the frailty of the American experiment in Puerto Rico: "But soon our doubts were entirely dispelled. The small boy, and the large one too, proved that he could make a noise as well as his brother in the States." The language of kinship, here, turns from "cousins" as seen in Hazelton Wade to "brothers"—the closer the perceived threat to imperial order, the closer the colonial relationship is pictured in this tradition of illustrated primers. Again, I note how kinship relations shift depending on an author's perspective on inhabitants as threat. The boy's ability to "make a noise as well" as a white, US child qualifies him to play American, but he is only pictured as emulating US children. The boy's action pictures US independence, yet this gesture is rendered as a failed act of liberation in the colonial script he, as a symbol for Puerto Rico under US rule, performs. This description of a young Puerto Rican boy facilitating relations between symbols of Latin American, Caribbean, and US independence and nation-building activities, also depicts the child as a kind of diplomat. Indeed, the yell proves to US spectators that he is capable of acts of imperial defiance, and is so depicted as a type of doppelganger for his white, US counterpart. This child of color is a near threat and thus must be hidden in plain sight and managed as an illegitimate "brother."

We see how ideas about Indigenous and children of color shift toward the turn of the century from the pickannies trope to a kind of dark doppelganger in terms of children of color acquired through US continental expansion. In particular, we see this shift toward dark doppelgänger as it becomes clear these children represent a close relationship and may be empowered through proximity of US rhetorics of revolution, liberation, and access. The doppelganger image, when contained, gives way to the notion of children of color as facilitators of diplomatic relations, though at the service of the US empire in Latin American and Caribbean relations. This tradition of US-illustrated readers suggests a predicament for cultural-producers and those imagining the future of US expansion in "far-flung America." Authors depict children of color to US white child readers as modeling and performing ideas about US progress and liberation, bringing together Latin American and US diplomatic relations, but do not allow these children to be viewed as participating in the full rights of citizenship. Readers are left with a caricature of Puerto Rican mixed-race brothers who are perfectly content with performing, but not possessing, America—a storyline I revisit in my final chapter by looking at Lin-Manuel Miranda's musical about the US revolution, *Hamilton* (2015).

**PART II**

**Juanito and Caribbean "Dick and Jane": Playing Normative Americans and Sovereignty in Picture Books and Illustrated Primers, 1918–1945**

When Keats's Juanito greets the US public on the pages of *My Dog is Lost!* (1960), he is attached to a history of US empire, non-continental land seizure, and the migration of hundreds of thousands of "brothers" acquired through conquest. Through this lens, we see how Keats portrays Puerto Rican children as isolated, docile, yet particularly suited for creating diplomatic relations even among other ethnicities. Keats's opening lines emphasize a deficit model approach to Juanito, while still humanizing him as a child meriting empathy and assistance: "Juanito was miserable. / Only two days before, on his eighth birthday, / he and his family had arrived in New York, all the way from Puerto Rico. / Now he was in a new home, / with no friends to talk to.

/ For Juanito spoke only Spanish" (1). Juanito is Keats's counter to popular culture portrayals of Puerto Rican youth which were central to how the US public imagined the urban metropolis by 1960, particularly ideas about juvenile delinquency (Lewis 1966; Sanchez-Korrol 1994; Gonzalez 2000). Latinx Studies scholars demonstrate how specific Latinx migrations form part of US culture, and how predominantly white audiences view certain groups as "assimilating" and participating in so-called upward mobility. As Puerto Rican Studies scholars such as Edna Acosta-Belen, Juan Flores, Sonia Nieto, and Lisa Sánchez-Gonzalez have shown, the Puerto Rican diaspora's significant presence and organizing in the urban metropolis, and cities such as New York, Chicago, Newark, and Philadelphia, shaped everyday aspects of US culture. The US popular imagination and public education reform and policy in the urban center was forever changed by Puerto Rican migration to New York. In *Harvest of Empire* (2000), Juan Gonzalez narrates the Puerto Rican migration's affect on the national consciousness:

> Until World War II, Mexican farmworkers were the most familiar Latin Americans in this country. True, a Latino might occasionally turn up in a Hollywood film role, or leading a band in a New York nightclub, or as the fancy fielder of some professional baseball team, but outside the Southwest, Anglo Americans rarely saw Hispanics in everyday life and knew almost nothing about them.

> Then the Puerto Ricans came. (81)

The Jones-Shafroth Act of 1917, which required all that US ships flying the US flag consist of crews made up of US citizens, was an act of Congress that established Puerto Ricans as US citizens. Prior to this, Puerto Rico remained under a military occupation governed by US military generals. Although illustrated texts such as *Greater America* mention the possibility of citizenship, this legal right is not extended until it becomes a question of maritime commerce though with restrictions. Puerto Ricans lived in the US as political exiles during Spanish rule, and after the US invasion, but the institution of citizenship and Boriken's seemingly endless economic upheavals sparked a massive exodus of this group of US citizens (over one million from 1917 to 1990; 470,000 from 1950 to 1960 alone). The presence of specifically Black and Puerto Rican youth in the urban metropolis was central to such influential thinking and policy with regard to race such as the *Moynihan Report* (1965) and Oscar Lewis's *La Vida: A Puerto Rican Family in the Culture of Poverty* (1967), and portrayals in popular culture such as the film *Blackboard*

*Jungle* (1955) and the stage show (and eventual film) *West Side Story* (1957). Puerto Rican youth were also seen as objects of intervention in studies which would later justify public programs such as Head Start and its televised counterpart, *Sesame Street* (Cooney).

I mark the centrality of Puerto Rican youth as objects of intervention in fundamental ideas about race, education, schooling, truancy, and juvenile delinquency in US national consciousness, as illustrated in Keats first attempt to populate the landscape of children's literature with an affirming portrait of a child of color through Juanito. Juanito represents a contrast to how Keats depicts Peter in *The Snowy Day* as mostly isolated and always in contrast with the images of whiteness, symbolized by snow, that surround him in the book (Martin; Capshaw Smith). Instead, Juanito reflects a desire for children of color as bridges. Before Peter, there was Juanito, perhaps the first child of color the US public would have encountered in a mainstream picture book: a mixed-race Puerto Rican child associated with ambivalence which is perhaps why we forget him. Juanito, regardless of his lack of proficiency in English, masters a campaign to mobilize representatives of Chinese, African American, and Italian communities in New York in order to find his lost "Puerto Rican" dog. The book's surprise twist comes when a policeman intervenes to help Juanito and this multicultural crew. The policeman tells Juanito, "We have been looking for you too!" This is a moment which 1960s audiences may have read as turning on its head. Perhaps, as a means of countering 1960s stigmas of Puerto Rican youth as vagrant criminals, Keats instead makes the policeman a hero. The policeman looks for Juanito because he wants to return his dog. Juanito's gifts of diplomacy make him and the policeman friends. As Keats pictures the group of kids, with a triumphant Juanito, marching back home, readers witness the coming together of a global village, perhaps a supposed end to police brutality and gang violence. As with the tradition of faux readers, Keats draws on a longstanding association of Puerto Rican youth as idealized for gifts of communication and diplomacy, yet always in tension with concerns about state power and overthrow, a central point in my analysis in chapter four of *Sesame Street* and Sonia Manzano's performance in, and writing for, the show. Keats's *My Dog is Lost!* works to humanize a Puerto Rican community that had been marginalized in a host of side-by-side contradictions—docile yet violent, deficient yet gifted.

Despite Keats's good intentions, the book repeats a pattern of how youth literature portrayals of Puerto Ricans primed the US reading public by the 1960s; these patterns were analyzed by Sonia Nieto, a forerunner in scholarship on Latinx children's literature, in her groundbreaking research and as part of the work of the Council on Interracial Books for Children. As Nieto writes in her chapter "Self-Affirmation or Self-Destruction: The Image of Puerto Ricans in Children's Literature written in English" (1987), "The dependence, helplessness, and passivity of Puerto Ricans are constant themes in many of the books. One is left wondering whether Puerto Ricans are capable of doing anything at all on their own without the help of the benevolent Whites who populate the books. These take the shapes of kindly cops, friendly store owners, helpful teachers, and understanding welfare workers. Passivity is perceived as almost a national characteristic, so that Whites are compelled to step in and help . . ." (216). Ultimately, Nieto asks these questions: "Who speaks for Puerto Ricans? Who defines our lives? Who are the guardians of the self-identity of our youth? And ultimately, who is responsible for determining to a large extent how others perceive us?" (215) As a transnational project, *Side by Side* focuses on the youth literature and culture of the Puerto Rican diaspora, and to a certain extent the role youth literature and culture has played in supporting a form of self-determination and cultural, creative sovereignty apart from political sovereignty. However, Nieto's questions guide my discussion of how Puerto Ricans imagined and formed the role of youth literature on the island, and the complex ways in which remittances from US to Puerto Rico continually travel (Flores 2001). Puerto Rico is a geographical location and an imagined community, as Benedict Anderson argues. However, Puerto Rico's lack of political sovereignty allowed Puerto Rican thinkers and cultural-producers to imagine a stateless, borderless nation, and a transnational movement including the island's subsequent diasporas and circular migrations (Capetillo 2011; Anderson 1983; Duany 2002; Flores 2001).

The Puerto Rican diaspora was originally considered a separate somewhat illegitimate literary and cultural tradition apart from the island by academics in Puerto Rico, but, with the shift in scholarship to transnationalism and the cultural riches and possibilities afforded by circular migration, authors in the diaspora have received recognition on the island. In youth literature, diaspora authors such as Pura Belpré and Nicholasa Mohr, however, were cataloged in tandem with island traditions since Flor de Piñerio de Rivera's *Cien Años de Literatura Infantil Puertorriqueña / 100 Years of Puerto Rican Children's Literature* (1987), a seminal bibliographic essay which I will return to throughout this book. Belpré's work, in particular, is gaining more visible recognition in Puerto Rico. Puerto Rican storytellers and writers on the island such as Teré Marchial Lugo feature moments of intertextuality with Belpré's popular *Perez and Martina* (1931) in their contemporary works for children. The University of Puerto Rico's graduate library school, in 2016, renamed their children's literature collection La Colleción Pura Belpré.

Along with Puerto Rico's over 400 years before US arrival, the US tradition of faux history books and illustrated primers about Puerto Rico works to erase the history of educational projects on the island before and after US arrival. These are projects which should be understood as transnational given the Puerto Rican community's history of circular migration, though there was an earlier movement shortly after US arrival in which island educators presented a much more insular curriculum and approach. US policy makers presumed that written texts were evidence of historical and aesthetic traditions and often. Even studies such as Felix Matos-Rodriguez's analysis of US tradition of writers, which seeks to recover how the colonial lens casts a deficient model on Puerto Rican culture, emphasize there were no Puerto Rican-produced or -written texts upon US arrival. Few discuss how Puerto Rican elites negotiated the process of colonial schooling and texts shortly after arrival. One such example which I will elaborate on here includes Manuel Fernandez Juncos's creation of a series of Spanish-language readers on Puerto Rican folklore and culture at the request of US officials (Villasante 1966). Scholars of this period in the turn of the twentieth century, and US officials looking at the history of education and culture also tend to presume that education and literacy was solely in the hands of official Spanish imperial schooling. Indeed, much of the archival history and scholarly work on Puerto Rican education rests on archival documents of US or Spanish officials (Del Moral 2013). Few analyses dwell on the writing and curricular work of educators and teachers, particularly women and Black Puerto Ricans, as imagining, writing, and implementing a curriculum, both for students and future Puerto Rican teachers, undergirding resistance in varying forms. However, the work of educators on the frontlines in creating pedagogies of resistance serve as seeds of Ethnic Studies movements and culturally relevant and sustaining pedagogies—such an impetus began in talleres and lower-grade classrooms, before the late 1960s in higher education, with the creation of curriculum materials for teachers and students. These texts serve as aesthetic and historical objects telling the story of imagined sovereignty, both its repression and development, through the island's many incarnations: as a Spanish colony, a US colony, a Latin American commonwealth under US rule, and a territory under US bondholder rule after environmental and economic devastation.

The 1920s–1930s marks a moment when Puerto Rican intellectuals and cultural-producers worked to preserve Puerto Rico's legacy as a Spanish colony, while the 1940s–1950s highlight a reinvention of the island as a colonial, Latin American commonwealth with a local government under federal authority. Youth literature provides a window into these processes of reinvention in relationship to ideas about formal schooling and literacy, and how texts function in nation-building and sovereign-thinking, both as inward and outward facing projects in Puerto Rico. After the US arrival, how would island educators and writers present a nation in transition between two empires? At the forming of the commonwealth, or Estado Libre Asociado (ELA), what sort of pedagogical project would undergird the creation of this new experiment in self-governance while remaining a US colony? In Puerto Rico, we see how educators and writers shift toward building a pedagogy of cultural nationalism which allows a sense of cultural sovereignty while upholding the US political status quo, though this is a much larger story than I can compose in any one chapter. My readings focus on how anti-Blackness and classicism shape official island pedagogy of the forming US colony, and the impending commonwealth, even as the African roots of Puerto Rico's educational and literacy practices undergird celebrated ideas about the persistence of a unique oral and performance local culture. I highlight differences between male and female pedagogies, yet regardless of generational, gender, and racial difference, one enduring concept about young people remains: Puerto Rican youth, unlike their adult counterparts, were uniquely gifted by subsequent colonial encounters.

## Juncos and Ginorio: Books for Proper Subjects

Prior to US arrival, Lola Rodríguez de Tío, a woman intellectual and author of the revolutionary "La Borinqueña" national anthem, published *Mis cantares (My Songs)* (1876), included in Piñerio de Rivera's *A Century of Puerto Rican Children's Literature* (1987), a historical bibliography (17). The famed Puerto Rican pedagogue and political intellectual, Eugenio Maria de Hostos, also published books such as *El libro de mis Hijos* (1878) and *En barco de papel* (1897), both of which featured childhood and children as central to the narrative, and which some critics have suggested were read to children (Villasantes 1966). In Puerto Rican Studies, more research is needed to recover the literate arts and reading practices of Puerto Rican children and families prior to US arrival, particularly those of non-elite children. However, what scholars gather about these habits is affirmed by many central figures in the development and preservation of Puerto Rican letters, including Manuel Fernandez Juncos, Ramirez Arrellanos, and Pura Belpré. The history of public schooling in Puerto Rico, analyzed brilliantly by Solsiree del Moral, highlights the efforts of Afro-Boricua educators and local teachers and intellectuals' resistance against US colonial pedagogy in which texts and readers for young people played a critical role. Within generations, Puerto Rican educators differed in terms of how they believed young people should remember the legacy of Spanish colonialism and the development of the US empire.

According to Carmen Bravo Villasante in *Historia y Antologia de Literatura Infantil Iberoamericana* (1966), US officials first intended to implement an English-only curriculum as a process of Americanization through school readers. The English-only policy was resisted by local teachers and intellectuals. Manuel Fernandez Juncos, who worked as a journalist, began a conversation with officials about the priority of Spanish as a language of instruction. Spain never instituted a normal or public school system in Puerto Rico, so there were no Spanish-language official curriculum materials and texts tied to such a system, apart from those associated with the Catholic Church and missions. The vast amount of Puerto Rican elites received instruction from private tutors, and some of these private elite tutors functioned through public-facing, community-based education, such as the legendary Maestro Rafael and Celestina Cordero (Del Moral, 60–66). Del Moral recovers this important story of Maestro Rafael in terms of how Cordero's taller-escuela (workshop-school) functioned as a public space for elites and working-class children alike, and how eventually Spanish officials provided Maestro Rafael with a salary to continue his work as a free educator. Rafael Cordero's taller-escuela began in his tobacco shop, which affirms the legacy of rich literacy practices of the *tabaquero* culture and public pedagogies for contemporary education (Acosta-Belen 1996).

One of Cordero's pupils was Manuel Fernandez Juncos, the creator of the first textbook tradition for Puerto Rican children in US colonial schools. Juncos's role in creating these illustrated readers causes historians of children's literature including Villasante and Pura Belpré to view him as a kind of guardian and preserver of language and culture. Villasante calls Juncos the "salvador del idioma" (or "the savior of the language"). Texts such as *Antología de Folklore Puertorriqueña: Prosa y Verso* (1911), as well as his translated-from-English primers, testify to Juncos's attempt to record and uphold a cultural and social ideology affirming Puerto Rican "national" identity while still supporting the US colonial educational project of Puerto Ricans as "Tropical Yankees" (Navarro 2002). Del Moral writes, "The process of consolidating US authority over public schools in Puerto Rico was deeply informed by the way US colonial officials conceptualized the relationship between race and education, both on the mainland and in the colonies" (51). Both Del Moral and Navarro discuss how past education models for Americanization and industrial education of African Americans and Indigenous communities in Tuskegee and Carlisle were consulted for Puerto Ricans. Both Tuskegee and Carlisle contained projects for training communities of color for domestic and military service and "killing" native and local cultures and languages, which helps access US policymakers' attitudes toward Puerto Rican youth and curriculum. However, Juncos's place as a Puerto Rican writer and arbitrator for a more culturally specific set of texts functions as both disruptor and upholder of status quo. According to Henry K. Carroll, the special commissioner to Puerto Rico, Juncos supposedly told US officials that "the chief fault of the Porto Rican is a lack of will force" (qtd. in Navarro, 37). Juncos rehearses the trope of will-less, vacant Puerto Ricans to officials and this carries over into his work for young people. Yet, I dwell on his position as pupil of Rafael Cordero, an aspect of his intellectual portrait that is undertheorized in thinking of traditions of Puerto Rican pedagogy, both written and oral. Two texts during the Spain to US transition which I will analyze in this section are *Antologia*, by Juncos, and *Lectura Infantil: Libro Segundo*, by José Gonzalez Ginorio. The preface to *Antologia* provides a study in Juncos's resistance to US colonial erasure and his adherence to status quo cultural nationalism, a doctrine that would prevail in much of the literature of the forming commonwealth and linger in the diaspora.

Piñeiro de Rivera asserts that folklore and poetry anthologies as textbooks constitute the beginning of a written tradition of youth literature in Puerto Rico. However, there is no critical reflection in her historical bibliography of why folklore and poetry function as founding genre and how they relate to linguistic and cultural preservation projects tied to colonial structures. In turn, such colonial structures connect with ideas about childhood. The turn to folklore highlights how terms such as "literatura infantil y juvenil" ("LIJ" as it is coded in Puerto Rico and other parts of Latin America) and "children's and young adult literature" were understood in the 1920s, which also impacts how early writers such as Belpré implement trend in the diaspora. Puerto Rican writers and thinkers in this moment struggled with what should be viewed as age-appropriate reading and/or literature. A common consensus at the time: literature should educate but at the same time remain playful. However, we should note that ideas about educational play are imagined by adults overseeing a change in imperial power. Puerto Rican authors' designs for writing and creating texts seem inseparable from the objective of refuting claims that Puerto Rico lacked any local culture, writers, and thinkers worth extolling prior to the arrival of the US. Puerto Rican elites take up an imagined mantle of documenting what they see as worth documenting and remembering about the local culture through folklore; this becomes a central tenant of teaching through texts in this critical period.

A close reading of how Juncos and Arellanos introduced their folklore anthologies for US colonial schools highlights the possible values and critiques shaping these texts. In his introduction to *Antologia*, addressed to children, Juncos writes, "En general esos trabajos no fueron hechos para niños y trata sobre ideas y sentimientos que no comprenden bien á vuestra edad; pero así y todo debéis leerlos y recordar con respeto los nombres de sus antores / In general these works were not created for children and deal with ideas and sentiments that you do not understand at your age; but even so you should read and remember with respect the names of your ancestors." Juncos describes the process of documenting folk life and culture as a process of archiving ancestral legacies which he then ties to deeply rooted ideas about culture and nation. Puerto Rican elites and folklorists, such as Juncos and Arellanos—having access to the cultural capital needed to address and petition US education officials—take on this kind of writing as a practice of nation-building for other elites and non-elites. At its core, Puerto Rican youth literature in this period is a study of demonstrating a sense of allegiance to colonial powers while asserting a separate culture. For example, Juncos writes that the Puerto Rican ancestors which young readers meet on anthology pages "impusaron el movimiento politico y educativo de esta sociedad en el siglo anterior y a ella debe Puerto Rico gran parte de la cultura que actualmente disfruta / where the impulse behind the political and educational movement in our society in the last century and Puerto Rico owes them a great part of the culture it enjoys in actuality." In these few sentences, Juncos references Puerto Rican revolutionary history, a period also referenced in US readers such as *Porto Rico: Its History, Products and Possibilities* (1898), a text which assured US readers that Puerto Rican revolutionaries, along with their ideology, were exiled by US arrival. Juncos reframes revolutionaries as educational and cultural heroes and heroines fighting Spanish oppression. In doing so, he allies nationalists such as Betances and Hostos with the US narrative of its status as the benevolent liberator of Puerto Rico. Juncos writes that these revolutionary ancestors were "en lucha con las institutiones nada expansivos del regimen colonial / in a battle with Spanish institutions that left no room for expansion by the colonial regime." He suggests two things: first, that he along with child readers shares a common struggle with these ancestors, specifically a struggle against the current colonial regime (the US); and second, that the US regime differs from Spain in that its institutions provide some room for expansion and dialogue.

Juncos narrates that Spain never instituted a system of public schools, therefore past Puerto Rican cultural heroes "No tuvieron como vosotros la gran ventaja de la escuela moderna/Did not have as you do the great advantage of a modern school." Nevertheless, Juncos instructs that stories of and for this *new* Puerto Rico—under US rule and under a banner of so-called

modern progress—should be seen as a progressive history starting with Puerto Rican cultural heroes. Juncos writes "Un sabio historiador ha dicho que las
nuevas generaciones parecen más grandes y lucidas, porque están sobre los
hombres de los generaciones anteriores. Con esto quiso dar a entender que la
cultura social no es obra única de la generación que la posse, sino productos
de herencia y de acumalciones sucesivas/ A wise historian has said that new
generations always look grander and more lucid because they are standing
on the men of former generations. With this, I want us to understand that
social culture is a not a unique, isolated feat of the generation which possesses
it. It is a product of inheritance and successive culmination." Here, Juncos
suggests that US officials may have introduced US public schools believing
they were tools of progress in the early twentieth century, but any sense of
progress from that historical advent needed to be attributed to Puerto Rican
cultural predecessors as opposed to Americanization. Indeed, US progress
would only happen on a foundation of Puerto Rican cultural preservation,
albeit in partnership with the colonizer. Juncos would also later rewrite the
Puerto Rican national anthem, revising the original, anti-colonial verses by
Lola Rodriquez de Tio into a hymn celebrating the island's beauty rather than
its resolve to become an independent nation. Interestingly, Juncos's act of
creating curriculum is somewhat subversive when we consider the implica-
tion of invoking revolutionary ideology and its potential to topple empires.
Yet, Juncos's selections in *Antologia* carefully underline a cultural nationalism
which maintains a status quo with US mythologies of freedom. For example,
there is no mention of Ramon Emeterio Betances, renowned for "El Grito
de Lares," the successful revolt against Spain in 1868, yet Juncos includes
selections by Maestro Rafael Cordero and Eugenio Maria de Hostos's "En
Barco de Papel"—both figures representing education as a path to liberation
under colonialism, though perhaps not as overtly nationalist as Betances. "En
Barco de Papel," read by Puerto Rican children during Spanish rule, revolves
around the Antillean desire for liberation in the Caribbean. It is interesting
to see how Juncos repurposes Antillean rebellion and Caribbean liberation
into simply symbolic works by cultural heroes. Alongside Hostos, however,
Juncos published "La Carta de Victor Hugo a los Alemanes," by Julian Acosta.
The letter celebrates the French Revolution as a predecessor for the American
revolution and centers "la lucha / the struggle" of Christopher Columbus and
Abraham Lincoln (33). Columbus and Lincoln, instead of being symbols of
colonial rule, represent noble leaders and liberators in "la lucha" for progress
in the Americas in Juncos's *Antologia*. This selection also highlights the beginnings of a tradition in Puerto Rican writing where revolutions enacted by
white Westerners are meant to inspire young Puerto Ricans toward ideas of

progress and liberation from tyranny; by contrast, local revolutionary lead-ers and acts are either erased or rendered innocuous. Miranda's *Hamilton: An American Musical* (2015), particularly, its performances in Puerto Rico in 2019 rehearses this similar trope, something I will discuss in chapter five.

Juncos appropriates terms historically associated with Latin American and Caribbean struggle against colonial oppression and applies them to Columbus and Lincoln, both representatives of the European and US em-pire. He successfully resists complete Americanization while containing the nationalist, revolutionary rhetoric of Puerto Rican and Antillean liberation fighters. Juncos and Arellanos's influence on Puerto Rican literature and art of the diaspora is evident in Belpré's work in New York from the 1920s to the 1930s, though Belpré's storytelling features more subversive tenden-cies. Through Juncos and Arellanos, however, folklore becomes synonymous with refuting Puerto Rican cultural inferiority in education, a problematic practice considering the genre's dependence on stagnant cultural tropes and potential stereotypes.

In tandem with anthologized folklore, a tradition of "Dick and Jane"-like readers were created by José González Ginorio for Puerto Rican colonial schools. These readers were meant to place Puerto Rican-authored texts upholding Puerto Rican culture and US ideals in the hands of students. Ginorio, a colleague of Juncos, was an educator and the president of the teacher's union in Puerto Rico when he began translating and adapting English textbooks into Spanish, emphasizing language instruction through verse. For example, in the first pages of *Lectura Infantil: Libro Segundo*, read-ers meet Luis who, pictured holding a replica of *Lectura Infantil*, narrates, "Este libro tiene muchos cuentos bonitos. A mi me gusto leer en mi libro. Yo leo los cuentos despacio y pronuncio bien todas las letras que tine cada palabra / This book has many beautiful stories. I love to read my book. I read the stories slowly and I pronounce all the letters well" (21).

*Lectura Infantil* pictures light-skinned, elite, primly dressed Puerto Rican children modeling and performing the "Tropical Yankees" ideal in a land of palm trees and haciendas. A close look at the illustrations in particular erases the mixed-race heritage of Puerto Rican children, and instead presents white, blonde-haired boys and girls, along with white teachers. The editors perhaps lift these illustrations from the English-language texts meant for white children, yet these images, with lessons on good behavior and diction in Spanish, also appear to model conformity to US ideals and supremacy. In one illustrated panel, two children, one boy and one girl, stand in front of "La Maestra / The Teacher" in a lesson that encourages respect and loyalty for teachers and colonial schools. La Maestra stands with one hand stretched out to the children while her other hand holds a book in almost religious contemplation. La Maestra's head is framed by an American flag, draped over the open door of the classroom. Outside the door, children fly kites and play in the school yard, reinforcing the idea of schools, as US institutions, as philanthropic spaces of safety and peace. Yet, the illustration also suggests peace as conditional on behavior and performance. Ginorio crafts the encounter between teacher and students as based on promises and mutual exchanges, writing:

> La maestra sonrío y miró a Ana. Luego los invitó a entrar y sento a Ana en su falda. Ella dijo que se alegraba de tenerla en la escuela y que le enseñaría mucho. Ana sonreía llena de alegría y prometio a la maestra portarse siempre bien y estudiar mucho.

> The teacher smiled and looked at Ana. Then she invited them to enter the classroom and sat Ana down on her lap telling her she was very happy to have her in school and was going to teach her a lot. Ana smiled, full of joy, and promised the teacher that she would behave well always and study a lot. (11)

As Luis, the little boy in the illustration, watches the teacher and Ana, he also reflects on the work he needs to do and how well he must behave: "He was sure that Ana would behave well. . . . He was also willing to study a lot and behave well." Student success and attainment in colonial schools is presented as dependent on how well children behave, which compares to images circulated after the Spanish-American War about the loyalty and behavior of colonial subjects in "the school" of Americanization. For example, "School Begins" (1898), published in *Puck* magazine, depicts the newly acquired colonies of Guam, Puerto Rico, Cuba, and the Philippines as children of color under the tutelage of Uncle Sam. The behavior is a performance of US cultural ideals of whiteness based on the incorporation of acquired lands into states. Considering Puerto Rico's status as unincorporated, the project of behaving and performing will never lead to incorporation but to allegiance and conformity to the US government. In this scene in *Lectura Infantil*, Ginorio affirms views present also in the faux historical readers authored by US authors: the success of colonial institutions is contingent upon how well Puerto Ricans perform as Americans. There is little confidence that US institutions themselves, as transplanted into Puerto Rican culture, will produce Americans. Ultimately, this scene with La Maestra and the children provides a Puerto Rican-authored version of Uncle Sam. The role transforms into a motherly, light-skinned Spanish-speaking teacher, though with the same characteristics of guardian, savior, and taskmaster. And administrator of white supremacy.

### Treintistas, Autora-cátedras, and Transnationalism

Ginorio's series of readers unite, as a schooling project, to the formation and rise of the Generación 30, a group of mostly male writers and intellectuals "committed to articulating a sense of Puerto Rican cultural identity in the face of US colonialism," as Vanessa Pérez-Rosario writes in her study of Julia de Burgos, *Becoming Julia* (2014). The Treintistas, positioned as those experiencing the shift in sovereignty, provide some of the hallmarks of Puerto Rican national literature, centering the novel and the essay as the chosen mode for contemplating Latin American existence. Antonio S. Pedreira's famed *Insularismo: Ensayos de Interpretación Puertoriqueña* (1934) is a definitive work of this time, with his concepts of Puerto Rican insularity, isolation, fragmentation, and, of course, his coined term "aplatanao," referring to what he saw as Puerto Ricans' dejection and despondency over their political and social relationship to the world. Scholars rarely consider reading practices and schooling alongside the development of Generación 30. How did US colonial schooling nurture a generation of writers for at least ten to fifteen years before Treintistas begin dominating literary circles with images of docile, isolated Puerto Ricans and colonialism itself as a malady? Trientista images were, to an extent, a reiteration of US writers' depictions of Puerto Rico and its people. School readers began priming young Puerto Ricans to uphold cultural, rather than political, nationalism as early as the first phase of US colonial schools, so it is no surprise why resolutions such as political independence and even statehood seem less palatable and sustainable options for Puerto Rican leaders and future generations. The 1930s also exhibited a trend in Latin American poetry toward the avant-garde or vanguardia, which Pérez-Rosario analyzes as "marked by autochthonous concerns, a focus on nationalist and Antillean cultural affirmation, African cultural influences, and an Americanist continental orientation" (17). Folklore was no longer privileged in conversations about youth literacy and pedagogy. Instead, readers and anthologies produced by Puerto Rican women educators became a space for experimenting with new styles of poetry. Into the 1930s and by the 1940s, women writers dominated the production of readers and anthologies diverting from Treintista preferences for essays and novels. Here, I reflect on the influences of vanguardia sensibilities for the cosmic, Antillean, Indigenous, and African undertones on women educators as opposed to the

Hispanic-centric curriculum tools of Juncos and Arellanos. The influence of vanguardia, and its turn toward a more highbrow tradition of poetry as education, might be traced to Juan Ramon Jiménez's history as a Spanish exile in Puerto Rico. The poet's influence on Boricua feminist pedagogies tell another story which encourages oral traditions and a transnational portrayal of Puerto Rico and its diaspora.

I use the term "autora-cátedras" to describe the work of women educators so as to emphasize the multifaceted role of these women as both writers and educators, and moreover as working in those roles simultaneously. Literary scholarship on Puerto Rican women has tended to erase women's work in newspapers, libraries, and the classroom, specifically as cuenteras and creators of curriculum materials, perhaps because school readers and curriculum often fall out of the radar of what is deemed as literature. At the same time, the aesthetic, political, and social value of women's writing for children in Latin American and the Caribbean often goes unnoticed. The work of Ángeles Pastor, Ester Feliciano Mendoza, Isabel Freire de Matos, Carmen Gómez Tejara, and Flor Piñerio de Rivera—all teachers and professors of education at the University of Puerto Rico—would be impossible to document and analyze in one chapter, let alone one section. However, I briefly address the ways these autora-cátedras counter, in the second half of the twentieth century, the supposed docility and dependency of Puerto Ricans demonstrated by the earlier group of male writers such as Juncos and Ginorio which reflected the US colonial project. When the University of Puerto Rico began offering degrees in education as part of a two-year teacher's certificate program in the 1940s, many of the professors who participated were former teachers who also wrote the textbooks for the program. This program became a way for many Puerto Rican women to partake in professional careers and generate income for working families (Del Moral).[1] This group emphasizes poetry and songs as the essence of literacy and the literary, as opposed to the essay and novel forms favored by Treintistas.

The endurance of poetry and music as the primary genres for youth literature continues in contemporary Puerto Rico. Poetry, both as a kind of ethereal concept and aesthetic, was instituted as *the* language of the Puerto Rican child in 1935 by a renowned Spanish poet, Juan Ramón Jiménez. Jiménez's intervention on youth literature in Puerto Rico came through his perspective on the relationship between creativity, art, and youth. His time as an exile in Puerto Rico, during the height of fascism in Spain and Europe, aligned him with questions of liberty and autonomy in the school of vanguardia. His famous work *Platero y Yo* (1914), an endearing tale about a young boy and his donkey, was frequently recited to children throughout Latin American and the Caribbean. Jiménez identified himself with the plight of impoverished Puerto Rican children, crediting these children as his inspiration while in exile, creating the first poetry festivals in Puerto Rico in 1935, El Festival de la Poesia y el Niño. The festival launched his series of free poetry anthologies, *Verso y prosa para niños* (1935), featuring renowned poets in Latin American and throughout the world, including Nicaraguan Rubén Darío, Chilean Gabriela Mistral, and Indian Rabindranath Tagore. This group of poets, as part of the education of Puerto Rican youth, grafted in revolutionary and nationalist sensibilities to the curriculum, emphasizing the aesthetic and performance of poetry beyond affirming proper pronunciation, as seen in Ginorio's texts. When considering the education and literature of Puerto Rican children, Jiménez, in the 1930s, creates a bridge in youth literature between a generation seeking to preserve Spanish culture while containing revolutionary thinking and a generation embracing the aesthetics of poetry as an ideal and metaphor for unification, transnationalism, and liberation. At the opening of the Festival de la Poesia y El Niño, Jiménez spoke of the Puerto Rican child as a creative force, breaking with the Hispanic tradition of representing the economically impoverished as also being culturally deficient. He emphasizes the culturally rich though economically impoverished:

> The Puerto Rican child, attracting all the color of Paradise, the poor child above all, has moved me profoundly. I have met this poor child often, walking that difficult road of his first life, in the city and the country; I have stopped him in front of me, I have stopped in front of him and I have asked him what he most wanted. "A book ..." (qtd. in Gull-on, 64)

Jiménez's approach to young people as readers is distinct from the paternalistic school of Juncos. Jiménez depicts children as teachers and leaders, the ones who know and originate the desire for books and stories. He places the child as in partnership with the adults, as opposed to simply standing on their shoulders, as in Juncos images of ancestry. Jiménez also positions the Puerto Rican child as containing the essential qualities of the nation and community—indeed, he represents these children as portals of history. In his vision, the child itself is a text:

> The old man and the old woman of Puerto Rico, with all the echoes of the life of their race, with all the colors and adornments of body and soul repeated by the years, their labyrinths grafted into their skin, all these things squeezed together, dry and final, they are impossible.

Inside, the child, as a synthetic prelude, reunites the possible and impossible. We cannot forget the material and immaterial vision, this
logical and illogical, this death and life of a child walking on a path,
through a door, under a palm tree, under the sun or rain or moon. All
of the paradisiacal oasis within this clear and nebulous exceptional
island of life and death, is still soft clay, a marvelous compendium,
within these little, indescribable beings . . . (22)

Jiménez's description demonstrates the complex ways in which literary figures have portrayed Puerto Rican youth in terms of contradictions. Yet, the
side-by-side contradictions, including violent imagery, in this child are the
very things making him/her "marvelous." All the fragments, mysteries, and
matters of life and death exist as possibilities in a "child walking on a path,
through a door, under a palm tree, under the sun or rain or moon." The
Puerto Rican child's ability to hold contradictions in tension and gather
limitless creative possibilities seems tied to multiracial identities, a stark
contrast to the ways in which US writers presented multiracial peoples as
savage mongrels. His perspective marks a movement—"a poetic harvest"—
according to literary historian and scholar Piñerio de Rivera, who cites him
as a "direct stimulus" and a figure "exert[ing] a powerful influence on the
development of children's literature. He set a high standard of excellence in
the literature for children" (25).

I suggest that a feminist school of thought developed around Jiménez's
harvest during a time when patriarchal traditions upheld essays, folklore,
and novels as the means to intellectual and artistic expression. This feminist
school, relying on poetry as an aesthetic of liberation and transnationalism, joined Puerto Rico and its children to the larger movements outside
the Americas and the world. Ángeles Pastor, Feliciano Mendoza, Piñeiro de
Rivera, Carmen Gomez Tejera, and Isabel Freire de Matos are responsible
for some of the most enduring and beloved books and treatise on Puerto
Rican education of the past generation, including countless manuals, textbooks, and philosophies on children's theatre, poetry, and art. Most Puerto
Ricans attending public schools between the 1940s and 1980s would have
read the Laidlow series of books centering on Pepe and Lola, many which
were written by Ángeles Pastor. The books were so ubiquitous that they were
also taught in New York City public schools during the second Great Puerto
Rican Migration of the 1950s (Jiménez-Garcia, "Old Forgotten Children's
Books at CUNY" 2016). The transnational aspect of these texts reflect a
creative exploration of Puerto Rican identity apart from the rigid tropes and
types offered by US and Puerto Rican authored rhetoric of the first part of

the century reflecting Puerto Ricans as broken. Indeed, I would argue that the sense of colonial malaise and brokenness was only presented as true for Puerto Rican adults. When referring to children, and writing about children and for children, Puerto Rican thinkers and writers presented young people as the hope of recovering and regaining what adults had lost. If anything, the trauma of colonialism seemed to advantage young people, transforming into almost exceptional poetic, gifted children.

Ideologically, the shift toward the creation of the commonwealth meant a reinvention of Puerto Rico a as land of American progress and a bridge to the Americas—in other words, a land of the future. The reinvention of Puerto Rico as a commonwealth was both US- and Puerto Rican-driven, and begin showing up in texts for young readers in the late 1950s through the 1970s. For the US, stories of island progress and industry are a quick contrast, and contradiction, to how US writers presented the island upon arrival—that is, as a primitive place of disease and chaos. Forty years later, Puerto Rico still functioned as a military occupation by the US, with governors elected by military rulers, many of whom had served in the Spanish-American War. Yet, Puerto Rico's elite leaders, such as Luis Muñoz Rivera, continued lobbying US Congress for a path to self-governance, which would lead to the creation of the commonwealth, or the Estado Libre Asociado, which ratified its own constitution in 1952. The US and newly elected Puerto Rican government, led by Luis Muñoz-Marín, the first elected governor of Puerto Rico, in 1947 began a series of initiatives meant to modernize the island through rapid industrialization and exportation of Puerto Ricans as cheap labor; this initiative would become known as Project Bootstrap. A major part of economic reform policy supervised by policy makers, including Teodoro Moscoso and Muñoz-Marin, was a kind of explosion of almost half the island's population by the Puerto Rican government—this was the largest Puerto Rican diaspora to the US metropolis, referred to by Gonzalez in *Harvest of Empire* (2000).

Outwardly, in the US, another tradition of readers for young people emerges around Operation Bootstrap in the 1950s and early 1960s, highlighting the creation of the Estado Libre Asociado and continuing the approach of writing youth literature as faux anthropological and historical. Edna McGuire's *Puerto Rico: Bridge to Freedom* (1963) was written well past Operation Bootstrap, but it perhaps best captures the celebratory rhetoric associated with US and Puerto Rican progress of the time. McGuire emphasizes a key theme identified by Matos-Rodriguez in US promises of progress: the characterization of Puerto Rico as an "experimental site for US capital." McGuire highlights an international consensus at the time of Puerto Rico as a "'bridge' or 'laboratory' between the US and Latin America" (Matos-Rodriquez, 40).

Matos-Rodriquez writes that "[t]he image of Puerto Rico as a bridge or a test case of US-Latin American relations—rendered with extraordinary power from the 1940s to the 1960s under the local leadership of the Popular Democratic Party (PPD) and recently resuscitated in a more Pan-Caribbean version—was created during the early decades of the twentieth century" (40). The image of the bridge, so prevalent in both US and Puerto Rican rhetoric (a bridge between the US and Latin America; a "middle way" between nation and state), extends into depictions of Puerto Rican diaspora culture. In the tradition of anthropological literature, McGuire's *Bridge to Freedom* opens with a dedication ("TO JOHN, whose faith in the ability of free people to solve their problems inspired this book"), an acknowledgment of "the time I spent doing research in Puerto Rico," and the prerequisite map. The inclusion of Muñoz-Marin's forward emphasizes US-Puerto Rico camaraderie, while also gesturing toward the tradition of a native informant who validates the narrative. The book claims to have been authored by several correspondents, although it is not clear if these are anthropologists or reporters sent to the island. The book features a sense of US-Puerto Rico camaraderie through a foreword from the governor at the time, Muñoz-Marin. Muñoz-Marin's writing contains equal amounts of hospitality and tension. To the US "young friends and readers," he writes, "your fellow United States citizens in Puerto Rico are very like you in their passion for liberty and love of democracy" (vii). Muñoz-Marin, however, centers his argument on the cultural differences rather than the similarities between Puerto Rican and US children. His stance is in tandem with Juncos's ideal of a Puerto Rican ancestral legacy while embracing Spanish and poetry, as opposed to folklore, as modes of cultural difference: "They differ from you largely in their cultural background. Puerto Rican children learn Spanish at their mothers' knees, are sung to sleep with Spanish lullabies, and—as they grow older—thrill to the cadences of poets like Rubén Darío, García Lorca, and their own Llorens Torres" (vii). The reference to poetry and culture advocates for a kind of cultural sovereignty which the new commonwealth would strive to possess while serving as a global village. Puerto Rico, according to Muñoz-Marin, acts as a "working-level United Nations," and as an experiment for developing agricultural nations into industrial modernization (viii). Muñoz-Marin romanticizes the Puerto Rican child's Latin American upbringing. At the same time, his description provides a rare glimpse for US readers of a distinct Latin American culture with a separate language and literary heritage. Muñoz-Marin, then, emphasizes a thriving, bilingual, industrial, and progressive society imagined during the years of Operation Bootstrap. His vision, however, participates in the US and Puerto Rican government project of denial and erasure surrounding narratives of progress. If Puerto Rico was such a land of opportunity, why had over 400,000 Puerto Ricans left for the US? If Puerto Rico was a land of progress, *who* had access to this progress and capital, besides US businesses?

In Puerto Rico, the reinvention as a Latin American commonwealth, I would argue, was culturally sustained by the work of the auto-cátedras. Indeed, the harvest of poetry credited by Piñeiro de Rivera precedes the formation of the commonwealth. Autora-cátedras planted seeds of resistance in these texts, fostering transnational thought and also fostering the idea of Puerto Rican culture as tied to the greater Americas, as even Muñoz-Marin implies in his forward to *Bridge to Freedom*. However, more than the previous generations of writer educators, taking cues from Jiménez's poetry anthologies, the generation of the auto-cátedras, such as Ángeles Pastor, craft stories through poetry, emphasizing orality and relying on the concept of children as sites for limitless possibilities. These texts seamlessly blend joyful stories, told in verse, about the Puerto Rican flora and fauna while also celebrating technological progress such as trains, roadways, and airports—yet they do so in a way which portray children as inquisitive participants in the stories about their land and as participating in imagining ways forward. Moreover, the auto-cátedras allowed for space to represent the reality of a "Puerto Rican nation on the move" into the 1960s and 1970s (Duany 2002). For the purpose of this section, I will focus on two examples from the later work of Ángeles Pastor and Carmen Gomez Tejera, *Amigos de Aqui y Alla* (1961) and *Conozcamos a Puerto Rico* (1972). The proliferation of books by these women writers means they educated school-age children at the formation of the commonwealth and into the time of neorican migration—that is, when thousands of Puerto Ricans who had migrated to the mainland US as children moved back to the island as adults.

*Amigos de Aqui y Alla*, to some extent, represents a primer on circular migration, what Luis Rafael Sanchez dramatized in 1994 in his story, "La Guagua Aérea" / "The Airbus" (1994). The staple characters of the series, Pepé, Lola, and Mota (the cat), make room for Dan, a young boy who arrives from New York and describes the city to his classmates. Dan's story portrays the benefits of modern transportation for conveying Puerto Rican children back and forth from two seemingly magical worlds: Puerto Rico and New York. In contrast to how Ginorio's readers presented Puerto Rican children as passive participants in schooling, Pastor and Tejara depict Dan, a boy recently arrived from New York, as teaching his classmates and his teachers about New York. The schoolchildren, who have never left the island, wonder at how he traveled from such a far-off place and he tells them he took "en avión / an airplane." In an interesting exchange, one of the children asks, "What are the airports like in New York, Dan?" To that, Dan responds as follows: "I imagine the are like the ones here in Puerto Rico." This line allows Pastor and Tejara to resist the idea of Puerto Rico as a stagnant place, seemingly frozen in a world of archetypes and folklore. In particular, the symbols of transformation and movement are associated with US initiatives. Dan himself is product of his circular migration, yet Pastor and Tejara break tradition with a dominant culture in Puerto Rico and the US of depicting migration as causing fragmentation, confusion, malaise, and even death (Flores 2010). The school children and the teacher also display curiosity and agency in their desire to learn more as opposed to expressing fear or passivity. Pastor and Tejara's depiction of the teacher clearly breaks from Ginorio's Maestra, as when they depict her asking Dan to lead a discussion about New York and specifically using a book which Dan brings about the city: "Dan, los niños no saben muchas cosas de Nueva York. / Dan, the children don't know many things about New York. No saben de su aeropuerto. / They don't know about its airport. Esta es una cosa nueva para ellos. / This is a new thing to them." Dan lifts up his book in front of the classroom and starts his lesson.

> (Dan) En este libro se ven muchas cosas de Nueva York. / This book has many things about New York.
> Miren que grande es el aeropuerto de Nueva York. See how large the airport is in New York.
> Se ven muchos aviones. / You see many airplanes.
>
> (La Señorita) Miren niños. / Look children
>
> (Dan) Aqui se ve la ciudad de Nueva York. / Here, you can see the City of New York.
> Es una ciudad muy grande y bonita. / It's a very large and beautiful city.
> Le llaman la ciudad / They call it the city
> De los rascacielos. / Of Skyscrapers.
>
> (Niños/Children) Rascacielos? / Skyscrapers?
>
> (Dan) Son casas muy elevadas. / They are like really tall houses.
> Trenes bajo tierra. / It has trains that go under the earth.
> Míralos en mi libro / You can see them in my book (50–51).

Pastor and Tejara represent children from the diaspora bringing important stories and ideas into the classroom, as opposed to empty receptacles that need to behave. Migration is portrayed as a magical journey in which one can take an airplane on a small island and journey to an enormous, beautiful city with otherworldly trains that are able to travel underground. The story perhaps functions as an effort to counter negative stereotypes which Puerto Ricans held about Nuyoricans coming to Puerto Rico. Indeed, the term "Nuyorican" begins as a way for islanders to mock the authenticity of migrants. Pastor and Tejara present the child from the city as being welcomed into the classroom; dialogue about his experiences is encouraged by the teacher and the other children.

Beyond this classroom scene, the book resists insularity through a trope of airplanes and stargazing. The children in *Amigos de Aqui y Allá* are often depicted as contemplating the possibilities and worlds away from Puerto Rico. For example, in one memorable story panel, children launch paper planes at the sky, wondering how far they will travel. Symbolically, in Puerto Rican youth literature, images of travel have also been used to contemplate the Puerto Rican nation. For example, Pastor and Tejara's paper planes joins with Hostos's revolutionary vision of the Puerto Rican nation, as an Antillean nation, in *En Barco de Papel* (in which Hostos tells the story of the struggle for Antillean sovereignty through the metaphor of a paper boat). Given the amount of time children have spent learning about planes in *Amigos de Aqui y Allá*, the paper plane—which the children begin imagining as a "cohete" or "rocket"—suggests a metaphor about the current Puerto Rican nation. Children dream about a plane/rocket that can touch the stars: "[El avion] se ve como uno estrella que va a la Luna. Se vein las estrellas y la Luna en el cielo" (88–89). Migration to the US is painted within the context of space travel and exploring the stars, making it serve as a metaphor for limitless possibilities. Simultaneously, this world of children's learning and play intersects with images of labor and struggle. On the next page, after Dan's story, an illustration invites young readers to recall objects and people from Nueva York. The illustration is of a tree with ten branches which hold illustrations of the airport, skyscrapers, the subway, and men working construction and doing carpentry, among other things (66–67). On the opposite page, a list of words is juxtaposed by illustrations of things like houses and Christmas stockings.

In *Conozcamos a Puerto Rico*, Pastor and Guzman introduce a series of tales that continue to trace the movement along Puerto Rico's many faces and reinventions including stories of Indigenous civilization, Spanish settler colonization, and African folk life. The work of Pastor, as with these primers, might be categorized as promoting racial harmony, while still relegating Black lives to particular places on the island (Flores 2010). For example, "Una fiesta de Loíza" tells the story of Diego, a child preparing for the Fiesta de Santiago Apóstol. Luis is depicted as a light-skinned Puerto Rican child, but the illustrations of the people at the festival center on Afro-Boricuas. In other words, the stories and illustrations depict dark-skinned Puerto Ricans and children as participating as festival entertainers, and light-skinned children as those who are entertained. Representations of Afro-Boricua lives may have progressed since the days of Juncos and Ginorio, but the tendency to relegate Black lives to entertainment and to certain places in Puerto Rico testifies to a persistent denial of Black centrality in Puerto Rican culture.

Pastor's highlighting of Loíza, however, as a location in Puerto Rican literary imagination also embraces a kind of Antillean, racial, transnational harmony, and aesthetic in tandem with one of the most famous, revolution-ary poems about Loíza, Julia de Burgos's "Río Grande de Loíza." Pastor's "Rio Grande de Loíza" literally runs through *Conozcamos a Puerto Rico*, as if purposefully dividing the primer in half. For too long, these texts have fallen out of the purview of scholarship without critical reflection on the choices and writing women educators brought to the pages of Puerto Rican textbooks, as well as the stories and counter-stories they brought to circulate in commonwealth classrooms. This reader tradition is certainly not radical for upholding a racial status quo, for example, we see how Blackness appears segregated from normative Puerto Rican culture. However, I suggest that these juxtapositions are purposeful and are one way in which autora-cátedras advocate for more radical politics for sovereignty in full view of the Puerto Rican and US governments. A revolutionary writer such as de Burgos would certainly have been edited out of the US tradition of readers. Here, while there is no mention of Julia de Burgos, nor of Pastor's intentions on including the poem, Pastor writes a version of the poem for this school-age audience. More than anything, Pastor chooses to capitalize on the symbolism of the great river as a powerful river of memories, pain, and stories. In particular, the river speaks of its access to the great and "deep" Atlantic Ocean and tells the children about the town's Indigenous past: "Recerda con dolor estas cosas y entonces since querer, crecen sus aguas. Corre veloz por cerros y plantíos, y barre todo lo que encuentra en su paso" / The river remembers these sad things and without warning its waters surge and grow. The water runs with great force through valleys and neighborhoods and levels everything it finds in its path" (105). The river's great force comes through its capacity to re-member painful memories, and through its pain, it can destroy anything in its way. The inclusion of this poem harkens to the revolutionary thinking of writers such as de Burgos and Hostos, respectively, which US writers and the earlier generation of Puerto Rican writers fought to contain.

Pastor's message about the power of stories and memories to destroy anything in their path—sweeping away human-made systems and structures such as houses and buildings—also speaks to the power of remembering an ancestral past tied to decolonization, or a time when neither Spain nor the US ruled Puerto Rico. It is an image I return to in my last chapter with an examination of contemporary works by the island's authors during the economic decline and since Hurricane Maria. In no small way, children, in Puerto Rican youth traditions, were idealized for their ability to imagine beyond the limits of adults and capitalize on the cultural gains of migration while maintaining and honoring the past in ways which could literally destroy the human-made structures of colonialism. Children were vehicles for all the contradictions of the Puerto Rican experience, and the experience made them stronger while still in this limitless stage of childhood. In this chapter, I have asked scholars to consider how traditions of US- and Puerto Rican-illustrated primers have served to prime Puerto Rican children to serve (and also potentially resist) as loyal US subjects, and, for white US readers, to inherit colonial possessions and people. I have also argued that while US and Puerto Rican male writers continued to present Puerto Rican children as docile and vacant through a tradition of school readers, Boricua women writers found ways for revolutionary thinking to survive in children's literature. Unfortunately, anti-Black racism also survived, clouding the contributions of Afro-Boricuas to youth literature and culture—the subject of my next chapter.

Chapter Two

# FROM THE GROUND UP

## Pura Belpré, Arturo Schomburg, and Afro-Boricua Pedagogies of Literacy and Resistance

In order to understand the literary and cultural work of Pura Belpré and Arturo Schomburg, one must uncover the roots of literacy and community education in Afro-Boricua thought. One must consider how Blackness and anti-Blackness have shaped Puerto Rican and US literary histories and pedagogies from primary through higher education. US and Puerto Rican texts for young people testify to the centrality of Black culture in Puerto Rican folkways and education, as much as they do about how Blackness was cast in the margins of what qualified as American and Puerto Rican. As a case in point, consider the hallowed careers of Maestro Rafael Cordero and his sister Celestina Cordero, who founded public education projects for young Boricua boys and girls, respectively. These two inspire reverence in Puerto Rican circles, but are often pictured as anomalies rather than as part of a larger tradition of Black intellectual mothers and fathers in Puerto Rico.

"AfroLatinxs," according to Eric Velasquez, the award-winning author and illustrator of *Grandma's Records* (2004), *Grandma's Gift* (2013), and *Schomburg: The Man that Built a Library* (2017) "are the most underrepresented people in history and children's literature."[1] The whitewashing of Latinidad is something that Latinx Studies scholars such as Arlene Davila and Miriam Jimenez-Roman and Juan Flores have theorized about in great detail (Davila 2008; Jimenez-Roman and Flores 2009). The ways in which Latinxs, as a substantial diaspora community in the US, have represented to the so-called mainstream has often meant the erasure of Indigenous and AfroLatinx stories and bodies. However, youth literature, perhaps more than any other kind of literature, is inseparable from AfroLatinx foundations, specifically Afro-Boricua, through the work of Pura Belpré and Arturo Schomburg. Yet, the erasure of Blackness from the roots of youth literature—and even more dreadfully, the roots of Latinx youth literature—is a particular predicament. This chapter seeks to render visible the Afro-Boricua literacies and

71

epistemologies which made Latinx youth literature a possibility and a tradition in the US. Belpré and Schomburg provide an opportunity to contemplate the politics of space and embodiment, and the failure to remember Black contributions and bodies converging.

The freedoms available to Boricua cultural-producers through talleres and library spaces, as opposed to traditional classroom spaces is central to my study. Theorizing and reflecting on community-based education is necessary in relationship to the development of children's literature on the archipelago, a literary tradition rooted in a school system at the service of Puerto Rican and US governments. The cultivation of spaces for creative expression and liberatory pedagogies makes for a fundamental part of Puerto Ricans' struggle for literary and cultural arts. Miguel Algarín, the poet and cofounder of the Nuyorican Poet's Cafe, writes in his essay "Nuyorican Literature" about the necessity of space for art and even healing, but more specifically, what he calls "transformation before the public eye." Algarín writes about how he and his colleagues sought to "create spaces where people can express themselves and create that space expressly for that purpose, and you open it three to four times a week, and you wait, and your public will come, and they will bring their writings. And if you, as guide of the space, have a generosity of spirit, you will find that you will have created a center for the expression of self and for people to transform themselves before the public eye" (Algarín, 92). Interaction with the public in this passage has as much to do with visibility as with creative transformation. Moreover, it calls attention to the oppression possible when denying people these spaces.

Youth literature and culture in the US is inseparable from the role of public libraries and the work of librarians of color. A discussion of children's and young adult literature is always a discussion of access to the literary establishment as an institution that functions much like a pipeline: Who had access to the publishing industry, literary salons, collections, and archives? For example, US military and government leaders invading Puerto Rico in 1898 denied literary value to anything outside of written English-language texts as historical documentation. More to the point, some children's texts were created for the sole purpose of standing in as historical documentation to the US public—even without eyewitness accounts or evidence. Simultaneously, texts authored in Spanish by Puerto Rican elite like Eugenio Maria de Hostos were invisibilized in this initial encounter. Further, writers and educators such as Juncos stepped in to create and translate a tradition of readers for Puerto Rican children by the 1920s and the rise of US colonial schools. Pura Belpré and Arturo Schomburg underline the importance of affecting social and political change to the literary establishment through

interdisciplinary means, utilizing written and performance-based pedagogies. Belpré and Schomburg also exemplify the public library, as opposed
to the school room or publishing house, as a space for establishing and
sustaining intellectual and cultural practices for communities of color. Scholarship on Belpré and Schomburg is currently in a resurgence thanks to the
foundational work of Flor Piñeiro de Rivera, Lisa Sanchez-Gonzalez, Victoria
Nuñez, and Vanessa K. Valdes. Previously, I have focused on Belpré indi-
vidually, though always in tandem with Schomburg, but this chapter delves
much more into a collective project Belpré and Schomburg participated
in, along with Augusta Baker, to create spaces and stories that documented
Black lives—a project that aims to counter historical erasure in US and Latin
American and Caribbean cultures.

Belpré and Schomburg, in concert with Baker, helped create a kind of
living archive and cultural renaissance that occurred for the communities of
color they served in 1920–1930s-era Harlem. Instead of presenting Latinxs
and African American history as running parallel, my approach interweaves
the literary and cultural histories of Latinx, US, and African American youth
literature and youth culture in order to render the contributions of Puerto
Ricans visible. This is especially important when locating Afro-Boricua
epistemologies. Linda Tuhiwai Smith, in *Decolonizing Methodologies* (2012),
reminds scholars that research itself is "a site of struggle between the interests and ways of knowing of the West and the interest and ways of resisting
the Other." Tuhiwai Smith underlines that especially in addressing research
on colonized populations "the collective memory of imperialism has been
perpetuated through the ways in which knowledge about Indigenous peoples
was collected, classified, and then represented in various ways back to the
West and then through the eyes of the West, back to those who have been
colonized" (2). As is the case in cataloguing literature and criticism in the
academy, terms such as "American," "Latino," "Black," and "African American"
have racialized national histories that are sometimes divorced from public and/or scholarly conversations about people of color. This tendency in
academic study to emphasize ethnicity and race as somehow homogenous
reflects colonial logics in terms of a void of historical context and specificity
which all of the writers and artists I center in *Side by Side* resist through the
creation of youth literature and culture (Mignolo 2007). Authors I discuss in
this book as Afro-Boricuas, including Arturo Schomburg and Pura Belpré,
are rarely analyzed in concert with African American and Latinx youth traditions due to long-standing approaches to Blackness as an organizing factor
in US and Latin American literary study, youth or otherwise. Authors were
incorporated into African American Studies and others into Latinx Studies,

but on the whole these writers lack visibility in US literature and culture. It should come as no surprise that individuals from marginalized communities, accustomed to erasure through categorizations, would consider cataloging and information services a critical place for intervention. The role played by libraries and archival collections, as testaments to historical memory, in the lives of young people, particularly during the formation of these kind of positions in the US, is also no coincidence.

Puerto Rican youth literature and culture is rooted in conceptions of history whether writers have viewed texts as documenting history, countering stereotypes, recovering the past, and restorying and reimagining the present. I draw a distinction between reimagining and restorying the past, though these two processes work together. Ebony Elizabeth Thomas and Amy Stornaiuolo argue that the restorying plays an important role in how communities take ownership of the narratives connected to their lived experiences (2016). Drawing on the work of Chimamanda Ngozi Adichie's important claims in her 2009 TED Talk about "the danger of the single story," Thomas and Stornaiuolo underline how

> Adichie emphasizes that storying is always connected to power—who can tell stories, how many, when, and under what circumstances—and that some stories, if told often enough, can become the sine qua non of a person, a group, or a nation. When people only have access to a single story—one that simplifies and flattens the complexity of human experience and excludes many perspectives from being represented—they can become constrained in what they imagine to be possible. However, when readers see themselves reflected in texts or read stories about people like them, they can more fully participate in the storying process.

Restorying provides communities with a sense of ownership and connects to imagining new possibilities. However, as Velasquez emphasizes, reimagining the past also depends on structural power; what is imagined may also result in erasure. Speaking of his own research into the Afro-Boricua past, Velasquez cautions against how reimagining may lead to "eliminating" knowledge(s) and peoples (interview). A community might reimagine a past that negates the contributions and centrality of Black culture. Reimagining and restorying depends on groups' seeking empowerment and whether such empowerment depends on the disempowerment of others, potentially replicating colonial and racist paradigms. The many reimaginings of Puerto Rico through colonial infrastructures, Spain, the US, and now, the Federal Oversight Board appointed by the US Congress, makes its potential for erasure at each of these reimaginings more dangerous for its most vulnerable communities, particularly those of color.

The Afro-Boricua epistemologies I highlight through Belpré and Schomburg pivot on the interrelationship between the past and future, in which restorying, through archiving, collecting, cataloging, storytelling, and publishing, function to empower youth of color for the generations. I focus on epistemologies that emerge from Schomburg and Belpré's work in conversation, considering Schomburg was the one who "pleaded" with Belpré to write for children (Piñeiro, 42). These epistemologies include an approach to collections and storytelling as Sankofa ("go back and get it" in Swahili), which centers Black wisdom and dignity in the process of restorying, as opposed to the false racial harmony of *la gran familia puertorriqueña*, a foundational narrative in Puerto Rican literature and culture. In Belpré's case, I also conceptualize how Sankofa as pedagogy is tied to a radical return to a precolonial past/present in her unpublished tales such as "Ines." For both, Schomburg and Belpré, I emphasize how they contributed to a collective renaissance of Black and Brown people in Harlem in the 1920s, providing young people with tools for decolonizing the imagination.

## DIASPORIC BLACKNESS, SANKOFA, AND THE REIMAGINING AND RESTORYING OF HISTORY: A MODEL FOR AFRO-BORICUA PUBLIC PEDAGOGIES

"AfroLatinx," as a term, challenges the false though implied racial harmony in Latin American and Caribbean concepts of race and *mestizaje*. Beyond Blackness as informing difference and othering, I emphasize Blackness as an aesthetic and critical set of tools in the lives of Belpré and Schomburg, which enabled them to build safe havens for young Boricuas navigating US institutions. In viewing Blackness as an aesthetic, a framework, and a practice, I am holding to what Miriam Jiménez-Roman and Juan Flores note in *The AfroLatin@ Reader* (2010):

> Afro-Latin@ also means the distinctive and unique phenomenological experience lived at a personal level by people who are both Black and Latin@ in all aspects of their social life. Aside from and lending human concreteness to the larger historical and structural dimensions outlined above, the way that Afro-Latin@s navigate their social identities as they intersect with other Latin@s and with other Blacks is unique to them. (14)

In terms of the storying and restorying of Puerto Rican history, Velasquez underscores how Afro-Boricuas—among the most literate and educated community during Spanish rule—have been silenced in historical portrayals and left out of definitions of the nation. Certainly, textbooks and readers for young Puerto Ricans tend to segregate Black life and culture to particular regions of the island, as seen in Pastor and Guzman's *Conozcamos a Puerto Rico* (1972). This kind of regulating fits with a paradigm of racial harmony that strives for a vision of equality, though not equity. In "Broken English Memories" (1996), Flores describes historical memory as a process that resembles restorying:

> Historical memory is an active, creative force, not just a receptacle for the dead weight of times gone by. Memory has been associated, since its earliest usages, with the act of inscribing, engraving, or, in a sense that carries over into our own electronic times, "recording" (grabar). It is not so much the record itself as the putting-on-record, the gathering and sorting of materials from the past in accordance with the needs and interests of the present. Remembering thus always involves selecting and shaping, constituting out of what was something that never was yet now assuredly is, in the imaginary of the present, and in the memory of the future. And the process of memory is open, without closure or conclusion; the struggle to (re)establish continues and to tell the 'whole' story only uncovers new breaks and new exclusions." (49)

Centering the work of AfroLatinxs calls for a consideration of the "breaks and exclusions" surrounding Black culture, particularly of free Black culture and enterprise in Puerto Rico. Velasquez suggests that Puerto Rico's continual historical re-imaginings often comes at the expense of Afro-Boricua intellectual and cultural contributions. For example, colonial histories and enterprises cast Black Puerto Ricans as ignorant, impoverished, and/or exceptional. A particular trope which emerges from the legends surrounding Maestro Rafael and Celestina Cordero—one that requires contextualization in any engagement with Afro-Boricua lives and literacies—is the exceptional Negro. A similar trend of using Schomburg and Belpré's legacies while suppressing their centrality to either Black or Latinx cultures repeats even in contemporary attempts to memorialize them. Either they are seen as exceptional and extraordinary, or they are not seen at all. Yet, just as Black culture is responsible for the rise of public education in Puerto Rico, Black culture is also responsible for the foundation of public literacy and archival projects for the Puerto Rican diaspora. This foundation supplemented the lack of visibility and care found in US classrooms, from primary through higher education.

Rafael Cordero and his family, including his father, mother, and sister Celestina, who opened a school for young women before Rafael, model the kind of strong literacy practices prevalent in the lives of free Blacks in Puerto Rico, practices that are deeply embedded in the fabric of Puerto Rican knowledge production. His own education and his taller-escuela provide a window into kinds of pedagogies arising from free Black culture. Jack and Irene Delano's bilingual picture book, *En Busque del Maestro Rafael / In Search of Teacher Rafael Cordero* (1994), published by El Editorial de la Universidad de Puerto Rico, is the only nonfiction picture book account of Cordero, among the few that exist, accessible to young readers. The Delanos based the book on historical documents and biographies written by Cordero's many students, among them author Salvador Brau. The picture book renders visible the lives of free Blacks in San Juan, Puerto Rico's large port city and an enclave for free Black culture and business during the Spanish Empire. Yet, as with any historical rendering, the picture book also offers opportunities to consider the omissions. Many accounts of Cordero's life exhibit the kinds of racist stereotypes about Blacks in the Caribbean tied to racial hierarchy. For example, descriptions of Cordero, even by his beloved students, as "negro pero con el corazón blanco" (Black but with a white heart) underline how Blackness is ascribed to depravity and deficiency while whiteness stands in for pure and good. As writers, the Delanos resist the idea of Cordero as an exceptional Black due to some kind of super moral character, yet the picture book is meant to spotlight the story as peculiar. Indeed, the narration highlights the almost unbelievable story of Cordero and his desire to open a free school for children of all races in his tobacco shop with almost no financial means:

> [A] cigarmaker by trade, stubbornly persists in trying to lift his people out of ignorance by teaching them reading, writing and human decency. For year after year, with the help of his sister Celestina, he keeps his school going, undaunted by poverty, a hostile slave society or the vagaries of a long line of aristocratic, military, Spanish governors. His pupils go on to become lawyers, doctors, and political leaders struggling to abolish slavery. (16)

The Delanos further a sense that Cordero's position as educated and as an educator at this time was exceptional in terms of Cordero's knowledge attainment as a free Black. Puerto Rico's free Black population lived in close proximity to the realities of enslavement, including skin-branding and auctions, in San Juan. San Juan itself is described by the Delanos as a city "in which everyone must know his proper place" (16). When the Delanos write that the Cordero household's educational aptitude and attainment was "the one thing distinguish[ing] them from most of their neighbors" and "an uncommon accomplishment for whites and even more so for blacks," the authors reveal how the vibrancy and contributions of Black culture remains veiled in Puerto Rican thought. More research needs to be done to recover the literacy practices of working-class Puerto Ricans before US arrival as a whole, but the field of AfroLatinxs studies and scholarly/public works, such as *The AfroLatin@ Reader* (2010) and Henry Louis Gates's PBS documentary *Black in Latin America* and *Finding Your Roots*, have academically and popularly helped shed light on the intellectual history of Blacks in the Caribbean. Illustrator and children's book author Velasquez attests that his research into the registers of his family in Santurce, Puerto Rico, during the Spanish Empire testifies to his Afro-Boricua grandmother's pride in her legacy of literacy and her insistence that he develop a love of reading and the arts. When he was struggling in design school, Velasquez said his grandmother told him, "'You come from a long line of educated, literate people. You are not going to be the one to mess up the chain' . . . I [Velasquez] am happy to report that every one of them [during 1870s–1880s] has a 'A'for 'Alfabeto,' marking them as literate in the registers" (interview).

My objective in bringing Cordero, and his pedagogical practices, in conversation with Schomburg and Belpré's work is to consider the centrality of Black thought in Puerto Rican cultural and literary projects for future generations, and to see it not as an anomaly, but as a tradition. Where did Rafael and Celestina's masterful teaching and knowledge come from? Delano illustrates Sotoreo Figueroa's biographical account of Cordero's education with a sketch of a young Black boy seated with an open book in front of him, encircled by his Black mother and father. In Figueroa's words, Cordero's parents took on Rafael's (and, we can presume, Celestina's) education after their Black children were denied entrance into the only school in San Juan that supposedly accepted white and Black children. Figueroa writes that these Afro-Boricua parents, "to the best of their modest abilities were solicitous and affectionate teachers" (27). The skilled proficiency in which Cordero's parents educated Rafael and Celestina, to the extent that they then became the most renowned educators of Puerto Rican children and the founders of public education, is admirable, but not an anomaly if we look into research on Afro-Boricua communities under Spanish rule who were business owners. In *En Busca del Maestro Rafael Cordero*, the Delanos ask the question: "How did they [Cordero's] parents learn how to read and write?" (26) They go on to speculate about white masters providing different kinds of instruction in "humility and obedience" for "field slaves" and "house slaves." However, birth certificates reveal that Rafael's parents were "free coloreds" (20). Regardless of how a Black person obtained free status, it remains that Rafael's parents were free Blacks teaching other free Blacks. In other words, his parents' learning and pedagogy cannot be attributed to white culture. Salvador Brau's account, in particular, gestures to Cordero's taller escuela as a tradition of community-based education led by women and free Blacks "all over the island": "Conducta observada en toda la isla por mujeres, algunas de ellas negras or mulatas manumisas, madres intelectuales de toda una generación de ambos sexos / [C]onduct practiced all over the island by women, some of them blacks or free Coloreds, intellectual mothers of an entire generation of both sexes" (40). This one glimpse is, however, not ever expounded on in Puerto Rican intellectual history. Such intellectual mothers, specifically Black women, stand veiled in our academic conversations about Puerto Rican intellectual life perhaps in a desire to see Black excellence as exceptional.

The tradition of Afro-Boricua literacy, autodidactism, and community-based education, in the face of racial discrimination and erasure, extends specific lessons about the cultivating of spaces and pedagogies for Puerto Rican youth. The Corderos symbolize a founding mythology of Puerto Rican education which various political movements in Puerto Rico have used to refute "US assertions of authority over the colonial school project" and "education by any means necessary" (Del Moral, 4). My intention is not to delve into the hypocrisies of how a Black teacher was used to sustain conceptions of racial harmony in Puerto Rico; Solsiree del Moral has already done a brilliant job at showing the nuances of how Maestro Rafael has been politicized and depoliticized. Instead, I am interested in teasing out a model of community-based education and methodologies rooted in Afro-Boricua lives. What sort of praxis emerges from cultures of free Black literacy which extend into the diaspora? Understanding that the Corderos form part of a larger tradition of community and family schooling, their example provides a glimpse into the Afro-Boricua pedagogies braided into Puerto Rican intellectual histories, advancing the futures of intellectual and cultural workers including Schomburg and Belpré.

One way to trace Cordero's intellectual imprint is to consider the intellectual work of his students and so begin tracing an intellectual genealogy of men and women through Afro-Boricua pedagogy. For example, Salvador Brau, José Julian Acosta, and Manuel Fernandez Juncos each took on distinctive projects of recovering history, whether through establishing archives, writing historical texts, or documenting folklore—all dedicated a considerable portion of their careers to historical preservation. Although Cordero's more privileged white students may have reproduced the study of history without an element of racial justice or revolutionary thinking, what if this attention to recovering history came through Cordero's tutelage? We know that Brau especially eulogized his old teacher, Cordero, as Vanessa K. Valdez writes, as "the right kind of black"—in other words, not as a subversive teacher or associated with the revolutionary thinking found in Haiti (48). Yet, I argue that Afro-Boricua pedagogies evidence transformative qualities which appear to transcend historical attempts to whitewash or define them. As scholars, we should examine the possibilities within these pedagogies beyond how an official canon of scholarship protecting a status quo decides to cast them. We might consider how these figures attached themselves to intellectual histories within and without the academy, pointing to the need for spaces outside the institution sustaining work inside institutions. Indeed, Valdés, writing about Schomburg, uses the term "intellectual genealogy" in referring to Cordero's students, Acosta and Brau. Schomburg writes in a letter in 1937 that the "works of José Julián Acosta and Salvador Brau have been my first inspiration to further an intense study of the Negro in America" (qtd. in Valdez, 27). Although Belpré attended the University of Puerto Rico, Belpré upheld the women in her family as her intellectual genealogy—perhaps the same group of "intellectual mothers" as those described by Brau—who trained her in stories and folklore she recounted at the NYPL. They were the ones who told her the stories she retold. However, Belpré also cites Juncos as a model for her written folkloric project. In her essays, Belpré praises Juncos's work in creating Puerto Rican authored texts and Spanish translations of US readers for young people in the early transition between Spain and the US empire. In her essay, "Writing for Bilingual Children," Belpré narrates Juncos's intervention:

> Finding the Spanish books inappropriate for the new teaching about to take place, the American government gave the island's educators three months to produce new class material exclusively in English, for English was imposed on the school system. The situation, which could have been tragic for the language, gave Don Manuel Fernandez Juncos—a Spaniard, poet, and scholar who loved Puerto Rico as his own country—the opportunity to compile a curriculum of literature written especially for children. (216)

Belpré notes how Juncos salvaged the Spanish language as a remnant of Puerto Rican culture, highlighting schooling practices as a way of sustaining local cultures. About Rafael Ramirez de Arellanos who wrote *Folklore Puertorriqueño*, Belpré wrote, "Don Rafael is more than a mere collector; he is a Puerto Rican interested in preserving the cultural legacy of his ancestors" (206). She continually deflected attention away from the formality of her role in folklore and placed it on a project of recovering ancestry and history: "I am neither a folklorist nor a collector, but like Don Rafael Ramirez de Arellano I also wanted to preserve for posterity the stories I heard in my home while growing up in Puerto Rico. I have retold them just as they were told to me by members of my family" (207). Her role in the US, as Belpré described it, would be "to preserve this folklore for the children in this new land. I knew that knowledge of his folklore would develop a sense of pride and identification in him" (209). Juncos's statement to child readers in *Antologia Puertoriqueña* underlines education through folk culture as a process of honoring antesores or ancestors. Could it be that when Juncos presents his anthology, in which he includes a selection about his beloved teacher to child readers as a means of honoring ancestors, Juncos is acting on Cordero's Afro-Boricua approach to education as intertwined with processes of revisiting and recovering history, cultivating a dialogue with, as well as honoring, ancestors? Juncos, Arellanos, and Belpré describe the role of folklore in twentieth-century Puerto Rico as a process of recovering history and, specifically, as a discursive strategy for marginalized populations taking control of historical narratives resisting assimilation and US empire. This is different from the cataloging of fairytales and folklore by European writers as a way of nation-building and asserting nationalism (Kidd 2011). Valdes writes in *Diasporic Blackness* on "the relationship between the creation of historical narratives and the collection and preservation of the documents that reveal these accounts as trustworthy was the critical imperative that motivated Black collectors and bibliophiles in the United States to engage in these activities since the nineteenth century" (93–94). The desire to provide and disseminate counterstories was also likely part of Black culture and pedagogy in Puerto Rico during the nineteenth century, weaving a strand of resistance into history as part of a young person's education. How successive generations reproduced this strand based on their subjectivity and relationship to Puerto Rico's racial hierarchy may vary, but I would still argue that the premise of history as recovery and providing counterstories stems from Afrodescendientes. Certainly, Juncos asks schoolchildren to treasure the published readings in *Antologia* as coming from a collective history of struggle before the "modern school"—specifically, the moment in which Cordero's taller-escuela served as guide, and instructs young readers to see their current access to schools as a culmination rather than as an improvement on the past. Could it be that, in searching for pathways to restory the Puerto Rican past, as Juncos stresses, Puerto Rican historical approaches work out of a pedagogy rooted in African diaspora principles of Sankofa ("go back and get it"), deeply embedded in the everyday practices of community education, instead of European, Hispanic lineage? Might Juncos's concept of "antesores," or ancestral legacies, stem from the practice of Sankofa performed by the Black men and women who created a culture of public pedagogies which grew into Cordero's taller-escuela as opposed to legacies of Spanish monarchy and nobility?

I phrase my centralizing of Black culture in Puerto Rican pedagogies for youth as a question due to issues of anti-Blackness in Latinx histories. "Hispanophilia," as scholar Marisel Moreno writes in *Family Matters: Puerto Rican Women Authors on the Island and the Mainland* (2012), "became a privileged site for the consolidation of the canon" (17). Moreno's book analyzes the concept of "la gran familia puertorriqueña" ("the great Puerto Rican family") that undergirds much of the rhetoric of national ideology in Puerto Rico. As Moreno writes, Hispanic culture as the locus of the Puerto Rican canon gave rise to:

> several totalizing metaphors, such as the family and the house, became instrumental in evoking the perception of unity that literary traditions often strive to achieve. The patriarchal myth of la gran familia re-emerged as a foundational narrative that continues to inform Puerto Rican letters even to this day. The myth has been conceptualized along three primary tenets: (1) a unified nation built on racial democracy and harmony; (2) the glorification of the island's agrarian, precapitalist past under Spanish rule; and (3) the cult of patriarchy, embodied by a benevolent father figure. (17)

La gran familia provides a "benevolent" framework in which one may easily exclude women and Blacks while still perpetuating racial harmony. Moreno argues that "*mestizaje* has served to perpetuate both external and internal racism, despite claims to the contrary" (Torres 1998; Rivero 2005; Santiago-Diaz 2007). A racial harmony, centering white European images and culture, as Santiago Diaz writes, "has in fact been used as a discursive weapon to silence the denunciation of racism by Afro-Puerto Rican sectors. The paradoxical coexistence of the discourse of racial democracy, embedded in *la gran familia*, and an abiding quest for *blanqueamento* has stifled the development of an Afro-Puerto Rican political consciousness" (53). Moreno credits the suppression of Afro-Boricua political consciousness to the colonial status of Puerto Rico as opposed to other Caribbean nations. Persistent internal and external anti-Blackness in Puerto Rican culture makes it difficult for scholars to locate Black culture, particularly free Black culture, as central to ideologies of education for liberation. However, in matters of Puerto Rican education and literacy, the persistence of public pedagogies rooted in Black culture, both in Puerto Rico and the diaspora, must be seen as foundational, not simply one of many parts.

## SCHOMBURG AND BELPRÉ IN DIASPORIC PARTNERSHIP: LESSONS ON CRITICAL LITERACY

Cordero's taller-escuela is an extension of a greater network of free Black literacy circles in Puerto Rico which also nurtured a young Schomburg and Belpré, both of whom went on to write about, and perform, these pedagogies in New York. The pedagogy founded during Cordero's day serves as a model for future generations of Puerto Rican thinkers and artists for how it works around apparatuses of Spanish colonialism and oppression. The four principles I see as emerging from this model include sankofa as an approach to education and history, public forums as ideal spaces for intellectual engagement, community and culturally sustaining pedagogies, and persistence outside of institutions—all principles we also see Belpré and Schomburg practicing in the 1920s and 1930s during the Harlem Renaissance.

Sankofa—the connection to ancestors and recovering of collective stories and objects, as a kind Afro-Boricua pedagogy of resistance and restorying—unites the work of Belpré and Schomburg as two Black Puerto Ricans founding and archiving the past at the New York Public Library. As Schomburg wrote in his essay "A Negro Digs Up His Past," these collections and "materials [were] not for only the first true writing of Negro history, but for the rewriting of many important paragraphs of our common American history." The Schomburg Center itself is a living monument to Schomburg ideas that centering the global Black experience allows us to see and know ourselves and others.

Weatherboard and Velasquez's picture book *Schomburg: The Man Who Built the Library* (2017) opens with a quote from Schomburg's essay, connecting the text to the interplay between past and future. Schomburg's words also emphasize history and learning as resistance: "The American Negro must remake his past in order to make his future. Though it is orthodox to think of America as one country where it is unnecessary to have a past, what is a luxury for the country as a whole becomes a social necessity for the Negro.

For him, a group tradition must supply a compensation for persecution, and pride of race the antidote for prejudice." Belpré also frames her work in librarianship, storytelling, and folklore as a means of recovering the past and countering prejudice projected at Puerto Rican children deemed "culturally deprived" by US-dominant culture. As Belpré writes in "Library Work with Bilingual Children" (1968):

> Often the term "culturally deprived" is used with bilingual children, as it is also used for all children residing in sections of the city considered "underprivileged." One can't call a culture that is 400 [years] old, culturally deprived. The fault of the term lies with those who lack the knowledge of the background, and the respect for the culture of these children. It is the knowing and understanding of it, that uplifts the child and gives him pride in himself. A child will be better prepared to understand the value of another culture when he knows the value of his own. (247)

Similarly, she writes in "The Folklore of the Puerto Rican Child" that "[t]o appreciate the present one must have a knowledge of the past, or in other words, to know where we go, we must know from where we come" (1). Belpré was also clear that her stories represented the Puerto Rican child's heritage to Africa, locating Black diasporic folklore as an equal source to Spain in her essay "Bilingual Storytelling at the Library":

> Just as Spain is one of the most important sources of our folklore, so is Africa. With the slaves that came to the island to replace the Indian workforce came African folklore. The popular trickster of African folklore, the Rabbit, soon made his home in Puerto Rico. Thus we have, with the usual variants in Spain and Europe, tales of clever animals (with their counterparts in Africa, Brazil, Haiti, and Mexico), tales of witchcraft and superstition, kings and queens, shepherds and shepherdesses, and regional stories from the highlands. Whenever these tales are told, either by mouth or on the printed page, they represent the unmistakeable imprint of our cultural heritage. (Sanchez Gonzalez, *The Stories I Read to the Children*, 205)

Actually, Belpré's published and unpublished tales tell the story of how the children's publishing industry, perhaps, decided to brand Latinx children's folk culture during her career, particularly in the 1930s when her tales were seen as filling a gap of "Hispanic" folklore for children. In *The Stories I Read to the Children* (2013), Sanchez-Gonzalez emphasizes that tales such as "Ines" and "Mariita" represent specifically feminist and Afro- and Indigenous-centered Boricua tales in Belpré's repertoire which are performed at different moments in her career. Yet, these are not the stories publishers centered in Belpré's collections. As Sanchez-Gonzalez writes, "I find it interesting that Belpré's most heroic stories about girls and women were never published. Perhaps not uncoincidentally, these tales were are also among the most magical. . . . Some of Belpré's heroines traverse realms and enjoy magical powers that are extraordinary, fantastic, even by fairytales standards." Even in wishing to represent "remnants of Native Caribbean and African diasporic" culture, how did these stories challenge what was deemed normative perhaps even to Juncos's generation of folklorist which Belpré credits as inspiring her? In particular, Sanchez-Gonzalez emphasizes that these stories "contain Arawak and African words, names, and phrases" (45). Cataloging Pura Belpré so often meant making her fit into colonial literary traditions centering European whiteness. Since publishers perhaps saw her as the first "Puerto Rican" or "Hispanic" storyteller, the literary industry neglected to embrace her Blackness and how that Blackness permeated how she enacted her many roles.

Belpré's position as a Black Puerto Rican woman in Harlem performing mixed-race folkways was a predicament for those looking for a champion for Latinx children, and it remains so. The Belpré Medal, named in her honor, has never bestowed its honor for "best Latinx children's literature" to either a AfroLatinx author and/or illustrator until recently. As Valdés writes, regarding Schomburg, that there is a "difficulty, for some, in conceptualizing AfroLatinx subjectivity; given that it defies how *latinidad* has been conceived historically, there is a temptation to bifurcate one's existence, so that an identification with one's nationality is perceived to be separate and distinct from one's racial and ethnic one" (11). Scholars writing about Belpré and Schomburg sometimes describe this period in Harlem as a crossroads for Black Latinxs, as if having to choose one side of their identity over another. For example, Efraim Barradas describes Schomburg's decision to uphold African diasporic culture as "assimilation" (Barradas 1999). Yet, Valdés's analysis of Schomburg's understanding of himself as a "diasporic man" is important in my reading of Belpré as well. Valdés writes that this diasporic Blackness "granted [Schomburg] access to multiple spheres. Contrary to the assertions that he abandoned his people, Schomburg augments the definition of the word *people* so that it included men and women across the African diaspora, including lands where they spoke Spanish" (11). Although Belpré clearly chose to name her work in service to communities cataloged at the time as "bilingual," "Spanish-speaking," "Puerto Rican," and "Hispanic" peoples, especially youth, her embodiment and the pedagogies she enacted at the New York Public Library center Afro-Boricua culture. Her constant references in her letters and essays to "seed-sowing" and "story-seeds" reflect her conception of a Puerto Rican diaspora which she saw herself as sustaining through Afro-Boricua epistemologies. Her embodiment and performance of stories did not interfere with her understanding of "lo puertorriqueño," though her representations of folklore and choices, at times, reflect an alliance with what was understood as Hispanic in the early twentieth century. For example, her decision to name her puppet players group, "The Cristobal Colon Club," as a message of empowerment for Boricua children, romanticizes the exploitative and violent nature of the colonial encounter, while her retellings of stories found in collections such *The Tiger and the Rabbit* and *Once in Puerto Rico* provide children with tools for resistance in a world in which they would not be in power (Jiménez Garcia 2014). The stories Belpré told and published contain the kind of epistemologies for disrupting institutional power and injustice rooted in Afro-Boricua literacy practices. In the realm of youth literature, the disruptive qualities of Belpré's work may seem veiled. Yet, as children's literature scholar Philip Nel has said, "What we learn from children's literature is the art of subversion" (Mickenburg and Nel 2010). Belpré's lessons on resistance were also perhaps more enduring given that she provided models both in the stories and through her embodiment of storytelling practices: She herself had to persist in arguing for the existence of a literary tradition as she was writing it in English and performing it in Spanish and English. Her approach was about children negotiating structural inequality and surviving with dignity as opposed to the more defiant tactics of successive generations of Puerto Rican writers and artists (though it is important to consider what her influence was on the children who became the Nuyorican movement, such as Piri Thomas and Nicholasa Mohr).

In this chapter, my emphasis on Belpré as collaborator with Schomburg represents a move toward scholars theorizing and celebrating her Blackness, and to consider how Blackness shaped the landscape of Puerto Rican youth literature and Latinx literature more broadly. For both Belpré and Schomburg, definitions and categories have marked what is memorialized about their legacies. How Belpré and Schomburg were both adopted and marginalized in multiple scholarly canons offers a study of how African diasporas challenge colonial categorizations. I argue that our current incorporations and even celebrations of these two figures often forsake the riches and nuance their careers might add to our understanding of access for people of color to collections, literature, and institutions.

Both Belpré and Schomburg converge in a public forum, spaces historically important in Afro-Boricua pedagogies—in this case, a library rather than a tobacco shop. The public library in New York, as in the days of the tabaqueros, functions as an intellectual space outside formal schooling institutions; Belpré and Schomburg build up the library as a space for future generations to foster critical thinking within and without texts. As Schomburg writes in "A Negro Digs Up His Past," about the development of his collection in Harlem: "Not long ago, the Public Library at Harlem housed a special exhibition of books, pamphlet prints and old engravings, that simply said, to skeptic and believer alike, to scholar and school-child, to proud black and astonished white, 'Here is your evidence.'" I emphasize Schomburg's inclusion of "school-child" in this list, which, although placed in opposition to the word scholar, suggests the separate spheres in which scholars and schoolchildren travel. Yet, in the public aspects of the library, these formerly oppositional relationships of scholar and "school-child" converge.

*Schomburg: The Man Who Built the Library* (2017) provides a window for young readers into the life and intellectual legacy of Schomburg and locates him in youth culture and youth spaces. Velasquez's cover illustration of Schomburg, up to his chin carrying a stack of colorful tomes in front of the 135th Street Library (today the Schomburg Center for Research in Black Culture), allows young readers to witness the man who devoted his life to "witnessing for the future"—they experience him not as bronze bust or plaque on a building but as a moving portrait who was also once a child looking for representations of his culture in school rooms. Velazquez recently donated an original print of the cover illustration to the Library of Congress's Young Reader's Center, making the Afro-Boricua intellectual icon a fixture of one of the most important children's reading centers in the US. Scholarly treatments of Schomburg rarely consider his work as cultivating youth culture and spaces. Children's librarianship is often invisible in African American and Latinx Studies, even in how scholars may dismiss librarianship as supporting intellectual pursuits rather than itself an intellectual pursuit. Therefore, we researchers may miss how the work of Schomburg and Belpré join in mission and intellect. We may miss the footsteps of a Black female children's librarian and storyteller next to a Black male archivist and historian memorialized as a scholarly powerhouse and namesake of the Schomburg Center for Research in Black Culture.

Victoria Núñez, in "Remembering Pura Belpré's Early Career at the 135th Street New York Public Library: Interracial Cooperation and Puerto Rican Settlement During the Harlem Renaissance," places Schomburg and Belpré, and the Black communities they served in Harlem, as cohabiting in a spirit of interracial cooperation, highlighting the importance of recovering how African American and Puerto Rican migrants in the 1920s converged and collaborated in Harlem. I analyze Schomburg, as a symbol and leader of intellectual life during the Harlem Renaissance, as working in tandem with Belpré in cultivating youth cultures and spaces. As Katherine Capshaw Smith (2001) has demonstrated, Harlem Renaissance writers as renowned as W. E. B. Du Bois created publications for young readers at the time, considering children and youth to be necessary co-revolutionaries in the struggle for liberation. Du Bois, who founded the National Association for the Advancement of Colored People (NAACP) and its publications, *Crisis* magazine (1912–34, containing an annual issue dedicated to children) and *The Brownies Book* (1920–21, centering on and for young readers), saw these publications as "cross-written," and as Capshaw Smith argues, the literature of this time often "blurs the lines between 'adult' and 'child' material, a sensibility that demands the child readers' interaction with adult political and social concerns" (2). As a contributor of *Crisis*, Schomburg would have been familiar with the mission and style of the magazine, as well as its inclusion of youth as readers and participants in liberation and the idea of the home as a place for training for the future of "race leaders" (2). Actually, Piñeiro de Rivera emphasizes that Belpré told her that Schomburg was the one who "implored with her" to write children's books, affirming the role of children's publications in building racial consciousness for the Black community in Harlem. Moreover, we know that other Afro-Boricuas, including the influential and vocal contemporary Jesus Colon, wrote plays for children which were then dramatized during Puerto Rican cultural festivities.

Eric Velasquez's illustrations of Schomburg in *Schomburg: The Man Who Built the Library*, along with Weatherford's brilliant poems, bring to life the public, working-class forum of the tabaqueros in which Schomburg began his career with words. Velasquez's images of a fascinated young Schomburg looking at the lector assigned to read to the tobacco workers contrasts with the pain in his face, on the opposite page, of Schomburg in his formal school room. Of his time in the shadow of the lector, Weatherford writes, "newspapers, novels, speeches, and politics. / Arturo took in the scent of the reader's voice. / Thus, Arturo not only learned his ABCs / but also to the love the written word." Velasquez's painting of Schomburg, first with the lector and then with the teacher, demonstrates a relationship of cause and effect, as Weatherford writes:

So when his fifth-grade teacher / told him that Africa's sons and daughters had no history, no heroes worth noting, did the twinkle leave Arturo's eyes? / Did he slouch his shoulders, hang his head low, and look to the ground rather than to the horizon? / No. / His people must have contributed something over the centuries, history that teachers did not teach. / Until they did, schoolchildren like Arturo would not learn of their own heritage, ignorance shackling them like chains." (3–4)

Velasquez and Weatherford imply that Schomburg's education was one based in autodidactism and public pedagogies of life among the tabaqueros. His access to the fountain of knowledge at the lectors' feet meant that he had access to creative and nonfiction literature that had been omitted in Spanish imperial schools. Velasquez paints the red and yellow Spanish flag in the background, as the teacher places her hand over young Schomburg's hand as if to stop his further investigation. The young Schomburg's ability to recognize the kinds of history he was taught in the classroom, then, illuminates his path to a more liberatory education through personal research and his ability to restory the narrative on African contributions. Velasquez paints young Schomburg, looking out at the audience of young readers, surrounded by white Puerto Ricans reading class reports about their histories, and asks: "Where is our historian to give us our side . . . to teach our people our own history?" On the next page, Velasquez chooses to show Schomburg with an open book and engaged smile, as he holds a book about Benjamin Banneker, "a self-taught inventor, astronomer, and draftsman" (5–6). Behind the young Schomburg is a clock, the same clock that had appeared in the classroom where he was previously. Velasquez renders the clock's face as set to 12 o'clock, implying that he studies this history on his own time—perhaps during the lunch hour—a fact which allows young readers to see the potential of self-education and research in an active learning process. This example demonstrates how, as students in a classroom under imperial rule, young people have a choice to question and search for alternative answers. Schomburg's collection provides tools to gaining information in a public space outside the school, thereby equipping youth to resist what Weatherford describes as the "shackles" of ignorance." Velasquez's illustrations of Schomburg and other Black leaders, including Frederick Douglass and Toussaint Louverture, function as a visual archive; flipping the pages allows young readers to enter Schomburg's collection.

Schomburg and Belpré constitute Afro-Boricuas who challenge the definitions of texts and knowledge, and provide young people with tools to do the same. The Puerto Rican diaspora begins its relationship with texts from the margins, creating literary and intellectual traditions which challenge what is valued as knowledge. Valdes underlines for scholars the value of accessing implicit knowledge production as opposed to explicit. She writes that "[scholars] are perhaps so accustomed to explicit modes of scholarly assemblage—e.g., pamphlets, articles, books, presentations, etc—all of which serve as examples of deliberation and reflection on a given subject, that at times we fail to consider what could be termed an implicit mode of knowledge production . . . the assembly of materials around a defined theme" (103). As a storyteller and performer, Belpré also often advocated for alternative modes of learning and production outside of formal institutions. Her multifaceted career makes her a shapeshifter of sorts. The process of recovering Belpré as a writer has been difficult for many reasons, including the "paperlessness," which Lisa Sanchez-Gonzalez discusses in her landmark study *Boricua Literature* (2001). Yet, it would be impossible to consider her a writer without seeing the way in which she chose to present her creativity to the world, and the way in which she resists the literary establishment's loyalty to published works. For example, the first time she told a story at the New York Public Library story hour, she did so without a published book since Puerto Rican folk tales were not available in English. The children's room, under the direction of legendary children's librarian, Anne Carrol Moore, operated as kind of mini-United Nations, where international folklore and fairytales stood in for the representation of a country (Jiménez Garcia 2014). Belpré advocated on behalf of the existence of a literary tradition without published books, although, in 1931, she would eventually publish *Perez and Martina*. As I have argued, the performances and exchanges taking place outside the book were just as important as the book, for Belpré, perhaps more so. Her puppet theatre and written plays, down to the costumes and traveling theater she created, represent a belief in impacting the world outside books. One of my favorite photos of Belpré is of her sitting surrounded by children of color, her arms raised mid-story, with a closed book in her lap.

For Belpré, in addition to connecting young people to ancestors, folktales stood for the testament of a mixed-race people that only survived due to *el pueblo*'s ability to recount, as opposed to academic and government interest and support. In a speech given at the New York Public Library, Belpré touted the ability of the Puerto Rican community to thrive without institutional apparatuses. This moment connects to what we know of Puerto Rican folk culture during the Spanish empire, and I suggest, also highlights particularly the free Black culture that persisted through autodidactism and family literacy. I suggest Belpré emphasizes the persistence of community literacy circles rooted in Afro-Boricua culture. In Spanish, Belpré writes "[this folklore is] preservada por generaciones y enriquecida por medio de la palabra oral, ya que por los tres primeros siglos de colonización española no había imprentas de la isla" / preserved by generations and enriched by way of oral culture, and during the first 300 years of colonial Spanish rule there were no presses or imprints on the island" (1).

Belpré and Schomburg worked to sustain and model the Afro-Boricua pedagogies—modes such as family and community literacies, personal research, and criticism of institutional knowledge—they had witnessed as part of their upbringing. They planted these critical approaches into the development of the Puerto Rican diaspora. Belpré and Schomburg used the institution of the library as a public space to curate and develop materials, but also to model critical literacy and agency for people of color. The skills they modeled and presented to young people were just as important as the tangible objects and books they helped create and preserve. From the space of the library, these skills included "reading" the world and envisioning oneself as having agency to look for and gain knowledge, approaching history as a process of recovery and restorying, critical literacy for narratives which served to empower youth of color, and an emphasis on literacy circles and community engagement as opposed to the superiority of the text. Like the stories and histories they told and retold, Schomburg and Belpré offered a counter-narrative to the schoolrooms and government agencies which proclaimed Puerto Rican, and other children of color, as problems. The next section deals much more extensively with the content of Belpré's stories and the context of both Belpré and Schomburg in the Harlem Renaissance. Considering the preservation of Afro-Boricua and Indigenous lifeways through the work of both, I submit that this renaissance provided a rebirth of a decolonial imagination for people of color in Harlem.

## A DECOLONIAL RENAISSANCE: LESSONS FROM BELPRÉ AND SCHOMBURG AT THE CENTER OF HARLEM'S RENAISSANCE

In this section, I focus more deliberately on Belpré's stories and the kinds of resistance strategies which she performed, told, and retold beginning in the time of the Harlem Renaissance. I also reconsider the meaning of renaissance or "rebirth" in terms of what it means for a migrant community of color in the US to experience a renaissance. Once again, Belpré and Schomburg provide a window into the tensions between embodied and literal practices, between the implicit and explicit, some of which coincides with key debates in performance studies and its intersections with literary and cultural studies which view archives as holding power and performance as resisting containment. Diana Taylor, in her essential work *The Archive and the Repertoire* (2003), argues for "shifting the focus from written to embodied culture, from the discursive to the performative," although she argues that these work in tandem. John Beverly, in *Against Literature* (1993), furthers an interesting theory on these tensions—as he says, "negating the literary," so as to take into account projects and perspectives that go against what is normally sanctioned as literary, including testimonial narratives. In "The Formation of the Ideology of the Literary (from Garcilaso to Greenblatt)," Beverly writes that desires for a national language and national literature permeate through the "over-valorization" of literature. When it comes to the roots of literature as a place of dissidence, he writes: "Difference could be tolerated even encouraged—but only within the centralized power system represented by the state and a national language, which existed like the literary text itself, both to make difference possible and to contain it" (26). Both Beverly and Taylor emphasize Latin America in their case studies. Like Beverly, I also argue that "[w]e tend to think of literature as a sanctioned space for the expression of social dissidence or marginality," but should consider that literary texts have served as vehicles to both "make difference possible and to contain it" (25). In the case of Schomburg and Belpré—particularly the latter, who created a host of artifacts such as puppets and costumes— consider the contribution of Robin Bernstein in *Racial Innocence* (2013) of "archive of repertoires" and "scriptive things" and how her analysis adds to our understanding of performance-based archives and also archives created from cultures outside the center (8–11). Bernstein's analysis also speaks to the tensions and breaks I emphasize in my approach to Latinx literature for youth as a politics of friendly, unassuming images and relationships "side by side" which veil colonial violence:

> However, a model of interaction, or even of harmonious cooperation, reifies a polarity between the two forms of knowledge.

> The heuristic of the scriptive thing explodes the very model of archive and repertoire as distinct-but-interactive, because the word script captures the moment when dramatic narrative and movement through space are in the act of becoming each other. The handkerchief is both an artifact of and scriptive prop within a performance— that is, simultaneously archive and repertoire, with neither form of knowledge preexisting the other. Within each scriptive thing, archive and repertoire are one. Therefore, when scriptive things enter a repository, repertoires arrive with them. Within a brick-and-mortar

archive, scriptive things archive the repertoire—partially and richly, with a sense of openness and flux. To read things as scripts is to coax the archive into divulging the repertoire. (12–13)

My decision to see Schomburg and Belpré as co-conspirators also serves to find ways to "to coax the archive into divulging the repertoire" and imagine how these embodied practices modeled for young people's relationships toward, with, and outside of literature. These embodied practices shape what we see in the archive and imagine those creating the artifacts, and those imaginings always engage with racial, gender, and class constructs. In the same way, Afro-Boricua epistemologies always invite us to see literature as a "scriptive thing"—an artifact with implied performances. Moreover, as an object in itself, agency and power are in the hands of those reading, to choose how they restory and who is empowered in so doing.

In many ways, the Harlem Renaissance in which Schomburg and Belpré began their careers provides a perfect example for revisiting the potential of restorying, artifacts, and performed practices. Every time we consider that moment in US cultural and literary history, the limitless potential of US people of color dreaming about, remaking, and reaching toward the future unfolds. This limitless potential connects us to other movements where people of color have sought to reframe the past and future, such as the Civil Rights and Black Lives Matter movements. Yet, how has "the" Harlem Renaissance," as a category of study, turned into a monolith? A renaissance brings the hope of renewal and rebirth, but what gets reborn and reinvented? As evidenced in some of the ways in which we celebrate Afro-Boricua culture, how we restory the past has the potential to divorce communities of agency and self-determination. However, when we consider the concept of a culture being reborn, it is important to see what artists and writers brought back to life in that era. In terms of my conversation of Schomburg and Belpré, and the role they played in organizing and providing literacy tools for the Puerto Rican community, I would like to suggest that the renaissance which they cultivated emphasized a rebirth of African and Indigenous lifeways, specifically.

I read both *The Storyteller's Candle*, by Lucia Gonzalez and illustrated by Lulu Delacre, and *Schomburg: The Man who Built the Library* as displaying the vibrancy and promise of the Harlem Renaissance, particularly in the ways Puerto Rican illustrators Delacre and Velasquez capitalize on images of light as a metaphor for rebirth. However, these picture books also demonstrate the difficulties of literally placing Belpré and Schomburg on the same page in contemporary youth literature which continually separates Latinx and African American communities who grew up together. In *Schomburg*, Velasquez brings to life Schomburg and a circle of writers, including Countee Cullen and Langston Hughes (24–25). Velasquez's painting of the group makes exquisite use of light, as two lit lamps are painted on either side of the room; a painting in the background also features a ray of sunshine piercing the darkness in the foreground as a group of enslaved people travel to freedom. Velasquez paints the light as touching each member of the group on the forehead and outlining their bodies like an aura. While the light is clearly pictured as emanating from the lamps, Velasquez's artwork suggests the light also emanates from the human and intellectual connections and conversations happening among the group. This portrait highlights the potential of dedicated, liberatory spaces for people of color in order to organize and participate in the intellectual and cultural work of social justice. Velasquez pictures Schomburg as something of a god, in the style of Michaelangelo, through his painting of Schomburg's pointed finger gesturing to the group, specifically Countee Cullen, who instead of holding up a limp hand, a la Adam, also points her finger at Schomburg; this is symbolic of the power of both genders in the movement. Weatherford narrates the moment, which is meant to illustrate the first meeting of the Harlem Writer's Guild:

> Arturo's acquaintances were a "Who's Who" of the Harlem Renaissance. He was invited to the first meeting of an informal guild of young black writers.
>
> Poets Countee Cullen and Langston Hughes Were members.
>
> So was novelist and poet Jessie Redmon Fauset, an editor of the NAACP magazine, *The Crisis*, and of the African-American children's magazine, *The Brownies Book* . . .
>
> Arturo loaned not only books to students, artists, and writers; he also lent interpretations, insights, and sometimes cash.
>
> With booklists full of texts that Schomburg found, his friends mined blackness and broke new ground. (24)

Weatherford's reference to "min[ing] blackness and br[eaking] new ground" emphasizes the centrality of Blackness as a rich, intellectual tradition, and ample field which Schomburg helped to frame and cultivate. This "mining of blackness and breaking new ground" forms the environment of the Harlem

Renaissance or the New Negro Renaissance—the stage on which Schomburg and Belpré's careers merge at the 135th Street Branch Library, and for Belpré, trickling into East Harlem and other Puerto Rican settlements.

Lucia Gonzalez's *The Storyteller's Candle* (2009), a celebrated picture book about Pura Belpré's career as a storyteller and librarian, also makes use of light as a symbol for rebirth through its motif of the lit storyteller's candle. On the cover, Puerto Rican illustrator Lulu Delacre emphasizes Belpré's lighting of this candle as a symbol of warmth and new beginnings. Interestingly, the cover includes an image of one of the main characters in the story, Hildamar, holding a copy of *Perez and Martina* (1931), indicating that this is Belpré in her later career at the 115 Street Library in East Harlem/El Barrio, as opposed to her earlier career in 135th Street during the period of 1921 to 1927. The candle was a tradition at the NYPL in which storytellers would light the candle at a story's beginning and a child would blow out the candle, and make a wish, at the end. Belpré began this tradition without a published book, a rule her supervisors essentially allowed her to break as she performed stories she had written down. This early stage of Belpré's career at the 135th Street Branch established within the NYPL and Harlem that a Puerto Rican identity within the US existed. The community's story took its place in Harlem's thriving environment of cultural pride. Belpré's storytelling could provoke the island's continual rebirth within the imagination of Puerto Rican children throughout Spanish Harlem. Indeed, Belpré continued telling her unpublished tales outside the children's room "in English and Spanish, throughout the library system, as well as in schools and PTA meetings" (Belpré, "Folklore," 2). However, we should remember that in the same library where Hughes, Cullen, and Schomburg gathered to celebrate a new Negro identity, and later at the 115th Street Branch, Puerto Rican migrants and their children gathered around Belpré's candle to renew and commemorate Puerto Rican cuentos, marking a beginning of their American story.

So, the beginning of Puerto Rican youth literature in the US opens with this performance of rule-breaking and a flickering flame on a lit candle, representing the place of Puerto Rican folklore, and history to a certain extent, on the children's bookshelf (Jiménez Garcia 2014). And the stories and traditions which were reborn in Harlem centered African and Indigenous modes of subsistence, survivance, and survival. However, the book begins with an illustration by Delacre of a Puerto Rican mother and her two bundled-up children walking through the cold streets of East Harlem. Gonzalez locates the beginning of Belpré's career as in East Harlem/El Barrio: "Winter was harsh for the people of *El Barrio* . . . [but] Pura Belpré brought warmth and beauty of Puerto Rico to the children of *El Barrio*" (2). Gonzalez's underlines the Great Depression and its affects on Puerto Rican migrants in El Barrio as the historical context for *The Storyteller's Candle*. The book distances Belpré from her beginnings as a Harlem librarian at the 135th Street Library, where she served the African American and Puerto Rican communities, and where her speciality in Spanish languages grew to the point that she was placed at the 115 Street (Aguilar) in El Barrio, as the Puerto Rican community grew in the area. Throughout her career at the New York Public Library, Belpré's placements followed the pattern of Puerto Rican migration to her final position at Seward Park in the Bronx, where she worked with a fellow Boricua librarian, Lillian Lopez. Victoria Núñez writes that "American memory" historically memorializes Spanish (East) Harlem, Brooklyn, and the South Bronx as "Puerto Rican," and Central Harlem as "African American." Yet, Belpré's "memories of the community in Central Harlem highlight the partiality of the existing memory" (63). Early Puerto Rican migrants of varying races may have seen Harlem as a welcoming neighborhood. Belpré, in an oral history she narrates to Lilian Lopez, describes the sense of cooperation:

> [At the 135th Street Branch] It was meeting an entirely different group of children. After having been acquainted with the blacks there . . . I did a lot of dramatic work. I had Reading Clubs, and I was very happy there. It was an enrichment that I've never forgotten. It was brand new to me coming from a Spanish tradition, to have this open door of black literature and black activities. (Belpré and Lopez, 10)

Belpré marks a distinction in terms of how she saw Black literature and culture opened up to her and the centrality in which it was celebrated "coming from a Spanish tradition." We know that she wrote about the African influences in Puerto Rican folklore and that she affirmed her Afro-Boricua family literacy practices as central to her development. Yet, while her comment might refer to language, Belpré's statement on "coming from a Spanish tradition" reveals the ways in which European settler colonialism, in this case through Spanish conquest and canon formation, marginalizes African traditions. Her work with Catherine Allen Latimer and Augusta Baker at the branch also serves to highlight how this collective of Black women librarians worked to render intellectually visible and sustain Black life in Harlem. In addition to Spanish bibliographies, Belpré created criteria for the selection and evaluation of "Black and biracial books for preschool through grade levels" using NAACP guidelines (Sanchez Gonzalez, *The Stories*, 262). In "Racism and Children's Fiction" (n.d.), Belpré writes "a major criterion was that no book would be listed if it was considered likely to communicate any *racist concept* or *cliché* about Blacks to either a Black or a white child" (262). She also emphasizes that she would exclude a book from a list if for "the pain it might give to even one Black child," stressing that the books according to the NAACP guidelines "had to be appropriate for use in: 1) an all-Black classroom; 2) an all white classroom, and; 3) in an integrated classroom." Belpré underlines "books marred by racial slurs"—one in particular which she refers to as "*Measure of Green* (Boston) by Knowe" is listed by Sanchez-Gonzalez as Lucy Maria Boston's *Treasure of Green Knowe* (1958) and was removed for its "deragatory descriptions of a Black boy's hair." In this collective of Black librarians, including Schomburg and Baker, Belpré had an ability for affirming Black culture as an integral part of her work with children of color as the first Puerto Rican and Latinx storyteller and librarian in the New York Public Library system.

Her training in the Black community in West Harlem during the Harlem Renaissance made an indelible mark on Belpré as she moved east to her post at 115th Street Branch or Grace Aguilar Branch. Narrating her arrival at the 115th Street Branch, Belpré portrays her 1930s-era East Harlem neighborhood as one in which it would have been difficult to ignore the professional and creative presence of immigrants and migrants. In East Harlem, she continued to bring to life the stories and characters that were part of a collective renaissance for communities of color at 135th Street. In her oral history, Belpré uses the term "renaissance" and connects the resurgence and movements in El Barrio to the momentum in West Harlem: "[The Puerto Rican migrant and Latin American immigrants 'barrio' covered] Eighth Avenue. Seventh. Lenox. And extending then almost to Fifth. But it was a Renaissance. It was the Renaissance, the Spanish Renaissance. . . . It was Hispanic America around there. . . . You walked the neighborhood itself. You walked up from that 116th Street, and you saw signs. You saw, you know, doctors, oculists" (Belpré, *Reminiscences*, 12). Her description of this early group contrasts with the tendency to portray Puerto Rican migrants as wholly impoverished economically and academically. Belpré's listing of the streets—particularly one such as Lenox Avenue, a well-known Harlem Renaissance center—signals her paralleling of the two communities' revivals. Her reference to this group as "Hispanic America" underlines the community's relevance to US literary and cultural history. This was a barrio in which both budding and renowned Latin American artists, poets, and actors shared their latest projects at the 115th Street Branch, the Grace Aguilar Branch, and other Spanish Harlem venues (such as El Club Obrero Chileno). With Rosa Zubillago, the adult librarian at the 115th Street Branch, Belpré "collaborated" in the creation of "magnificent" theatre, poetry, and storytelling programs for Latino/a patrons. For example, she helped to organize poetry readings by Chilean poet, Gabriela Mistral (19). Delgado emphasizes that "it was not uncommon for such popular figures as . . . muralist Diego Rivera, or Puerto Rican tenor Antonio Paoli to visit the library and provide free public lectures" (430).[2] A 1940s-era flyer from Belpré's personal collection announces the reading of "la gran poetisa / the great poetess) and Puerto Rican "mensajera/messenger" Julia de Burgos.[3]

Yet, Belpré brought a specific skill set for creating racially and culturally inclusive environments for young people and their families. *The Storyteller's Candle* emphasizes Belpré as the founder of Spanish-language services in the NYPL system, something that makes her a heroine for working-class Puerto Ricans in the book and in real life; as the young girl Hildamar runs into the local Bodega Santurce in East Harlem, she exclaims, "They speak Spanish at the library!" (15). However, I suggest the categorization of Spanish has historically distanced scholars and educators from critically engaging with the racial diversity she embodied and practiced. Why do we have difficulty seeing Belpré's Blackness, and her roots in African American community, as part of a Latinx tradition? Moreover, why do we have trouble seeing Blackness as more than a cultural component but indeed an intellectual one? Belpré's legacy—as we have come to know it through practices such as the awarding of the Belpré Medal and even her published works, which remain out-of-print—perpetuates a tendency of reading her as "Hispanic," the term guiding the NYPL collections and the publishing industry during her beginnings. During Belpré's rise as a published author of "Spanish" folktales, the New York Public Library and the publishing industry were invested in international folklore. Belpré's folktales, as some of the first published English language texts of Puerto Rican folklore in the US, stood in for all Hispanic cultures on the children's bookshelf. Publishing houses working with Spanish translators and content supervisors who were mostly from Spain may have policed the nature of what would be represented as "Spanish" to the white mainstream. Nicholasa Mohr later writes about her schooling experiences with "Spanish" in the public school classroom, and the shaming of those with Caribbean accents in *Nilda* (1973).[4] For example, publishers may have asked Belpré to perform a Castilian accent for the earliest Spanish audio recording of *Perez and Martina* for an industry expecting a certain linguistic register. Discussions of ratio-sociolinguistics, or how language is coded socially and racially in US society, apply when considering how an Afro-Boricua storyteller at home in Harlem was commodified for publishers and the reading public in the 1930s (Rosa 2019). I submit that Belpré's Blackness and Caribbean Spanish were aspects the publishing industry had difficulty locating and marketing. Today, the way we memorialize Belpré through traditions such as the medal continues to edit out the centrality of Black and Indigenous traditions in her work, and simultaneously, in Latinx literature for youth—an astonishing reality given that the founders of library and literacy practices for young people of color in the US were AfroLatinx and worked out of epistemologies rooted in Blackness.

The cultural politics of children's literature medals have historically excluded people of color from their ranks, something which is repeated even in a tradition that was founded for the purposes of rewarding and amplifying voices of color. The Belpré Medal, until Elizabeth Acevedo, has never been awarded to an AfroLatinx writer in its twenty-year history—a fact that could relate to the books available and the stories publishers choose to view as reaching and representing a Latinx market. In the contemporary discussion focused on "own voices," which is usually directed toward Anglo writers who benefit from writing "diverse" stories, who and what is considered "own voices" in a community of color may actually surprise some and needs more critical nuance in order to further equity. Through a politics of space, Lisa Sanchez-Gonzalez in *Boricua Literature* reflects on the legacies of Schomburg and Belpré, and the respective spaces that house their archives today—namely, the Schomburg Center for Research in Black Culture and the Centro de Estudios Puertorriqueños Library and Archives, Hunter College, CUNY. "The Schomburg Center," Sanchez-Gonzalez writes, "[unlike the Centro Library] was much more inviting . . . [and] was teeming with activity every day. . . . seeing local children doing their homework in the reading room, I felt even prouder of [Schomburg's] legacy . . ." Sanchez-Gonzalez's observations touch on how these spaces mirror both visible and invisible racial and linguistic categorizations, yet also how such categorizations affect contemporary youth of color in these public spaces founded with them in mind:

At first I was saddened to think that, despite Schomburg's commitment to the Puerto Rican section of his collection, the current holdings had few texts by or about Nuyoricans for me to spend time reading. Then I reasoned that his vision had been African diasporan, his collection indeed followed that foundational vision, and AfroRicans form only a relatively small part of the larger diaspora. Still, whenever I saw the children doing their homework, I felt an acute sadness that more young Boricuas were not there too, thinking hard and feeling that immense sense of pride the building inspired in me. After all, I thought, the Schomburg Center is a public library that services Harlem as its immediate constituency, and Boricuas are one of Harlem's longest-standing communities. (Sanchez Gonzalez, *Boricua Literature*, 73)

Belpré and Schomburg, and the spaces they left behind, represent, to an extent, an "archive of repertoires" in which we are the performers—contemporary scholars and the public perform the racial lines, ideas, and behaviors we have learned about these literary histories, even when those we are studying provided alternative epistemologies. We perform exclusion in our research and analysis, and in our keyword searches for "Latino," we drop off Blackness. Weatherford beautifully narrates Schomburg's legacy as an AfroLatinx when she writes:

> *Arturo Alfonso Schomburg may have felt kinship*
> *With African Americans and their cause of equality*
> *And even worked to build pride among them.*
> *He may have adopted the Anglicized version of his name—*
> *Arthur—and insisted that his children speak only English*
> *And not Spanish, his own mother tongue.*
> *But he never lost his love for the Caribbean*
> *Or his longing for Puerto Rico the island of his birth. (39)*

Belpré and Schomburg's legacies speak to the interrelationships of language, race, and culture, and how these interrelationships reach across Caribbean, Latinx, Africana Studies, Latin American, and American Studies.

## LESSONS FOR DECOLONIZING THE IMAGINATION

Through embodiment and published texts, Belpré's storytelling models specific lessons about resisting colonial oppression. The core of Belpré's published folklore collections, *The Tiger and the Rabbit* and *Once Over Puerto Rico*, suggests her centering of Indigenous and African forms of resistance. Here, I focus on her use of Indigenous survival and the African trickster. Reflecting on the concept of renaissance, I want to think about what it means to resurrect these Indigenous and African traditions in the Harlem Renaissance. In particular, the Harlem Renaissance was a moment in which Schomburg's archiving and Belpré's stories provided children of color with tools to rout the colonizer in everyday life and in the imagination. Even her most popular tale, "Perez and Martina," I argue contains a warning to the colonizer regarding his ever-present greed; it is, after all, Perez, with his perfect Castilian accent, who falls into the pot, digging for more and more of Martina's rice. His greed costs him his life, no matter how refined his culture. The unpublished Belpré further centralized Black culture in her storytelling repertoire through her youth protagonists. Her unpublished tales, such as "Inés" and "Mariita," emphasize a decolonial lens and an imaginative landscape in which Indigenous and Black culture played an active role in the present, particularly in routing colonial oppression. Moreover, a story such as "Inés" lingers on the possibilities of a world without colonialism.

Stories such as "The Tiger and the Rabbit," published in Belpré's first collection of folktales in 1941 and with an introduction from Augusta Baker, demonstrate the rebirth of the trickster character, a type found in Indigenous and African folklore but one to which Belpré attributes African ancestry in her essays. Ann Gonzalez writes about the prevalence of the trickster character within Latin American culture, a character whose marginal position causes him/her to create alternate "avenues" of success within the dominant culture: "[T]rickster characters and the texts that portray their deceptions in Latin America all find ways to cover their tracks and hide what they do; they speak on multiple, sometimes even contradictory, levels to multiple audiences: children, adults, colleagues, and peers. Yet the message is always fundamentally the same. How to get what is necessary without direct confrontation or open resistance" (8). The presence of the trickster in Latin American and Caribbean literature and culture speaks to how Indigenous and African diaspora peoples persist under Spanish colonialism. Through US conquest and colonization, scholars may observe how these characters, reborn through a new generation, shift depending on communities' interest and location. Additionally, a tale such "The Tiger and the Rabbit" might be read alongside a text such as "The Tale of Brer Rabbit and the Tar Baby" by Uncle Remus.

In the political allegory of "The Tiger and the Rabbit," a clever rabbit, representing the Puerto Rican population, finds himself living side by side with his colonizer, the powerful yet dumb, Tiger:

> Long, long ago all the animals were friends and lived in peace with one another, except the Tiger. For the Tiger had promised himself to eat small animals, especially the Rabbit if he ever crossed his path.

> But the Rabbit was very clever and known for his quick wit. He knew that the Tiger wanted to eat him, and though he considered the beast stupid, clumsy, and a fool, he managed to keep away from his path and thus avoid trouble. But this was not always possible, since both them liked to roam about. (Belpré, "The Tiger and the Rabbit," 1)

In the "The Tiger in the Rabbit," I outline what I see as the first mode of resistance Belpré's stories offer young readers through representations of

African and Indigenous cultures: outsmart the colonizer. Indeed, the trickster rabbit uses his local knowledge of complicated power dynamics between other animals and the Tiger's own strength as leverage. The Tiger, as the highest in the food chain, functions as a symbol of the oppressor in Latin American folktales (Ann Gonzalez). The Tiger and the Rabbit participate in dysfunctional partnership mirroring the US relationship in Puerto Rico and thereby suggesting the ways colonialism functions to alienate the population against each other in order to survive. For example, the Fox and the Rabbit have one of the more curious relationships in the story:

> Long after this adventure with the Tiger, the Rabbit paid a visit to his friend the Fox and the conversation fell on the subject of the Tiger. The Fox was a great admirer of the Tiger and thought he was clever and intelligent. He said the Tiger could do anything he wanted; nothing ever stood in his way. The Rabbit, who knew better, began to laugh.
>
> "He is a fool, that's what he is," he said. "A big fool. Why, he is such a fool that he lets himself be used as a horse by his friends."
>
> "I don't believe it," said the Fox.
>
> "I will provide it to you," answered the Rabbit . . . (16)

The Fox, a fellow predator, aligns himself with the Tiger's interests, believing that the Tiger's strength resembles his level of intelligence. Because he is a predator, the Fox might symbolize the ruling classes who benefit from the colonizer's exploits while the less privileged fall prey. The Rabbit eventually tricks the Tiger into letting himself be tied up, convincing him it will help the Tiger survive an oncoming hurricane. The Rabbit climbs on top of the Tiger and rides him away from other little animals, as the Fox looks on. Yet, as the story ends, we learn that the Tiger and the Rabbit "*were ever the best of friends.*" This story illustrates the importance of knowledge and wit, as Belpré teaches, as a means of leveraging the colonizer's strength against him. Belpré also implies that in a land in which colonialism reigns, the most vulnerable must learn to cultivate answers.

The second mode of resistance young readers may discern in Belpré's stories emphasizes how one might negotiate with those in authority. Belpré's portrayal of the Taino characters in her stories perhaps best displays this mode. Tainos, once the Indigenous population of Puerto Rico, represent a kind of Puerto Rican Adam, gentle and innocent though present in a paradise that will ultimately fall due to oppression. In the 1970s, which is when *Once in Puerto Rico* was released, Tainos became the symbol of the nationalist revival, and they continue to occupy a space in Puerto Rican imagination regarding sovereignty. Through the Taino, however, Belpré's retellings invoke rhetorics of Indigenous survivance, both in principle and imagery. Belpré models survivance through her emphasis on storytelling, even in academic discourse; her essays and papers often rely on her analysis—of folklore, Puerto Rican culture, race, migration—as a cuento/story. This discursive strategy of storytelling as academic discourse is important to mark considering Belpré gave some of the first talks on Puerto Rican culture in the history of Puerto Rican Studies. Her remarks on the persistence of el pueblo in telling stories, even without printing presses and support from government, align with survivance and the way survivance also coincides with a kind of warning. Indigenous writer Leslie Marmon Silko writes in her novel *Ceremony* (1977) about the formidable power of stories, "These stories aren't just for entertainment. / Don't be fooled. / They are all we have, you see / all we have to fight off illness and death stories are carried in the body / in the belly / where they live and grow" (2). Mármol Silko's poem speaks to the literal survival and witness of stories despite violence and even rumored extinction, and how those ascribing to Eurocentric ideals of power and authority may mistakenly interpret Indigenous negotiating as an act of submission. This reframes the noble tale of "Ivaiahoca" in Belpré's collection *Once in Puerto Rico* (1973), the story of a Taino woman who makes a noble plea for the life of her son, who is imprisoned by the Spanish. Ivaiahoca's speech to General Salazar illustrates a kind of civil disobedience founded on sacrifice and empathy, through images of femininity and matriarchy:

> Señor Salazar, I know you must have a mother. Because of her you can understand my suffering. My son is young and loves his liberty. He should live to enjoy it. I am old. If he were in captivity, my last remaining days would be in agony. But if I knew he was free, I could pass those days in peace, whatever tasks and trails might come to me. Take my life and my services for his liberty. Heaven will reward your good deed. (39)

Ivaiahoca wins her son's freedom through this speech. She then risks her life for General Salazar by delivering a letter to Juan Ponce de Leon. Her bravery leads to Salazar's praise of Ivaiahoca's "nobility" instead of deterring him from the war on the Tainos. Belpré's retelling of "The Rogativa" combines trickster and civil disobedience tactics. In the story, thousands of Puerto

Ricans assemble in the streets, curiously enough, with lighted candles to deter British fleets in San Juan Harbor, as Belpré narrates:

> The English spies on watch sent an urgent message to Abercrombie's headquarters. Great movement could be seen within the capital. They heard a loud ringing of bells and could see strange glimmering lights toward the west.
>
> "They must be getting reinforcements from the country," said the English general. (70)

The British interpreted the lighted candles as symbols of conglomeration and resistance. The mass of people, each with a candle in hand, symbolized the importance of each protester.

In considering the Afro-Boricua literacy circles that trained Belpré and Schomburg's generation, we see how the stories Belpré told were rooted in sustaining life. Stories have the power to permeate and transcend generations even in the face of genocide and slavery, and as is clear from Rafael Cordero's example, denial of sanctioned schooling spaces. Gerard Vizenor describes "[t]he character of survivance" as "creat[ing] a sense of native presence over absence, nihility, and victimry. Native survivance is an active sense of presence over absence, deracination, and oblivion." The third mode of resistance Belpré provides young readers is perseverance/preserve—in other words, that survival is in itself an act of resistance. In "The Legend of the Royal Palm," young Milomaki transforms into a tree in order to save himself from an attaching tribe. The narrator tells young readers how "the voice" of Milomaki still resides in Puerto Rico's royal palms. Similarly, in "Amapola and the Butterfly," a teenaged Amapola learns that many of Borinquen's stones are actually victims of a witch's spell (Belpré, *Once in Puerto Rico*, 16, 33). The Taino, then, is represented as a kind of monument of the past preserved inside Puerto Rico's resources. Belpré's retelling of this legacy in the English language reconstructs these "monuments" in a US urban center, simultaneously making this folklore a part of US heritage while always keeping the young reader's gaze on Puerto Rico as a place of origin. She suggests that no economic or political oppression would ever disrupt the Puerto Rican child's tie to the land. The Taino is a presence in everyday Puerto Rico which, as Belpré is keen on reminding readers, remains such through the rocks and trees, and to a certain extent the Taino is reborn once more in the readers' keeping of the lessons and tools they left behind. This sense of perseverance through word and embodied practice, for Belpré, seems the utmost form of cultural preservation; this was the kind of preservation she sought to reproduce through the public institution of the library, not because this preservation was dependent on the institution, but because she knew, as did Schomburg, the power of public spaces to reproduce knowledge for communities of color.

In her essays, Belpré wrote that stories had to be preserved for "the Puerto Rican child in this new land." It was a cultural and literary heritage that would continue to reproduce in each generation, regardless of tangible means. I have argued previously that Belpré's—who wished to be remembered as "the Puerto Rican Johnny Appleseed"—planting of stories was a deeply nationalist project creating a remnant of children, themselves story-seeds, which would reproduce Puerto Rican culture and resistance abroad and on the mainland. Some of those children might even return to Puerto Rico and take up the cause for independence. She has written that she believed that, in receiving these stories, the "collective psychology" of the Puerto Rican child on the archipelago would join with the child in diaspora. We see her stressing this quality of persevering and outlasting sources of oppression. Belpré ends her telling of "The Stone Dog," about a loyal dog who never left his master and is still waiting for his return in the form of a stone, by telling readers that stone "it is still there to this day." The Taino is a relentless presence that cries out for justice, and through young readers, knowledge of them remains; even if the dominant group fails to recognize what these markers mean, those with the knowledge of Puerto Rican cultural typology will know and never forget. And remembering, memorializing, persevering is a form of resistance. This sort of resistance contrasts with the unpublished Belpré, and also with the contemporary legacy of Tainos in new superheroine mythologies such as those by Edgardo Miranda-Rodriguez's *La Borinqueña* (who I analyze further in the final chapter).

Given the importance placed on preservation, my analysis now turns to what has most often gotten edited out of Belpré's portrait: her stories. Belpré's books remain out-of-print for young readers, although Sanchez-Gonzalez's 2013 book *The Stories I Read to the Children* made a tremendous contribution by making available many of Belpré's essays, stories, and unpublished works. In particular, I want to conclude this chapter with a discussion of two young female protagonists that never made it to bookshelves, Inés and Mariita. The absence of young protagonists from books young readers could access is significant, particularly in the case of a writer whose published repertoire includes mostly animal tales and folk characters. Belpré's only published young protagonist came late in her career, through her last book *Santiago* (1969), the only story about a Nuyorican child that is set in the US as opposed to an imagined Puerto Rican landscape in folklore. Even in *Firefly Summer* (1996), a book published posthumously by Arté Publico, Belpré presents readers with Teresita, who is a young woman dreaming of making it to the Feast of the Cross in her hometown in Puerto Rico. Borrowing Rudine Sims Bishop's metaphor of "mirrors, windows, and sliding glass doors," Belpré's mirrors, through her published fiction, asks young people to see themselves through characters tied to particular tropes of Puerto Rican culture, but always with an eye toward Puerto Rico, as opposed to the United States. What does that mean today, and what does that mean to the generations of Nuyorican children she told her stories to? Her unpublished folklore emphasizes a feminist vision and magic, a world much more ethereal than the perhaps more tangibly "Hispanic" folklore which tastemakers such as head children's librarian of the NYPL, Anne Carrol Moore, and publishers such as Frederick Warne saw as representing "Spanish" readers in the US. In "Inés," we find a "determined" young woman whose abilities to commune with nature make her almost a deity of spiritualist traditions:

> Long, long ago, on the edge of the Luquillo forest, there once lived a girl called Inés. She lived with her father, a woodcutter, whose work kept him away from home for days at a time.
>
> Any girl would have been lonely under such circumstances, but not Inés. She turned to the forest for company and had made it her friend. (149)

The details of the "Inés" story place her in a past which seems exempt from colonial violence and injustice, although it is clear that Belpré locates this tale in Puerto Rico. For example, the names of "El Yunque" and "El Toro," and the names of the plants such as "Dama de la Noche" and "Flamboyan," tell us this is still the Puerto Rico which remains for contemporary readers. Readers familiar with folklore know that many folk stories turn on a danger or crisis of some kind, or a perilous journey to find a key object or item. Yet, Inés walks in a world which is seemingly void of peril, at least for her. Inés is a young girl who receives wisdom and help from plants, as she works to bring "more color" to El Yunque, suggesting the reality of magic and spiritualism for the everyday in order to protect and cultivate communities. The "Dama de la Noche" plant, opening up her vines and blossoms, teaches Inés about the "scarlet Flamboyán," whose red flowers are synonymous with Puerto Rican flora and fauna.

Inés embarks on a quest to find the Flamboyán and plant its seeds throughout El Yunque, something the Dama de la Noche tells her she must be "brave" to do since "the tree is guarded day and night." Indeed, arriving at the tree, Inés is challenged by both a bull and a toad protecting the tree, but the objects she receives on her journey from a farmer, an old woman, and the Dama de la Noche help her swiftly conquer these barriers. Inés is seemingly fearless, as even the wind comes to her aid and blows the red flowers all throughout El Yunque. As she does in her published folklore in the modes of resistance she modeled, Belpré suggests youth might accomplish bold feats by listening to elders, mostly women, and implementing local knowledge on any challenge and barrier. When Inés returns, surrounded by a whirl of red flowers, the personified El Yunque and El Toro become fearful, as Belpré writes:

"Oh Inés save yourself!' said El Yunque. 'The forest is on fire!' shouted El Toro."

And when Inés heard their warning, she began to laugh. Smiling at the mountain peaks, she said. "Hush. That is not fire. That is the wind carrying the red blossoms of the Flamboyán. They are my gift to you." (155)

This image of a young female of color, a Boricua women, laughing at the idea of danger and potential colonial violence (who would set the forest on fire?) is an image which never made it to shelves. Inés, as youth protagonist, represents a confident female of color in a land of imagination and joy, something that is still a rarity in our contemporary youth literature. Could it be that this child was not seen as being in keeping with what publishers and the general public pictured at the time? What would the impact of having access to such a story have been for young Puerto Rican readers? I ask because my next chapter will take up the issue of writing one's self into existence as a young Puerto Rican, as is the case for Nicholasa Mohr—a child growing up during the time when Belpré told her stories and who later became her colleague and friend. "Inés" ends on a note of survivance, blending the possibilities of the imagination and young women, with the reality of contemporary Puerto Rico; as Belpré adds, "Even now, every June their branches come into full bloom, bright as the sun and red as fire, sharing Inés's gift of glorious color for all to see" (155). The red flamed flowers of the flamboyán also recur as a feminist image for Puerto Rican writers on the island, such as Georgina Lázaro, challenging the rigid constraints of cultural nationalism in the commonwealth, a topic I return to in my last chapter.

In chapter three, I consider how the Nuyorican generation of writers responded to the challenge of filling in literary history and the children's bookshelf using both Anglo and Latinx typologies. However, in this current chapter, through my discussion of Belpré and Schomburg, I have presented the kind of epistemologies, rooted in African and Indigenous rhetorics and literacies, which provided youth of color in the 1920s and 1930s, at the formation of library services and children's book publishing, with tools for recovering the past and resisting colonial oppression. In particular, drawing on the epistemologies rooted in free Black culture in Puerto Rico, I found that Maestro Rafael Cordero, Belpré, and Schomburg cultivated public spaces for gaining knowledge, providing a critical eye toward formal institutions. To a certain extent, Belpré and Schomburg provided young people in the diaspora with access to tools for decolonizing knowledge and the imagination, including the ways we should approach history, literature, and formal study. As Weatherford writes:

> *Arturo Schomburg studied the past /*
> *But he did not dwell in it. Quite the opposite.*
> *His mission looked to the future.*
> *I am proud, said Schomburg, to be able to do something that may*
> *mean inspiration for the youth of my race.*
> *Then young blacks would hold their heads high*
> *And view themselves as anyone's equal.* (32)

Contemporary youth literature, such as *The Storyteller's Candle* and *Schomburg: The Man who Built the Library*, renders the lives of these Afro-Boricuas visible during a time of renaissance, yet there is still difficulty with seeing how Black and Latinx culture and knowledge coincide and tell parts of the same story. Belpré and Schomburg attempted to restory the past and provide ways for young people to do the same, but I have tried to draw attention to the ruptures that occur when restorying results in erasure. Moreover, the imagination proves the hardest place to decolonize, as Nicholasa Mohr demonstrates in her groundbreaking fiction and novels, apart from poetry and traditional folklore.

## Chapter Three

# NICHOLASA MOHR WRITES BACK

## Imagining a Diaspora Child in
## the Garden of Multiculturalism

The history of Puerto Rican youth literature highlights how the book industry, in the form of public and corporate influencers such as the New York Public Library and Frederick Warne, chose to interpret ethnic descriptive categories such as "Hispanic." For the most part, "Hispanic" meant non-Black and rooted in Iberian culture. For all the depth of Belpré's career and characters, the decisions of publishers meant that her most celebrated characters in contemporary memory were Hispanic-performing animal characters, Perez and Martina, as opposed to the youth protagonists she created and cast in a noncolonial, magical realm. Though characters such as Ines were published posthumously in Lisa Sánchez-González's *The Stories I Read to the Children* (2013), the breadth of Belpré's repertoire remains inaccessible to young readers. In the gap between Belpré's generation of los pioñeros and Nicholasa Mohr's generation of the Nuyorican movement, what did the lack of human characters and protagonists, authored by stateside Puerto Ricans, mean for youth in the diaspora? How would a child of the diaspora, the very children Belpré and Schomburg so earnestly attempted to reach, respond? A child or young person of color protagonist is a rarity—as part of a world shaped by a writer of color even more so. Belpré and Schomburg provide youth of color with ways to survive and thrive in the US through lessons and models from African and Indigenous culture. However, Nicholasa Mohr's work stand outs for how she reinvents the present without necessarily seeking to transcend the cityscapes and streets which, for Nuyorican writers, represented new pathways for the imagination.

In a world in which folk characters from island lore and witty animals served as mirrors, Nicholasa Mohr chose to elevate to novel form the language and culture she witnessed growing up in 1930–1940s-era Puerto Rican communities. Youth literature, in particular, has been idealized by scholars and writers alike as itself a kind of a project of decolonizing the imagination.

For example, Shaobo Xie (2000) writes on the possibilities of children's literature and scholarship as reordering the consequences of colonization: "Children . . . are most violently subjected to colonialist ideas of racial-ethnic Otherness at the most formative years of their lives. If children's literature and the criticism of children's literature take upon themselves to decolonize the world, they will prove the most effective project in the long run, for the world ultimately belongs to children" (13). The imagination, then, as opposed to the physical and digital spaces where literature, as an object and "scriptive thing" dwells, seems the logical place for challenging inequity. As "scriptive things," Bernstein might remind us to consider the kind of performances of equity and/or inequity that objects and media ascribed to youth culture inspire.

Something we learn from Mohr about attempts to decolonize the imagination and literature—understanding that decolonization is more than "a metaphor"—is that we should be mindful of telling children where they belong and what creative influences they should draw from for cultural authenticity (Tuck and Yang 2012). For example, in this chapter I emphasize how Mohr rehearses and revises some tropes from the so-called classics of children's literature as a means of highlighting inequity. How do authors of color seek "mirrors" some might deem to be outside authentic culture? How do traditions shift generationally in relationship to ideas about authenticity, liberation, and transformation? Women writers in the diaspora ask us to think beyond rigid, stagnant attempts to define culture in essentialist terms. This is evident in Nicholasa Mohr's novels and essays starting in the 1970s and reaching into Sonia Manzano's career on *Sesame Street* from 1970 to the 2010s. It is also evident in the contemporary, post-Hurricane Maria Puerto Rico of Ada Haiman, a writer who returned after living in the US for most of her life. Contemporary fantasy fiction writer Zetta Elliot writes in an essay for *Horn Book*, "Decolonizing the Imagination: AfroUrban Magic and the Door of No Return" (2010), on how, as a young Black reader in North America, she approached the "windows" provided on the children's bookshelf:

> I am an immigrant. I grew up in a former British colony, dreaming of magical wardrobes and secret gardens. Doors figured rather prominently in my imagination, and books were indeed windows into other worlds. They were not, however, much of a mirror for my young black female self. I learned early on that only white children had wonderful adventures in distant lands; only white children were magically transported through time and space; only white children found the buried key that unlocked their own private Eden. Perhaps the one benefit of being so completely excluded from the literary realm was

that I had to develop the capacity *to dream myself into existence.* My imagination went into overdrive trying to picture a girl like me living inside my beloved books.

Elliot connects writing to dreaming beyond a dreamscape populated by Anglo literature. She describes the writer's journey as one in which writers must contend with their own subjectivity in this imagined space. Elliot also resists those who would have her perform out of essentialist framework for Black readership, writing, "Why would a plump, brown-skinned girl with an Afro embark on a quest to read all the books she could find by Frances Hodgson Burnett? Was I an Anglophile in training, or was my taste in books (and music, and clothes) a way of rejecting popular representations of blackness, which fit me just as poorly (if at all)?" (1) Elliot insists that she wants "African American youths to know that they need not look to a castle in England to find magic: there are wonders to discover and adventures to be had right here at home (and in other parts of the globe)." She offers a young person's everyday life and US neighborhoods as the ultimate dreamscape, contending that young people do not require a far-off land—even one some might consider to be more culturally relevant—in order to have a fantastic voyage. Elliot, however, marks familiar tropes of children's literature such as gardens and magic doors as remnants of the colonial past. More specifically, Elliot highlights the way in which children's literature has served to colonize the imagination and shape the way people of color dream, while also viewing herself as contributing to a rich tradition of African "wayfinding" literature.[1] This sense of locating oneself, of dreaming and writing oneself into existence, and writing back to children's literature classics is a project which Elliot shares with Nicholasa Mohr, and no doubt, many writers of color who wish to occupy the children's bookshelf.

The late 1960s and early 1970s was a time when photo books and documentary footage of youth of color rose to popularity, something Katherine Capshaw Smith brilliantly examines in *Civil Rights Childhood* (2014). For example, Puerto Rican youth were among the youth poets in June Jordan's *The Voice of the Children* (1970) and were filmed in Bert Zaltman's television production, *Miguel: Up from Puerto Rico* (1971). The Puerto Rican child was also a longstanding fixture of the US imagination as a symbol for dependency and anxiety through depictions by US authors of imperial projects in Puerto Rico and countless studies. Belpré's only child character, "Santiago,"[2] and Keats's Juanito dominated the kinds of images circulating in media—children casting a backward glance at Puerto Rico. A displaced child, a fixture in an attempt to document ghetto life, a child with no sense of authorship in her own narrative—such was the typical portrayal of Puerto Rican diaspora children in popular culture until Nicholasa Mohr published her landmark novel, *Nilda* (1973). Mohr's literary works confront a literary landscape vacant of Puerto Rican youth protagonists.

As an artist, Mohr challenges readers to see the artistry in everyday life in communities of color, specifically East Harlem/El Barrio, interweaving Nilda's observations of her world with color, light, and darkness. In "On Being Authentic" (1987), Mohr notes that her writing career began as an act of intervention in the tradition of Belpré. Mohr, recalling the literary worlds she encountered as a child, emphasizes, "I, as a Puerto Rican child, did not exist in North American letters." She contends in another essay that "if I as a woman and my ethnic community did not exist in North American letters, then [through her writing] we would now." If Mohr's fiction reacts to what she perceives as an absence in US letters until the 1970s, then her work critiques not only Anglo literature, but those literary portrayals erasing Puerto Ricans from US culture. Though Belpré toured New York libraries and schools, offering tales of Puerto Rico's imagined past, Mohr states that she "never found a book [at the library] that included Puerto Ricans or, for that matter, other Latinos. My family, my friends, and all of us in my community did not exist."[3] Like Belpré before her, Mohr sought a representation of herself on library bookshelves, something animal fables and tales of jíbaros were unable to provide. Belpré's project in folklore and storytelling promoted critical readings of US history that were continued by Nuyorican authors like Mohr, though her published works, and to an extent, what the publishing industry allowed to circulate, did not speak to the lived experiences of Nuyorican life. Mohr is the voice of a generation of diaspora children[4] born and bred *en Nueva York*.

Mohr's early fiction is characterized by her poignant and complex presentation of diaspora children. I remind readers that her work is indeed fiction since there has been a tendency to categorize Mohr as an autobiographical writer. I shift attention to Mohr's artistic and experimental talents, such as the satirical and playfully subversive ways in which she challenges traditional Puerto Rican and Anglo-American texts and imagery. Reading Mohr should involve the consideration of multiple literary and cultural traditions, inherited through the US colonial project, which she both relies on and resists. Her Nuyorican perspective offers reinterpretations of certain myths of childhood present both in Puerto Rican and Anglo-American culture. Mohr remixes familiar children's literature tropes: "once upon a time," imagined wonderlands, secret gardens, and so on. Her focus on diaspora children contributes to both Puerto Rican Studies and Children's Literature Studies by offering alternate readings of the American dream, the lure of Puerto Rican nostalgia, and the portrayal of minoritized children in literature. Reading Mohr might cause us to reconsider vital questions in the study of youth literature and culture, such as, for example: What separation, if any, exists between adulthood and childhood? Between children's worlds and adult worlds? How do people of color provide alternative readings, challenging the Anglo, privileged perspectives on which such notions of childhood were popularized through children's classics?

Mohr's representation of childhood in early texts like *El Bronx Remembered* and *Nilda* invokes a discourse of political orphanhood and adoption which touches on notions of child subjectivity in relationship to colonialism. She also provides alternative perspectives to ongoing debates in Children's Literature Studies about the idealization of children as innocent others.[5] Mohr's child protagonists exhibit tremendous amounts of agency and authorship inside colonial subjectivities. These protagonists root themselves in the US and oppose the traditionalist view that they are in exile, such as the kind of displaced child employed by Belpré in *Santiago* (1969). Though Belpré imagined fantastic children in an imaginary, decolonial world, she often failed to imagine functional children in US society and literary life. However, Mohr presents her child characters as castoff, stateless children or orphans contending for their right to a place (or adoption) in the US imaginary.

Some critics—such as Barbara Roche-Rico,[6] who argued for a "critical reassessment" of Mohr's work—may view my discussion of Mohr in terms of "children's literature" as counterproductive. Roche-Rico rightly argues that Mohr, as one of the first US Latina authors, has received relative critical silence when compared to other Latina writers such as Sandra Cisneros or Julia Alvarez (3). With the exception of critics such as Roche-Rico, Lisa Sánchez-González, or Eugene Mohr, literary discussions of Mohr are dominated by interviews and book reviews in education and library journals touting the importance of multicultural education.[7] These sources often feature Mohr as a kind of interpreter of her own work, suggesting a tendency to view her writing as testimonials of life on "the mean streets"[8] rather than as narratives that aesthetically and historically form part of US fiction. Roche-Rico believes that classifying Mohr's texts in the "reductive" category of children's literature limits her scholarly consideration and places unrealistic expectations on her work by those looking for library books containing "role models" for children (161). Even Mohr has said that while only two of her works, *Felita* (1979) and *Going Home* (1986), were intended for children, the majority of her works have nonetheless been marketed and reviewed as children's literature, something she has discussed within the context of censorship. Mohr implies that marketing her works as "for children" stems from publishers' perspective of "a Puerto Rican female as 'perpetually juvenile'" (109). Mohr is clear: "Hispanic" literature is largely unread in the US "because it is not being published!" Diverting her fiction from an adult readership and publishing it as juvenile fiction, Mohr suggests, may serve as a form of imperialist control: "The best way to censor a people is to ignore them. In this way there is not even the possibility of confrontation. And, those enjoying such eminence and affluence need have no fear that the literature of the people of color will in any way impinge or threaten their well-guarded empire" (109).

Indeed, lumping Mohr's fiction into school library projects celebrating diversity and US multiculturalism evades her unsettling accounts of US colonialism. It is also worth noting the trend of publishing women of color as "children's literature" in the 1970s and 1980s. Her categorization as a "young adult" author during the post-civil rights multicultural movement suggests a stifling of her political critique on US colonial relations. However, my study views youth literature not as a "reductive category," but as an important platform for subaltern resistance employed by Puerto Ricans since the community's inception. Youth literature is a political medium that has shaped how dominant and minority cultures imagine childhood and how these cultures imagine the development of their narrative histories. Mohr has expressed frustration with being categorized as a children's author. However, in a 1999 essay titled "Freedom to Read" published in the children's literature journal *The New Advocate*, Mohr revised her "I did not exist in North American letters" statement. Instead, she said, "My family and I did not exist *in children's literature*" (emphasis mine). Children's literature forms part of the literary tradition to which Mohr "writes back," and this includes Belpré's folklore and Anglo children's literature. In Mohr, traditional children's literature tropes function as a kind of frame which helps us focus on inequities and how children of color dream through and around them. First, I examine how Mohr's *El Bronx Remembered* challenges the concept of folklore and displaced children in her creation of a kind of urban folklore for Puerto Ricans. Mohr's stories elevate Nuyorican folkways and center a new tradition of intellectual mothers. They also reconsider notions of childhood and citizenship vis-a-vis the metaphor of adoption and resist barriers between the child and adult world. Second, I read Mohr's *Nilda* as incorporating elements of Frances Hodgson Burnett's classic work, *The Secret Garden* (1911), a text known for its exploration of exile and postcolonial relationships.[9] While no one has studied this connection between Mohr's garden and Burnett's, Mohr's treatment of this classic, and its central image of the garden, reframes how Nilda transforms her urban spaces into a kind of wonderland and imagines her agency and subjectivity in the world. Mohr's weaving in of folk traditions and children's classics form a narrative about the diaspora where she argues for "a bit of earth"[10] in the US literary landscape.

## A NEW GENERATION OF INTELLECTUAL MOTHERS: URBAN FOLK-LORE AND REMNANTS OF ISLAND LORE IN *EL BRONX REMEMBERED*

A notable shift occurs between the 1920–1930s Spanish Harlem Renaissance, which I proposed in my previous chapter, and what Sánchez-González calls a 1960s–1970s "Nuyorican Renaissance": the emergence of the novel as a medium for representing the diaspora. The novel evolves into a space for elevating Nuyorican interiority, folkways, and dialogue and for employing, as Sánchez-González writes, "modern discourses of anticolonial resistance and civil rights" (103). Novelists such as Piri Thomas and Nicholasa Mohr inherited a dialogue of resistance from earlier writers employing less traditional mediums, including storyteller Belpré or newspaper columnist Jesus Colón (103). As a self-professed "daughter of the Puerto Rican diaspora," Mohr draws from a variety of narrative discourses representing US, European, Latin American, and Indigenous island cultures. Her diverse narrative perspective functions as a kind of collage of cultural difference. For example, she frames *Nilda* with a poem by Spanish poet Frederico García Lorca and organizes *Nilda* as a sort of Euro-American *bildungsroman*, but, as Roche-Rico suggests, she includes elements of Latin American magical realism (170). *Nilda* also fits in a "larger enunciation of dissent" during the civil rights era by US groups of color, Sánchez-González writes (106). Many scholars, including Sánchez-González, Pilar Bellver Saéz, and Roche-Rico focus on how Mohr and other Puerto Rican writers, among them Thomas and Esmeralda Santiago, revise the *bildungsroman* by presenting social situations "not as a given, static set of conditions, but rather as a contradictory and flexible situation in which characters not only can, but must create new models of social agency in order to situate themselves more comfortably and integrally in the existing social order" (Sánchez-González 106). The novel also works in the form of what Roberta Trites has analyzed as an *entwicklungsromane* or a young adult novel—by the novel's end, readers witness Nilda as a young woman, though still a teen as opposed to an adult (27–30). Given Mohr's emphasis on art and creativity as a tool for transforming social situations, perhaps *kunstlerroman* better describes her narratives of development; however, a continual emphasis on her work as "novels of development" may perpetuate autobiographical readings of her work. I am more interested how Mohr "writes back" to Euro-American traditions beyond *bildungsroman* such as canonical children's texts and Puerto Rican folklore. Folklore, in particular, may reproduce elitist, pro-Spaniard standards governing the Puerto Rican national canon.

Flor Piñeiro de Rivera in *Un Siglo de Literatura Infantil Puertorriqueña / A Century of Puerto Rican Children's Literature* (1987), published by El Editorial de la Universidad de Puerto Rico, Puerto Rico's elite university press and longtime guardian of national culture,[11] identifies Belpré and Mohr as the first and second generation of diaspora children's writers, respectively. It is significant that, in representing El Editorial, Piñeiro offers an extensive review of Belpré's publications as "authentic Puerto Rican juvenile literature" (42). However, Piñeiro makes a distinction between Belpré and Mohr:

> The first generation of writers found its inspiration in memories of the folklore, the scenery, the history and personal experiences of the Puerto Rico of its childhood. The second generation bases its writings on memories not of the island, but of the Hispanic areas where its life is rooted. This present generation is interested in social problems, searching for new structures to replace the depressing conditions of the Barrio. (42)

Piñeiro also highlights Belpré's use of Spanish (her texts were published both in Spanish and English) and Mohr's use of English as a distinguishing factor. In comparison with her four-page analysis on Belpré, Piñeiro includes just a single paragraph on Mohr, listing only *Nilda* and *El Bronx Remembered*. There is an element of authenticity in these two texts endorsed by Piñeiro as Puerto Rican, though not in the same way she sanctions Belpré. Using an insular paradigm of authenticity focusing on flora, fauna, and folklore limits Piñeiro's ability to analyze Mohr, along with many diaspora writers.[12] Yet, if we return to the lessons of the autora-cátedras, the transnational nature of Puerto Rico and its diaspora has also been seen as a strength in feminist traditions. Interestingly, we see how adhering to particular notions of Spanish folklore restrict this transnational, feminist vision. Standards of so-called authenticity have shifted in contemporary, transnational Puerto Rico, but it is clear writers of Mohr's generation were marginalized by insular academic traditions. Yet, Mohr, in many ways, is the transnational feminist child the auto-cátedras and Belpré dreamed of—tracing her path in a world of magic, except her inspiration would be New York City rather than solely El Yunque.´

The limited visibility of diaspora writers in insular literature and the marginalization of Puerto Rican literature in the US canon designates diaspora

texts in a kind of orphan category of literature.¹³ Mohr assesses this sense of
orphanhood in her perspective of the Puerto Rican predicament, calling herself, and Puerto Ricans, in general "adopted citizens." These adopted citizens,
Mohr states, do not "look like that family and long [] to know who his or her
parents really are." The adopted child-adoptive parent relationship—portraying Puerto Rico as a child, specifically an orphaned child-nation—was perpetuated in the New York City schools Mohr attended, possibly from the US
tradition of illustrated readers: "I was taught that Americans adopted Puerto
Rico, it is not a real country. So, am I supposed to be forever grateful because
someone adopted us and took us in? The Spaniards first and then the United
States? How does a child, then, form an identity?" (90) This moment allows
us to imagine how writers of the Nuyorican generation, as young people,
reacted to the distorted mirrors offered by US fictions of Puerto Rico. Mohr's
fiction functions as a means of remapping of migrant origins. She resists this
sense of political orphanhood by presenting Puerto Ricans as legitimate heirs
to the US. Diverting from Belpré, Mohr offers the diaspora child a new folk
culture that locates and grounds diaspora characters in the US metropolis.

The distinctions Mohr draws between adoption, belonging, and citizenship for Puerto Rican children coincide with important debates in childhood
studies. As Carol Singley has analyzed in *Adopting America: Childhood, Kinship, and National Identity in Literature* (2011), US discourses of adoption and
kinship tie to ideas about bloodline and citizenship. Singley analyzes how
US authors from Benjamin Franklin to Edith Wharton explore adoption as
a means of also looking at the US as promoting a different kind of national
belonging from Europe beyond blood kinship. Adoption fiction, for white
males in particular, implied US ideals of "self-reliance-or self-adoption—and
resiliency" (Singley, 7). However, Singley is also clear in her study of Harriet
Wilson that the adoption narrative failed "antebellum black and mulatto
children," and, instead of offering hope and incorporation into a new society,
signaled "their undesirability in the white society" (134). Indeed, Mohr emphasizes how adoption motifs, when referencing communities of color and
unincorporated territories such as Puerto Rico, instead present communities
as a burden to the adoptive parent, the US. Bernstein's racial innocence argument, of course, tells us how children of color were excluded from humanity,
childhood, and citizenship for the sake of the slavocracy, whereas Saguisag
analyzes how depictions of unruly and well-behaved children sustained
ideologies of sorting immigrants and migrants into citizen and noncitizen
categories. Race continued to shape ideas about childhood, citizenship, and
belonging in the mid-to-late twentieth century, and Mohr's comments on
adoption implies her disqualification, as a child of color, from US citizenship

and to an extent, the US imaginary. However, Mohr found ways to revise US tropes of resiliency through community-based storytelling and arts.

Texts like *El Bronx Remembered* present a radical reimagining of Puerto Rican history. I read *El Bronx* as the literary presentation of a new folk culture, complete with characters, landscapes, and moral lessons. In Belpré's and Juncos's generation, though publishing Puerto Rican folklore served as a strategy for resistance by purporting that migrant children were not culturally deprived, these traditions contain a portion of racial, classist, and linguistic prejudices—some that were resisted by Belpré, others which, without the balance of her unpublished work, appear to be even more magnified. For example, the racial and class hierarchies of the Spaniard, the Negro, and the Indigenous Taino, the lower status of woman, and the romanticization of the Spanish settlers, are all problematic elements in retold folktales like *Perez and Martina* (1932). Martina rejects and mocks each of her native-born island suitors since they do not speak the Queen's Spanish, favoring the Spanish-born courtier Perez. Belpré's employment at the New York Public Library, an institution Mohr calls "her university,"[14] means that Puerto Rican folklore, through storytelling and texts, were available to children like Mohr in 1940s–1950s-era Spanish Harlem and South Bronx libraries. Mohr affirms that "el cuento puertorriqueño, storytelling" was "an intrinsic part of Puerto Rican culture," yet she emphasizes storytelling as a ritual and strategy for survival grounded in migrant homes: "When our family faced difficulties, an adult would say, 'Don't lose hope, sit back and relax, and I'll tell you a story.' Our family would gather around the storyteller, fascinated by the ancient folk tale or modern adventure. Our problems and burdens began to seem lighter, and life appeared promising." For Mohr, "the ancient folktale" and the "modern adventure" complement each other; she does not privilege Puerto Rican folklore over family-originated stories rooted in New York City landscapes. Such family tales may even center on the daily struggles with prejudice and poverty in the city, perhaps serving a similar function as the traditional folk tale in terms of cultural transference.

Some examples of family survival tales occur in Mohr's *Felita*, when "Mami" and "Abuelita" transform a traumatic event into an opportunity for a story. After relocating to a wealthier neighborhood, Felita seems inconsolable when a group of white children and their parents physically and verbally assault her. "Mami" evokes a cultural legend by diverting Felita's attention from her torn dress and toward her turned-up hemline: "The hemline is turned up. You are lucky this day . . . when that happens the very first time a person wears a dress, there's a true saying. It's a custom I heard, that if that person kisses the upturned hemline and wishes for a new dress, she'll get

one!" (38) After kissing the hemline and making a wish, Felita finds a yellow
party dress, "sparking like the sun," on her bed: "My wish had come true!"
Abuelita has a similar reaction to Felita's assault, asking Felita if she would
like to "hear a story" (55). When Felita turns down her offer, Abuelita then
urges Felita to tell *her* story. Felita recounts her victimization, reframed by
her grandmother's wisdom and consolation. Abuelita also reinforces Felita's
pride in her cultural heritage through stories about the island's foliage: "Why,
you never saw so many marvelous colors." The women alter Felita's trauma
into a site of magical myth-making. Folklore for Mohr, then, combines the
urban experiences of the migrant community with a sense of magic. When
she writes that the library books and popular culture portrayals such as
*West Side Story* did not contain representations of her community, Mohr
underlines the absence of the everyday barrio heroes and heroines from
the US imaginary:

> Where were my mother and aunt? All those valiant woman who left
> Puerto Rico out of necessity, for the most part by themselves bringing
> small children to a cold and hostile city. They came with thousands of
> others, driven out by poverty, ill-equipped with little education and
> no knowledge of English. . . . This is where I came from, and it was
> these women who became my heroes. When I looked for role mod-
> els that symbolized strength, when I looked for subjects to paint and
> stories to write, I had only to look to my own. And my source was
> boundless, my folklore rich and the work to be done could consume
> an eternity. ("Journey Toward a Common Ground," 83)

In this passage, Mohr essentially argues for rewriting Puerto Rican lore from
the perspective of those often left out, calling for the recognition of a new
generation of intellectual mothers thriving in New York barrios. In other
words, stories of heroes and heroines did not end with New York Public
Library's story hours, but continued in the roles that men, women, and children played each day in breaking new ground as a community in the US. If
the Puerto Rican diaspora consisted of some of the poorest, working-class
islanders, why should they inherit a folklore celebrating Spanish classism?
Instead, the hero and heroines of the diaspora, mainly women and children,
would form the locus of culture in Mohr's narratives. She continues a Puerto
Rican tradition of centering and elevating intellectual mothers citing them
as knowledge producers on the page.

In *El Bronx Remembered*, Mohr chooses to incorporate elements of children's narratives such as fairy tales and folktales in her piercing commentary

of urban life. The collection of short stories reframes the diaspora community as a group with established US roots. Her dedication to *El Bronx* unites the text to a myth of storytelling: "To the memory of my mother, for those days of despair when she shared her magic gift of storytelling, making all things right." Through this dedication, Mohr associates herself with a matriarchy of storytellers (the Mamis and Abuelitas) capable of providing strategies for community survival. A new generation of intellectual mothers were alive and at work in New York City, and the stories they told also drew from everyday life in the US metropolis. Mohr's storytelling contains an allure of magic and fantasy existing side by side with violence and injustice. She prefaces the collection with a short narrative on Puerto Rican history for those unfamiliar with Puerto Rican New York (which may include US readers and island Puerto Ricans). Mohr's opening sentence—"There have been Puerto Ricans living in the mainland USA since the middle of the last century"—designates these stories as the heritage of a longstanding US community, countering those who might view an influx of Puerto Rican narratives[15] into US fiction as a sudden occurrence.

It is significant that, in recapping and remapping Puerto Rican history, Mohr weaves in folkloric tropes which transform the epoch, landscape, and people of US culture. For example, she contrasts basic information about Puerto Ricans' legal entry into the US against a kind of rhapsodic image of their arrival: "As citizens they did not face immigration laws or quotas . . . and so they arrived by the tens of thousands, first by freighter and later by planes" (x). Her use of ellipses denotes a silence in the narrative—a moment which dramatizes the migrants' travel through time and space. This is a story where humble villagers, instead of setting off for their quest on foot, board airplanes and ships to reach their promised land. Mohr also locates the narratives within a fabled time of US progress; the stories concern the "everyday struggles for survival" of Puerto Rican migrants "during that decade of the promised future 1946 through 1956, in New York City's 'El Bronx.'" The "promised future" refers to the post-World War era of economic and political advancement that, arguably, catapulted the US into a dominant world power. Mohr situates the diaspora community within the nation's greatest metropolis, New York City, during its greatest period of progress, the years following World War II. The elements of myth and nostalgia at work in her collection heighten when, reading in retrospect, readers know that few of Mohr's migrant characters enjoy the promises of the nation's future.

Readers enter the world of *El Bronx* understanding that they are encountering a passed generation. They remain frozen within a sense of promise, regardless of whether mid-twentieth-century promises of US progress and optimism would be borne out. Mohr also outlines a new landscape which Belpré, for the most part, veiled by keeping the child's gaze on the island. Rather than cafetal plants or tropical rainforests, Mohr introduces the reader to the urban spaces of El Barrio and El Bronx within New York, a city with a level of notoriety and expectation rivaling any fantasyland. Mohr explains how areas like the South Bronx are "known to Puerto Ricans as El Bronx." Renaming major areas of a modern US city through Nuyorican ways of knowing lays claim to the city's history. However, as Mohr emphasizes, only Puerto Ricans "know" these Hispanicized names, denoting the community's political subjectivity rather than dominance. Mainstream readers, some for the first time, must grapple, simultaneously, with Puerto Ricans' right to and erasure from US history and culture.

By imagining Puerto Rican characters on US soil, Mohr radically presents the concept of a Puerto Rican "America." *El Bronx*, in particular, features Mohr's vivid sketches of characters and caricatures of the types and personalities one might encounter in 1940s–1950s-era Puerto Rican Nueva York. The heroines of this folk culture are working-class, urban city dwellers as opposed to the rural *jíbaros* and animals with Spanish alliances. Mohr allows readers a window into the life of characters, among them Graciela Fernandez in "A Very Special Pet," a typical diaspora mother looking to feed her children; Hector in "Shoes for Hector," the valedictorian who cannot afford new shoes for his graduation; and Alice in "Hector and Alice," the pregnant teenager with broken dreams. These are characters never found before in US fiction. It is also significant that these characters, as Sánchez-González writes, "speak and signify completely in Boricua and other urban vernaculars" (107).[16] Mohr upholds the Puerto Rican community as its own culture, customs, and language.

Mohr's characterization of diaspora children, in particular, contrasts with previous portrayals by Belpré. Mohr's heroes and heroines navigate their quests in the US and not an imagined island landscape. Though Mohr's child protagonists wrestle with their subjectivities, they are not in perpetual limbo. Indeed, her aim is to present children, particularly her female children, working toward wholeness. Diaspora children, instead, vie for a place within US culture, and at times challenge their categorization as ethnic other within the system. For example, in "The Wrong Lunch Line," Yvette willingly contests the school's system of organizing lunch lines by ethnicity and color when she decides to stand in line with her Jewish friend, Mildred. She is kicked out of the "Jewish" lunch line by school administrators for looking "Spanish" (Mohr, *El Bronx*, 107). The administrator reprimands Yvette for "taking someone else's place" and "going where you don't belong." However, the administrator's act of rejection highlights that a place does exist, albeit a subjugated place, for the "Spanish" diaspora child even in a faulty US system.

Mohr's take on the diaspora child's marginality differs greatly from Belpré's published works. For example, Belpré's character Santiago in the book by the same name (1969) remains in a state of exile and isolation while living in New York City. The only remedy for such feelings of displacement in the displaced child model is a return, either literal or imagined, to the island. Instead, Mohr views marginality as an opportunity for creativity. Mohr's interpretation of marginality coincides with a pattern which I highlight in Puerto Rican youth literature and culture: the significance of the children's bookshelf in forming concepts of nationhood and global community.[17] Many authors and artists speak of confronting this shelf and attempting to fill it. Within this metaphor of spacelessness or shelflessness, a displaced child is a nonexistent child in children's literature. Without a nation and without a representative book, children and their communities lose a place in the imagined global history and landscape of the bookshelf. The children, like their nation, are orphaned from the world of literature. Mohr's characters are symbols of marginality, yet it is not their destiny to stay in the margins, but to transform their subjugated spaces into productive arenas through self-authorship and artistry. In fact, *Nilda* presents us with how marginality functions as a training ground that develops the child into an artistic and poetic (even prophetic) figure, a concept that will be developed in later chapters. Marginality as the substance of creativity and defiance coincides with Bill Ashcroft's statement about postcolonial communities when he writes that "the alienating process which initially served to relegate the post-colonial world to the 'margin' turned upon itself" and created an atmosphere where marginality could "bec[o]me an unprecedented source of creative energy" (12). Latina feminist scholars have analyzed this creativity, particularly in *Nilda*, as offering a space to transform trauma into healing (Garcia 2018; Rodriguez 2019). Sonia Alejandra Rodriguez, for example, analyzes Nilda's drawing as a means of understanding her own agency in which "creativity forges a path toward healing that impacts [her] and her communit[y]" (9). Mohr's child characters search for wholeness found within and in relationship to their community—a community which children participate in building along with adults.

Mohr distinguishes herself from writers like Jesus Colón or Belpré by highlighting diaspora children as forerunners alongside adults in her stories. Her short stories and novels recognize the work of immigrant and migrant young people in supporting their communities, as translators, errand runners, and, at times, representatives for non-English-speaking adults. In the preface, Mohr identifies the daily interactions of children as prominent, if not the most prominent, locations of cultural exchanges within migrant and immigrant communities: "[Migrants] moved into congested neighborhoods inhabited by the children of earlier immigrant groups" (xi). Her stories can actually serve as an argument for how these diaspora children, along with immigrant children, experience greater consequences (e.g., identity confusion, humiliation) than adults as a result of migration. In addition to adult-governed realms, such as the principal's office, children must negotiate power among competing immigrant groups within child-governed realms, such as on the playground or the lunchroom. Children, such as Elba in "The Wrong Lunch Line," who continually reminds Yvette that she is standing in the wrong line, police some of the societal boundaries within the school and neighborhood.

Roche-Rico writes that Mohr's description of "these migrants and their children" as "strangers in their own country connects the narratives of her characters to a shared cultural myth . . . these terms at once connect Mohr's writing to a tradition of immigrant fiction and establish a clear distinction from it" (164). However, Mohr's migrant mythology contrasts with immigrant or American Dream mythologies in that, instead of simply traveling to the US in search of, as Mohr writes, "a piece of the good life known as 'the American Dream,'" these voyagers were translated to the US by the dark side of the American Dream: US expansionism through colonization. Also, though critical, the close association between folklore and nationalism suggests Mohr's desire to unite Puerto Ricans with US national mythology.

*El Bronx*, then, presents a kind urban folklore that inverts classic folkloric and mythological structures, such as the class and gender hierarchies, heroes, and landscapes that Anglo and island readers have come to expect from this tradition. Though she resisted publishers' desires to sensationalize Puerto Rican life, what she sarcastically termed "the whole chilling spectacle of ghetto existence," her texts still expose an underbelly of urban life that does not, as did Belpré and the NYPL, draw the curtain on war, death, and poverty.[18] Mohr exposes societal turmoil from the domestic realms of home and school. She plays with reader's expectations of folklore as a means of exposing hypocrisy within agents of socialization such as the school and the nation, particularly through her use of the phrase "once upon a time" and her treatment of the island's jíbaro mythology.

"Once Upon a Time," the disarming title of a short story in *El Bronx*, is a tale in which Mohr ushers readers into a world where it is not uncommon for children to encounter a dead body during play time. The familiar folkloric phrase frames a story about child's play set against the backdrop of street brutality. The story opens with a children's rhyme, one of three recited by the three girl characters. Like the title, the rhyme contributes a playful though eerie quality to the narrative. Mohr's use of these rhymes seems to invite readers to look behind a shroud of simplicity and innocence covering the child's world: "Bouncey, bouncey, bally, / My Sister's name is Paulie / She gave me a smack, I gave her one back / Bouncey, bouncey, bally" (Mohr, 58) Each girl, varying in her degree of street smarts, recites a different rhyme as she takes a turn bouncing the ball. Mohr refers to these girls simply as "the first girl," "the second girl," and "the third girl"; their namelessness perhaps signifying that these are typical diaspora children one might find playing in the streets and on the rooftops. "The first girl" and "the third girl" exhibit the most street smarts, corresponding to the rhymes they recite. For example, "the first girl" recites a rhyme about receiving and returning a "smack" from her sister, which correlates with the self-preservation she exhibits in the story. "The third girl," who maintains complete composure when the girls stumble upon the body, recites a rhyme that hints at her past experiences with violence and death: "Once upon a time / A baby found a dime. / The dime turned red, And the baby fell down dead!" (58) Interestingly, "the second girl," who exhibits the greatest innocence through the story, recites the most patriotic rhyme: "One, two, three a nation. / I received my confirmation / On the Day of Decoration / Just before my graduation. One, two, three a nation!" This rhyme suggests her attachment to certain social apparatuses, such as the Catholic Church ("my confirmation") and the US government ("Day of Decoration," or Memorial Day), which may prevent her from processing the brutality of the scene the girls later encounter. For example, while the other two girls alternate between thinking the man is dead or asleep, the second girl never diverts from the illusion that he is asleep. Also, by reciting the words "nation" and "Day of Decoration" in the midst of a game, "the second girl" demonstrates how diaspora children are intimately acquainted and tied with a discourse of American patriotism during the war. The patriotic words, recited nonchalantly in a children's rhyme, underscore Mohr's ability to craft social critiques which a reader cannot assess without breaking from an idealist view of children as apolitical or children's literature as a politically neutral medium.

As examples of Mohr's child protagonists, the girls in "Once Upon a Time" are not the traditional, Anglo child characters with assigned children's spaces such as a nursery. Mohr's children have remarkable access not just to the adult world, but also to the underworld of gang and street life; this is exemplified by the facility with which the girls, simply by looking for a more comfortable place to play, encounter the body of the "tough guy" leader of the

Puerto Rican Leopards "curled up, facing the wall" (65). "The first girl," who hatches a plan to inform the Leopards about their leader's death, knows the exact location of the Leopards' club house: next to the candy store. A gang clubhouse beside a candy shop highlights the almost symmetrical existence of the underworld and child's world. As they observe the body, the girls stand in a dark hallway which could represent the societal darkness of urban life encroaching on these children. In order to comprehend the gruesome site, the girls "concentrated as they stared at the body, trying to make things out. After a while, their eyes adjusted to the dark and he became more visible" (62). Mohr upholds children as innocent, since the girls' sight must adjust to the abnormal image of a dead body. The adjustment (or maturation) happens only after prolonged exposure to societal darkness which seems both unjust and inevitable. Yet, Mohr depicts the girls as slipping easily between child's play and this confrontation with death. By the end, the girls revert into a kind of childlike reasoning, deciding that the man was probably "sleeping and has woken up by now." Mohr implies that diaspora children unavoidably encounter societal darkness; however, this moment of "their eyes adjusting to the darkness" does not necessarily forsake innocence. "The second girl" suggests "another game of ball," and the girls begin bouncing the ball to each other again, the narrative ending with the third girl's ominous rhyme "Once Upon a Time / A baby found a dime / The dime turned red / And the baby fell down dead! (67). Like William Blake[19] before her, Mohr highlights innocence and experience as inseparable, symmetrical realities for urban children. Her portrayal of childhood resists the "Child of Nature" model, one which has been extensively analyzed and challenged in Children's Literature Studies and which enforces a distinct barrier between adulthood and childhood, usually understood to be innocence (Gubar, 5). Though usually discussed within the context of nineteenth-century British authors, as in the work of Gubar and Jacqueline Rose, this paradigm still drives much of our discussions of child-hood and children in the field, whether we subscribe to it or not. However, here, precocity or an urban child's interaction with societal maladies does not have to result in ruin or monstrosity, such as in Charles Dickens's portraits of London street children. Indeed, the innocence ascribed to white normative childhood seems ever in peril and is contingent on a reasonable amount of sheltering in order for childhood to persist, underlining the amount of affluence and access needed in order to raise such children, which, in turn, highlights the exclusion of racialized others. Mohr's take on childhood in-nocence speaks to a kind of inner joy, creativity, and wholeness possible for children of color in relationship to their communities which shatters deficit paradigms about so-called at-risk youth in the inner cities.

In *El Bronx*, Mohr also dispels some of the mystique surrounding the fabled island jíbaro, arguably, the most prevalent metaphor and symbol of Puerto Rican folk life. Some of Puerto Rico's earliest published rhetoric—including Manuel Alonso's *Gibaro* (1849), as well as fundamental articulations of national character such Antonio S. Pedreira's *Insularismo: Ensayos Sobre el Caracter Puertorriqueño* (1926)—revolves around the mythical jíbaro, a kind of Puerto Rican Adam. As the emblem for the Partido Popular, the democratic, pro-commonwealth party in Puerto Rico, the jíbaro continues to thrive as a modern articulation of national, political ideology.[20] Accompanied by symbols of rural life (straw hat, bohio, hen, and machete), jíbaro folktales such as the *Juan Bobo* (*Simple John*), tales included by Belpré in her repertoire,[21] feature the innocent farmer partaking in a type of sinless, abundant paradise. By "sinless," I imply that tales such as Belpré's *The Rainbow Colored Horse* (1978) present jíbaros like Tano enjoying the beautiful landscape as he plays his quarto. The intense poverty in rural Puerto Rico—the lack of education, food distribution, and income produced by Spanish and US colonization which propelled the diaspora—never disrupt farm life in these tales. Instead, Puerto Rico represents an Eden untouched by the kind of societal darkness so prevalent in stories about El Barrio or El Bronx. Belpré's Santiago[22] reflects the jíbaro type in his inability to acclimate to city life and his desire to reclaim his pet hen in Puerto Rico. Considering the prominence of jíbaro mythology within Puerto Rican national typology, Mohr's "A Very Special Pet," "A New Window Display," and "Uncle Claudio" read almost like anti-Santiago or anti-jíbaro tales demonstrating the devastation awaiting city dwellers who cling to the jíbaro myth.

"A Very Special Pet," in particular, resists the jíbaro myth through its central premise: Graciela Fernandez, a diaspora mother desperate to feed her family, nearly slaughters Joncrofo, the family's pet hen who lives in a box under the kitchen sink. Joncrofo, a Hispanicized pronunciation of 1940s film actress Joan Crawford, represents the rural island fantasy which Mr. and Mrs. Fernandez and their five children cherish as a family. Though Joncrofo is pampered and "cantankerous," often nipping the children on their arms and legs, like the Fernandez's dream of buying an island farm, the family continues feeding it (the hen/the dream) even though it never lays an egg (materializes). Joncrofo symbolizes the fantasy, as well as the absurdity, of returning to an idyllic island past: a coddled, sterile hen eating cockroaches along the floor of a New York tenement. Joncrofo is also an anachronism representing the impossibility of maintaining a national identity based on the island of old in the contemporary US metropolis. Through Mr. and Mrs. Fernandez's dream of buying an island farm, Mohr expresses the disillusionment which many working-class migrants experienced as hard work failed to reward the sacrifice of leaving the homeland:

> "Someday I am gonna get that job . . . and we could make a lotta money. Why I could . . ." Mr. Fernandez would tell his family several times a week.
>
> "Oh, wow, Papi, we are gonna be rich when you get that job!" the children would shriek . . .
>
> "We gonna get everything and we gonna leave El Bronx," Mr. Fernandez would assure them. "We even gonna save enough money to buy our farm in Puerto Rico—a big one! With lots of land, maybe a hundred acres, and a chicken house . . . And Joncrofo don't have to be tied up like a prisoner no more—she can run loose." (Mohr, 6)

Mr. Fernandez imagines Joncrofo, a symbol of the migrant dream of returning to jíbaro roots, as confined within the US metropolis but liberated within the island. The hen acts almost as an extension of the family itself; it represents a piece of the family they strive to become after sharing in the American Dream. However, once Mrs. Fernandez begins reflecting on how "things are not going that well" and that "they had not saved one cent toward their farm," the reality of a coddled hen living under the kitchen sink becomes incongruous with life in El Bronx: "Lately, she had begun to worry; it was hard to put meat on the table" (6). Contemplating the barren hen, Mrs. Fernandez reaches a decision: "Tonight, her husband would have a good fresh chicken broth for his cold, and her children a full plate of rice with chicken. This silly hen was really no use alive to anyone, she concluded" (8).

Mrs. Fernandez's decision to slaughter the hen actually uncovers a level of brutality within rural farm life which rarely enters the jibaro fantasies. Interestingly, Mrs. Fernandez's decision emphasizes an unromantic truth about rural life: "It had been six years since Mrs. Fernandez killed a chicken, but she still remembered how" (8). The idyllic Puerto Rican island past is suddenly ruptured by images of survival; without productivity, the hens on an actual island farm were not coddled as pets, but prepared as food. As Mrs. Fernandez begins preparations to kill the hen, she still worries about disturbing the innocence of her city-raised children regarding killing animals for survival: "She would tell the children that Joncrofo flew away" (9). Indeed, the children are horrified to find their mother twirling the hen by the neck. As Olga, the oldest, exclaims, "You killed her! You're bad, Mami!" Mrs. Fernandez remembers her island childhood, "[w]hen she was Olgita's age she was already helping her mother slaughter animals for food" (14).

Through Mrs. Fernandez, Mohr emphasizes a type of violence and basic survival in the rural farm for which city children are unprepared—something perhaps even more horrifying than their exposure to drugs or gangs. However, after Joncrofo survives the attack, Mrs. Fernandez decides to continue the children's fantasy of Joncrofo/the farm/the island by telling them that the hen simply "got sick and went crazy" and that sometimes those "things just happen." The children leave the kitchen and Mrs. Fernandez places a traumatized Joncrofo under the sink. The story ends on an unsettling note as the children hear their mother "singing a familiar song . . . about a beautiful island where the tall green palms trees swayed under a golden sky and the flowers were always in bloom" (18).

Though Mrs. Fernandez, in the face of her children, struggles to give up the fantasy, Mohr implies that a migrant's survival in El Bronx may depend on the death of the island fantasy, which cripples migrants between two impossible dreams—the American and the Puerto Rican. The theme of island fantasies and attachments as crippling to the migrant recurs in "Uncle Claudio" and "A New Window Display." For example, Uncle Claudio, as his nieces and nephews recount, returns to Puerto Rico shortly after his arrival because he cannot give up the social status he enjoyed on the island: "At home, when he walks down the street he is Don Claudio. But here in New York City, he is Don Nobody" (136). Uncle Claudio, as his Nuyorican brother tells him, "is always dreaming instead of facing life." His return outfit, which the children notice is the same outfit he arrived in, pictures Uncle Claudio as the epitome of Puerto Rican masculinity, reminiscent of the jíbaro: "a white suit, white shirt with a pale-blue tie, white shoes, and a very pale beige, wide-brimmed, panama hat" (141). The image of jíbaro masculinity contrasts with a kind of emasculation perceived by the children in an earlier scene when Uncle Claudio, stating his reasons for wanting to return, "buried his face in his hands and was crying out loud" (134). "A New Window Display" centers on the death of an island boy, Little Ray, who dies as a result of the terrible New York winter, which he seems biologically incapable of withstanding. Little Ray never learns English; in fact, as one of the children comments, he "talks Spanish as good as my grandmother and parents" (24). Little Ray is a tragic figure since he rejoices in the freedom of El Bronx (he tells the children that Puerto Rico has stricter code of conduct for children), yet, as readers, we know he will not go on with the next generation of diaspora children (28). His inability to acclimate, both linguistically and physically, to his new environment makes him weak and prone to disease, costing him his life. Little Ray is also a kind of fantasy child in that his close association with Puerto Rico, like Joncrofo, inches him closer to his death in El Bronx.

His kindness and manners, possibly associated with his island upbringing, cause the children to see him as "a little angel" as they observe him lying in his coffin, seemingly the only fate in El Bronx for such a child (35).

In the narratives of Joncrofo, Uncle Claudio, and Little Ray, Mohr implies a generational shift. A culture had formed which was no longer displaced and not merely an extension of the old, but a new phenomenological and literary existence. Mohr's framing of this new culture and its heroines presents an alternative Puerto Rican mythology resisting the myths of the island, though it is not without a degree of romanticism. Even the title *El Bronx Remembered* hints at a sense of nostalgia and loss in this portrait of a generation. However, in *Nilda*, Mohr highlights the Puerto Rican narrative as a separate existence from Puerto Rico, and an experience deserving a rightful place in US letters. She addresses the silences around the diaspora in relationship to island literature, while also directing her critique toward Anglo literature. Mohr's portrait of the diaspora child in the US literary landscape is further nuanced when reflecting on her decision to transpose *Nilda* with a canonical children's text like *The Secret Garden*.

## MAKING MAGIC IN NILDA'S WORLD: BARRIOS, WONDERLANDS, AND SECRET GARDENS

Puerto Rican youth literature and culture, in part, responds to Anglo narratives of childhood. Researching childhood as a cultural construction and subject of contention in US literature requires the inclusion of narratives representing varying discourses of "American" childhood with regard to issues such as race, nationality, and ethnicity. Critics should consider that authors of color might choose to incorporate and revise white normative childhood tropes, using those tropes as a means of expressing subversion but also ownership and agency.[23] For example, in *Nilda*, Mohr sought to create the first Puerto Rican child protagonist in US literature, but in doing so she spoke to how Anglo children's literature informs, as Zetta Elliot suggests, how writers of color write and dream up worlds. Nilda is the story of a misunderstood girl (and an orphan by the story's end) who locates a secret world which provides her with a sense of purpose and freedom. The plot, present in Burnett's *The Secret Garden* and, in varying degrees, in other Golden Age children's texts such as Lewis Carroll's *Alice's Adventures in Wonderland* (1865), enables Mohr to highlight the unique experiences of diaspora children while also locating Nilda Ramirez within a familiar literary world populated by Anglo heroines such as Burnett's Mary Lennox or Carroll's Alice Liddell.

Secret lands or spaces in children's literature are certainly not a British or North American invention; however, the privileging of an underdog child hero (a child who overcomes all odds to gain success) occurs more commonly in North American than Latin American literature. As Ann Gonzalez writes, trickster characters are prominent within Latin America (as seen in Belpré's folktales), and though "both [underdog and trickster] figures are socially disadvantaged characters who succeed in the end," the methods toward their success distinguishes the two: "The American underdog [I would also consider England and Canada in this motif as a result of colonial relations] is an individual who, against the odds, achieves success, defined in terms of the American Dream, through perseverance and strength of character. In Latin America, however . . . the underdog is . . . an astute figure whose deceptions represent the unconventional ways that the periphery uses to satisfy basic needs (hunger and survival)" (7). The trickster creates alternative strategies for "success," hides "their deceptions," and teaches children "how to get what is necessary without direct confrontation or open resistance" (8). Interestingly, *Nilda*, reflecting an interwoven discourse of colonialism, incorporates elements of the underdog, through Nilda's perseverance in improving her craft, and the trickster, through the private fantasies Nilda forms around her oppressive environment. Nilda, then, represents Mohr's creation of an "American" girl imprinted by Latin American culture; she is not simply an extension of a Latin American nationality.

Nilda's encounter with a hidden Eden, like so much in Mohr's work, foils readers' expectations of a story about urban children: "[Nilda] noticed . . . a thick wall of bushes. Curious, Nilda went towards it and started to push her way through. Struggling, she pushed away the bushes with her arms and legs and stepped into an opening of yards and yards of roses delicately tinted pink" (Mohr, 154). Much of Nilda's story takes place within the confines of a six-room tenement (she shares the space with eight other family members including an infant) or within inner-city classrooms that restrict her on multiple levels (e.g., physically, linguistically, creatively), but the secret garden is a welcome moment of relief at the center of the tale for both Nilda and the reader. For E. Mohr, Mohr's secret garden distinguishes the novel as a "memorable comment on womanhood," making "*Nilda* particularly satisfying . . . both within and without the context of Nuyorican writing" (77). Yet, given Mohr's interest in childhood, Nilda's secret garden, a central image within the novel, also links *Nilda* with Golden Age typology and a critique of empire. Humphrey Carpenter asserts the importance of garden imagery within the Golden Age of children's literature by writing that Burnett's *The Secret Garden* represents "a work of fiction which, more clearly than any other single book, describes and celebrates the central symbol [the garden] of the Arcadian movement in English writing for children" (188).[24] Carpenter, like Jerry Phillips, interprets Burnett's garden as a symbol of adult desire for utopia—a return to a paradise lost. However, apart from the tradition of garden imagery within literature concerning womanhood and childhood, Phillips emphasizes *The Secret Garden* as a powerful commentary on empire and healing through nature. More specifically, it is Burnett's meditation on "the possibility of a blowback" that underlies her representation of the consequences of imperialism (343). By blowback, Phillips refers to the unsettling of domestic British society caused by the "return of the imperial program" (e.g., the return of British settlers to the homeland). Burnett's text deals with the "predicament" of settler children, like Mary Lennox, who experience identity confusion while attempting to find a place within their "native" land (345). Similarly, Mohr's "secret garden" offers an interpretation of the consequences of US empire, this time for the children of Puerto Rican diaspora. Like Belpré's harvests of story-seeds, Mohr's garden captures the image of scattering seeds—in this case, wild, unwanted seeds. The garden scenes also contain Mohr's plea for the acceptance of diaspora children within US culture. However, though Mohr's child characters share similar interests with their Anglo compatriots, she presents them as developing in fundamentally different ways. As Sánchez-González writes, "Nilda's life [is] similar to most children's lives. . . . However, at each turn in Nilda's childhood she is faced with oppressive structures of power that continually interrupt her world and impose themselves in obnoxious and threatening ways" (122). Through a postcolonial lens, Mohr's garden allows readers to see *Nilda* as a study in difference from the ways Anglo narratives present a child's voyage into an imaginary or secret realm and a child's, especially an orphan child's, search for an individual, creative space in the actual world.

Nilda's secret garden enables Mohr to comment on a diaspora child's journey into a kind of wonderland experience and how that journey differs from an Anglo child's. The garden scene suggests a splitting of the novel into two sections (Nilda, before the garden; Nilda, after the garden) with regard to Nilda's ability to "journey" into a secret realm. Pre-garden, Nilda's secret realm or wonderland exists only within her imagination and creativity; it is not a physical space, but, rather, a state of mind. Readers filter the story through Nilda's perspective, which means incidents are sometimes scattered and characters are often exaggerated. Nilda's "box of things," a container with cardboard cutouts, paper, and crayons that she keeps under her bed, exemplifies her ability to project her imagination around moments of oppression or embarrassment: "[S]he began to divide the space, adding color and making different size forms. Her picture began to take shape and she lost herself in a world of magic achieved with some forms, lines, and color. She finished her picture feeling that she had completed a voyage all by herself, far away but in a place she knew quite well." Ever the artist, Nilda continues this strategy of coloring around and reshaping disturbing situations, as when she imagines pricking Mrs. Heinz, a social worker who humiliates Nilda and her mother over the child's "filthy nails." Nilda "wants to stick her with this stupid nail file," given to her by Mrs. Heinz. She imagines the death of Mrs. Heinz, dramatizing what others would say after she disappeared: "No blood would come out of her because she hasn't any. But just like that . . . poof! She would begin to empty out into a large mess of cellophane . . . First her eyebrows disappeared . . . And now she is all gone. Disappeared, just like that! Poor thing. My what a pity" (71). Post-garden, however, Nilda remembers the "secret garden" as a tangible experience, one she chooses to conjure during moments of transition and loss, such as her stepfather's death. Nilda also shows her cousin, Claudia, a drawing of the garden, and the trail leading to it, at the very end of the novel. This moment cements the garden as representative of an actual place of purpose and opportunity beyond simple fantasy and the constricting social conditions of the barrio (Mohr, 292).

Mohr emphasizes child agency through creativity and imagination, suggesting that diaspora children can and must transform subjugated spaces into what Sánchez-González calls "an alternative space" (123). However, Nilda envisions this space as a kind of proactive, self-fashioned wonderland. If Nilda is going to experience a journey into a fantasy realm, she must take charge of the experience, drawing her wonderland over and around the actual world as a kind of graffiti.[25] For example, in the novel's opening, Nilda and many El Barrio residents feel as if they are "baking alive" in the summer heat. Jacinto and some of the other men break open a city hydrant, creating a momentary oasis for adults and children. Some children even wear bathing suits or jump into the water naked, a moment that Nilda sees as transforming the street into a "magical waterfall" (4). Then, Nilda, through her imagination, "erase[s]" the white policemen who break up the crowd: "If this happens again, one more time, I'm going to arrest all your asses! The whole . . . bunch of you spicks" (6–8).

This sense of Nilda drawing over and around the actual world contrasts with Anglo texts such as *The Secret Garden*, which present a child's entrance into and out of their secret, magical spaces as happening with relative ease. Though fantasy realms may reflect an author's commentary on social issues, in traditional Anglo children's tales, the child and the reader generally experience an uninterrupted voyage into the other world with clear boundaries between the magical and actual, such as a garden door, a rabbit hole, or a wardrobe. In *The Secret Garden*, for instance, Mary Lennox finds the key to the secret garden and takes possession of the space with little opposition: "[Mary] was inside the wonderful garden and she could come through the door under the ivy any time and she felt as if she had found a world all her own" (Burnett, 95). Mary, Colin, and Dickon, the central child characters, spend several uninterrupted hours within the garden as if it were their own private kingdom. Mary actually considers the garden her "secret kingdom," and carefully considers to whom she allows entrance. Colin, the master of Misselthwaite Manor in his father's stead, demands that the adult staff of Misselthwaite keep away from the children's space: "I will not let anyone know where I go . . . Everyone has orders to keep out of the way" (Burnett, 302). Similarly, characters like Alice or C. S. Lewis's Pevensie siblings, remain in their magical spaces over the course of several episodes, awakening from a dream or walking out of the wardrobe at the end of the tale.[26] Additionally, like Mary and Colin, Alice and the Pevensie children are portrayed as conquering the fantasy worlds they encounter (e.g., Alice is crowned the queen of the Looking-Glass World, the Pevensie children are the kings and queens of Narnia). Arguably, the drama in these Anglo children's stories centers on a child's ability to subdue the magical world. However, Nilda's fragmented adventures suggest that a prolonged wonderland experience, where a child quickly accesses a portal and persists within a secret space for a long period in the text signals luxury and even imperialistic entitlement.

Phillips highlights the "class politics" of Burnett's interpretation of the British Empire in India and her characterization of lower-class areas of England such as Yorkshire. Although Mohr ultimately likens Nilda's ambiguous national identity with Mary Lennox's position as an Anglo-Indian, I suggest class politics have also figured into the way Burnett (and, arguably, other "Golden Age" authors) mark the separation between child and adult spaces in contrast to Mohr. Gubar has argued that Golden Age authors like Burnett thought of children as much more socialized and connected to the adult world than has been suggested (5).[27] Regardless of Burnett's ability to create child characters that were intellectually and culturally on par with adults and keen to the realities of the adult world, class is still an imperative issue in Burnett's idealization of children's spaces. Mohr's narratives suggest that the ability to access a separate child space or to maintain a barrier between adult and child worlds depends not so much on a child's ability to maintain innocence, but on class. Class and race governs space, whether it is space to maintain or to feign a children's innocence. Mohr presents Nilda as imagining, dreaming, and living differently from an Anglo child; this impacts the construction of a secret world, particularly with regard to space and time.

In Nilda's world, privacy is a nonexistent commodity. As in *El Bronx*, *Nilda* contains none of the nurseries or playrooms prevalent in classics like *Peter Pan* or *Mary Poppins*.[28] The economic instability of the Ramirez family compromises Nilda's physical space; her home experiences several additions and losses in family members as the story progresses. Nilda must give up her room to both her aunt and later her brother's girlfriend and the new baby: "Nilda had Frankie's cot in her parents' bedroom. She missed her bed and her room, especially her window. Her own bed used to be by the window and she could look and see the sky anytime she wanted. She missed the privacy she had been used to. . . . Nilda was constantly aware of the fact that she could not make any noise" (72). Nilda's lack of physical space compounds with the frequent violent and social interruptions which inhibit the linear progression of Nilda's imaginary adventures. For example, on a walk in the neighborhood, Nilda's mediation on the shapes and colors in the concrete lead her to a gruesome discovery:

> The different shapes of the worn-out surfaces of concrete and asphalt developed before her eyes into dragons, animals, oceans, and planets of the universe. She continued looking for the new and wonderful worlds that lay hidden underneath the concrete.
>
> Nilda was completely absorbed when she saw tiny red dots all about the same size of a dime. She bent down to examine the shiny surface and as she touched the dot with her shoe, its spread. It's liquid, like paint or something, she thought . . . The red dots led Nilda to a doorway and beyond, into a pool of glistening red liquid inside the hallway of a building. 'Ay, ayyy,' someone moaned. . . . Looking up and into a corner, she saw a man clutching his stomach. His light blue shirt was streaked with crimson and his hands were drenched in blood. His face twisted in pain, he looked at Nilda, his dark eyes pleading for help. (36)

Nilda's first impression of the blood ("like paint or something") is oddly beautiful, a moment of innocence suggesting a deeper reality: transforming blood, shed in violence, into an artist's tool. As in *El Bronx*, the moment also suggests Mohr's conception of childhood as an equal relationship between innocence and experience, never a forfeiting of one over the other.

Recalling the Joncrofo narrative of *El Bronx*, Mrs. Fernandez explains Joncrofo's would-be slaying by telling the children that the hen had a moment of madness—a "thing that just happens sometimes." Those "things" that "just happen sometimes," like the persistent inequality and darkness surrounding Mohr's characters, are recurrent ruptures in the diaspora child's dreamscape, preventing linear journeys into a dream world. Nilda's adventures into the secret space of her imagination are sporadic and must occur between interludes of city noise, adult reprimands, and violence.

The narrative's interruptions, along with Mohr's illustrations, help lead the reader into Nilda's world which Sánchez-González believes forms part of Mohr's "woman-centered prose" and "hermeneutic co-participation with the reader" (121). Living in Nilda's world means that even moments of play, daydreaming, and sleep, often considered sacred childhood activities, are interrupted, as illustrated in Nilda's experiences at an Irish Catholic charity camp, a free summer camp for Puerto Rican and other minority children. As Nilda and the children board the train to the camp, signs of the city slowly fade from Nilda's window view. She sees "no tall buildings at all," but, instead, the unfamiliar landscape of upstate New York:

> White churches with pointed steeples. Barns and weather vanes. Neat patches of grass and flowers. It reminded her of the movies . . . the Andy Hardy pictures, she almost said out loud. In those movies Mickey Rooney and his whole family were always so happy. They lived in a whole house all for themselves. She started thinking about all those houses that so swiftly passed by the train window. Families and kids, problems that always had happy endings. A whole mess of happiness, she thought, just laid out there before my eyes. . . . Nilda smiled, losing herself in the happy plot of the story. (Mohr, 9)

Yet, though Nilda begins getting "lost in the happy plot of the story," a nun's interjection quickly prevents her fulfillment: "Don't pick your nose. You'll get worms . . . You! You! I am talking to you." Mohr's allusion to the 1940s-era Andy Hardy films, and the image of Nilda and the other "Brown" children, looking out of the train window at a world apart from the inner city, also probes at the class and racial division that color a diaspora child's dreamscape. "The happy plot" belongs to the images of whiteness that Nilda sees on the movie screen or outside the train window, not to the children heading for the charity camp. Nilda's pleasure in fantasy, something which momentarily erased her awareness of onlookers, is interrupted by the nun and the "embarrassment spreading all over her face as everyone laughed" (9). Indeed, the charity camp scenes resonate with images of alienation and humiliation. Continuing the trend of orphanhood, the scene where the campers line up to receive their nightly meal from the nuns resonates with *Oliver Twist*, complete with a serving of gruel. Nilda and the other female campers fall asleep to the sound of their own sobs: "Pulling the covers over her head, she began to cry quietly . . . until she fell asleep. During the night the sounds of sobbing and whimpering coming from the other cots woke her, but each time she closed her eyes, going back into a deep sleep" (16). Mohr depicts Nilda as a continually awakening from a "deep sleep," which parallels Nilda's inability to "lose herself" in fantasy. Nilda's intermittent dreaming also occurs during another episode in which she imagines "building a neat fortress of snow in Central Park" as the voice of her teacher, Mrs. Langhorn, fades "far, far away." Nilda's thoughts about the snow fort ("Maybe Nilda thought, we could build an igloo house like I seen in them pictures about Eskimos") are interjected with Mrs. Langhorn's lecture about the importance of hard work in America ("Nobody gave you anything for free those days"). The reader gains admission into Nilda's secret places much in the same way that Nilda does, by editing out the interruptions (54).

More than mere escapism,[29] a wonderland experience in children's texts often serves as a critique of the social order, protocol, customs, and mythology of the actual, governing world. Carroll's *Wonderland* does this through Alice's encounters with characters who continually ask her to recite or obey arbitrary rules, as in "The Mad Tea Party" scene that satirizes the politics of order at the tea table. Similarly, by inviting the reader into one of the most notorious and marginalized US neighborhoods, deciphering Nilda's world involves the reader's descent into an underground world that pokes fun at the sometimes nonsensical politics of order, particularly within the US-Puerto Rico colonial relationship. Because many critics treat *Nilda* as an autobiography, they miss the experimental and satirical aspects of the text. Mohr evokes this descent into the barrio during a scene where Nilda walks home during her lunch hour and must pass through a series of dark, urine-infested tunnels on Park Avenue: "The tops curved into archways; inside each tunnel a single bulb shone, giving off very little light. Nilda squinted her eyes as she stood at the entrance trying to see inside" (58). Ten-year-old Nilda, who sometimes sings in the tunnels, already has an awareness of crime and keeps her money in her shoes, advice from her brother who told her not to "be a sucketa, stupid." The image of a little girl singing and walking through dark tunnels in order to reach home underlines East Harlem/El Barrio's illicit reputation in upper-crust New York society, represented by Park Avenue, a symbol of the city's wealth and power. Mohr's spiraling illustrations,[30] containing both words and pictures, also enable the reader's sense of descent into El Barrio's underground. On *Nilda's* original 1973 book jacket, a Harper & Row reviewer is quoted as saying that "the more you look at these pictures, the more deeply you enter Nilda's world." Mohr's illustrations do not "create scenes" or "convey moods," but "combine representational art, symbols, and words to express the essence of the characters and to make a statement about their interrelationships." For example, the opening fire hydrant scene, the novel's first illustration, pictures a mangled mess of barrio residents (women, men, and children) as they float in the ripples of the "magic waterfall." Mohr's illustration of Nilda and her stepfather, Emilio, pictures one of Emilio's obscene lectures to Nilda on the US government and the Catholic Church. A row of East Harlem buildings is sketched in the upper periphery of the drawing. Nilda's image is sandwiched between the buildings and Emilio's image. Nilda, lying on her stomach, her hand pressed to her chin, drifts into daydreaming, presumably another "happy plot" considering the words, "No BIG Buildings??? . . . all about People who live in little houses. Everybody does?" sketched above her head. Emilio's smoke rings, like those of Carroll's caterpillar, spiral before Nilda's face. The smoke rings read: "Ok, think Nilda . . . racists . . . war killing . . . Nilda listen . . . bunch of garbage . . . basura" (207).

Inside El Barrio's underground, readers engage with a series of caricatures and contradictions that poke fun at the power structures in Nilda's world. Nilda's story highlights that anyone from adults to children, "Spanish" or Anglo, can represent an agent of power policing the spaces of Nuyorican children. For example, Nilda's white teacher, Mrs. Reilly, and Olga, a young girl from Spain, both ridicule Puerto Rican Spanish as a class marker (155). Even Nilda's mother slaps her for defying Mrs. Heinz: "If I make that woman angry, God knows what she'll put down on our application. We have to have that money in order to live" (70). Everyone is "a little mad" in Nilda's world; she really has no one to provide her with direction or validity.

Mohr captures the oppressive forces in Nilda's world through her caricatures of El Barrio's white authority figures, such as Mrs. Langhorn and Mrs. Reilly, both of whom represent a project of internal colonialism within US education. Mrs. Langhorn is a teacher obsessed with locking the supply cabinet so as not to "tempt a thief." The thieves: her classroom of Nuyorican children. Mrs. Langhorn lectures against what she perceives to be the children's inherent, habitual thievery: "'That's how it all starts; first it's a pencil, then perhaps a fountain pen. It's so easy why not open somebody's purse? Oh, no! Start right from the beginning and you'll get into the habit of being honest. H-O-N-E-S-T-Y,' she said, spelling out the word" (52). Mrs. Langhorn's "loud sandpaper voice" causes the children to call her "Foghorn." Mohr's description of Mrs. Langhorn exaggerates the teacher's features:

She was a short plumpish woman close to sixty years of age. Her thin-
ning grey hair was cut short and done up in a tight permanent wave.
She had a sallow complexion and small eyes surrounded by puffy
skin. . . . The loose-fitting dresses she wore were made of crepe materials, usually dark in color, and most had stains that years of dry
cleaning had permanently set into the fabric. Her bosom caved in
and her stomach extended out. She always wore low-heeled shoes in
need of a shine. (51)

Mohr's emphasis on color in Mrs. Langhorn's description enables the reader
to see the teacher as Nilda does, all "grey," "dark," and "in need of a shine"—she
is the antithesis to Nilda's visions of shape and color.

Mrs. Langhorn, a caricature of the US education system, seeks to impart
children with idealist notions of US progress, history, and the American
Dream. Mohr, through Mrs. Langhorn, highlights the impossibility of this
dream particularly since this idealist vision offers no place for children who
look and speak like Nilda. Mrs. Langhorn lectures Nilda and the class about
the potency of the imperial project: "Brave people they were, our forefathers.
. . . They were not going to permit the Indians to stop them. This nation was
developed from a wild primitive forest into a civilized nation. Where would
we all be today if not for brave people? We would have murder, thievery, and
no belief in God?" By mentioning "thievery" in her list of consequences of
an uncivilized nation, Mrs. Langhorn implies that she perceives the children
(thieves) as challenges to American imperialism, making her instruction
part of the civilizing process. Like a cartoon villain, Mrs. Langhorn smiles
through "discolored teeth from smoking," and wears stained clothes, all while
reprimanding the children "for coming into class unwashed." She seeks to
transform the children into "good Americans," something which she demands not only through her lectures but, further symbolizing the imperial
project, through violent force (52). Nilda and the children continually get
"rapped on the knuckles" by Mrs. Langhorn for disobeying one her "most
strict rules"—speaking Spanish within the classroom. Mohr depicts Nilda,
who is both beaten on her hands and made to wear a "dunce" cap for speaking Spanish, as literally coloring around the abuse: "[Nilda] hated when
the skin broke and the knuckles swelled; her hands stayed sore all day and
hurt for a long time. This was especially upsetting to Nilda when she looked
forward to working on her cutouts and drawings for her 'box of things' at
home" (53). Nilda's injured hands, a disturbing image within Mohr's portrait
of diaspora childhood, represent Nilda's defiance of the rules as well as the
opposition she must endure in creating her secret place. Nilda's injured hands

also reflect the combination of trickster and underdog models at work in Mohr's characterization. Nilda defies social order both publicly (underdog) and privately (trickster), but she does not always "hide her deceptions." More the underdog, Nilda represents strategies for confronting and pushing past injustice. Spanish, within Mrs. Langhorn's context, corresponds with a child's degree of assimilation and acts as a hindrance to American progress: "You will never amount to anything worthwhile unless you learn English. You'll stay just like your parents. Is that what you people want? Eh?" Through emphasizing the children's parentage and home life as dishonorable, Mrs. Langhorn renders Puerto Rican parents as void within the criteria for raising good Americans. Without proper parentage, the children are, in a sense, wards of the state in need of proper upbringing made possible only through the US school system.

Mrs. Reilly, a "petite woman" with neat silver hair, also highlights the US education system's tendency to alienate diaspora children, this time by undermining Latin American heritage. Mrs. Reilly, the Spanish teacher, teaches the children Spanish with "an American accent [that was] so thick that Nilda had a hard time understanding what she said." For Mrs. Reilly, whose "favorite country was Spain," the children's Puerto Rican Spanish ("that dialect") hinders their status within an ideal of Spanish and Latin America culture (213–14). She tells the children that in Spain "they speak Castilian, the real Spanish; I am determined that this is what we shall learn and speak in my class; nothing but the best!" Mohr's caricature of Mrs. Reilly highlights the nonsense of a teacher speaking with an American accent while demanding that her students annunciate as Castilians: "Accent! Remember, proper enunciation diction" (215). The scenario becomes even more ridiculous as Nilda observes Edna, a student "born in Puerto Rico," faulting as she tries to speak "with the accent that Miss Reilly required." Mrs. Reilly responds to Edna: "Very well, Edna, you are doing a little better. However, you must practice and stop speaking that dialect you speak at home; it is not helping you. . . . We mustn't forget what the Spanish tradition is and means . . . pride" (216). Mohr underlines the burden of children like Nilda, who, as colonized individuals searching for identity and place, negotiate between varying sets of nonsensical, cultural standards established by the colonizer. Like a mad tea party of sorts, Nilda and the other Puerto Rican young people are incapable of performing as proper Americans or Latin Americans. Nilda and the children, like Alice, are left with no space at the metaphorical table.

Nilda's secret garden helps us evaluate the political and social intricacies of Nilda's search for a space within US culture. *Nilda* contains Mohr's assertion of a US identity, so Nilda's secret garden represents more than an imaginary wonderland; it is also a symbolic place of exploration and dialogue, within the US, for diaspora voices. Mohr's garden, like Belpré's story seeds, fixates on the literal seed scattering within the concept of diaspora. While Belpré speaks to planting a harvest, Mohr speaks to cultivating something already planted creating an intriguing connection between these women writers. Is Mohr's garden a representation of the kind of planting done by Belpré and the older generation of Puerto Ricans? As with her desire to build a new folklore, Mohr's garden contains anxieties about national origin, specifically proclaiming the US as a new point of origin outside of the Island paradigm. Roche-Rico also highlights Mohr's interpretation of the diaspora as regeneration: "[Diaspora for Mohr is] more than 'scattering'—geographical and cultural dispersion; it is also a 'sowing'—a propagation of new forms, new opportunities for artistic expression and cultural exchange" (172). Mohr, like Belpré, emphasizes the difference between those Puerto Ricans migrating from the island and those born stateside; however, unlike Belpré, Mohr interprets this difference as a gain and not a loss. Belpré hoped that diaspora children would foster a love for Puerto Rico, which would, eventually, return them to their homeland. However, Mohr claims the US as the homeland, and through her narratives, holds her homeland accountable for its parentage of diaspora children.

Nilda's secret garden also gathers themes of marginality and orphanhood present throughout Mohr's portrait of diaspora childhood. As Nilda finds the trail to the garden, she attempts to connect the scenery to her mother's stories about the island; she "remember[s] her mother's description of Puerto Rico's beautiful mountainous countryside covered with bright flowers and red flamboyant trees (153). Mary Lennox's first vision of her garden also connects her to a memory reflecting her own ambiguous national identity. She remembers the roses of India, a country which she left for her "true" nation, England. Nilda's second-generation memory of the island also reflects a sense that she is distancing herself from one country (Puerto Rico) in order to pursue another (the US). Considering Phillips's point about *The Secret Garden* as a critique on returning to the homeland after empire, Mohr inverts the traditional narrative of the homeland. In Puerto Rican literature, the homeland is usually the island, yet Mohr emphasizes a child embracing the US as her homeland. Nilda's first memory of national foliage and landscape—something she associates with ideas of belonging and place, and a memory carrying her to the end of the text—happens not on the island, but in a rose garden in upstate New York. The garden is specifically a "wild" rose garden, which, as in Burnett's classic, has been left unkempt and unwanted. Like Burnett's Mary, Nilda must push the overgrown branches and shrubs in order to behold her discovery: the "scattered" roses "growing wildly on the shrubs" (154). As in *The Secret Garden*, the rose garden can represent Nilda's position as an unwanted, "contrary" child. Nilda is "contrary" within a US metropolis where national origin is almost synonymous with social and geographical order (e.g., Chinatown, Little Italy, and Spanish Harlem). She is not American enough for the Mrs. Langhorns of the city, but not "Spanish" enough for the Mrs. Reillys of the world, who demand distinct cultural boundaries from children in terms of national identity. The parallel between these two texts enables Mohr to liken Nilda to Mary by placing Nilda within the role of orphan. The child orphan, as Phillips writes, may actually figure as "a metaphor for the instability of identity, the crisis of representation in certain social relations" in nineteenth century culture (345). Nilda's orphanhood, however, is specifically a political orphanhood—a child without a nation to claim her as its own. Perhaps, Mohr desires readers to see Nilda as Mary, who, before finding the secret garden, lamented about her lack of parentage and place: "[Mary] had begun to wonder why she had never seemed to belong to anyone even when her father and mother had been alive. Other children seemed to belong to their fathers and mothers, but she had never seemed to really be anybody's little girl" (Burnett, 14). As Nilda walks into her secret garden, she is, figuratively, also not "any [nation's] little girl."

Once in the garden, during a visit to a camp, Nilda finds a sense of order and belonging that seemed impossible in the city.[31] In upstate New York, Nilda experiences the kind of spiritual renewal and healing that Mary, Colin, and Dickon enjoy in the English countryside. Mohr depicts Nilda as "inhaling the sweet fragrance of the flowers." The sun shines down on both Nilda and the roses, "enveloping her . . . as was part of them . . . they were part of her." By blending into the roses, Nilda exhibits a freedom from the literal signs of physical and creative restriction that continually encroach on her life: "DO NOT WALK ON THE GRASS . . . DO NOT PICK THE FLOWERS . . . VIOLATORS WILL BE PROSECUTED" (Mohr, 154). Furthermore, Nilda models this belonging within the garden through a highly symbolic act: "She took off her socks and sneakers, and dug her feet into the earth like the roots of the shrubs. Shutting her eyes, Nilda sat there for a long time, eyes closed, feeling a sense of pure happiness; no one had given her anything or spoken to her. The happiness was inside, a new feeling, and although it was intense, Nilda accepted it as part of her life that now belonged to her" (155). Like Nilda's injured hands, digging her feet into the earth proclaims Nilda's (and Mohr's) defiance of the societal boundaries that would render her and her community mute and nonexistent. Nilda positions herself as an American rose, growing wildly in a scattered garden, which, though ignored and perhaps unwanted, continues to form part of the New York landscape. Once again, there is something about marginality that somehow privileges Mohr's characters with insight and an artistic, almost prophetic gift. Nilda can see the future in the garden; it leads to her first feelings of "happiness," which she claims as part of her new life. It is Nilda, the orphaned diaspora child, who finds the secret garden and then leads two other female campers into that secret space. She brings the two girls up the path to the garden, saying, "You are going to have to push the bushes and the branches out the way." The girls, both white, stand with Nilda in the garden, a gesture which reveals, as E. Mohr writes, her "offering [of] a deeply personal gift—offering them, as it were, herself" (77). The girls ask Nilda questions about living in El Barrio, a place they know for its violent reputation. Nilda tells the girls a story about "seeing a man knifed," even as she talks about returning to the camp and visiting her new friends. By inviting the girls into the garden, Nilda offers the garden as a platform for dialogue and storytelling. The garden may even hold some potential for racial harmony. Mohr's illustration of the three girls in the garden (each girl blending into the other, arms outstretched, playing, and a rose at the feet of each girl) further emphasizes Nilda's position as an American little girl. Upon returning to El Barrio, Nilda uses the garden as a point of reference; it is the evidence that a productive, nurturing place where she can thrive does exist: "The perspiration began to run down the sides of her face and, for a moment, she remembered the camp, the trails, her garden, and the silence. That is happening, she thought, right now too, someplace real far, where I was this morning" (168).

## "A BIT OF EARTH": ART, CREATIVITY, AND BELONGING IN A GARDEN OF MULTICULTURALISM

Because the garden is a site for creation and dialogue, Nilda's secret garden also contains Mohr's advocacy for the arts as an outlet for the cultivation of diaspora children. Like Burnett's garden, Mohr's garden is a place where the child can govern and take action. When Mr. Craven asks what Mary wants for amusement, Mary asks for "a bit of earth." The request reveals her desire to beautify and remake the unwanted garden. Mr. Craven grants Mary's request, saying, "take it, child, and make it come alive" (143). Through *Nilda* and texts like *El Bronx*, Mohr essentially makes a similar request of the US literary establishment: a "bit of earth" that testifies to the existence of her community and its children within US culture. Nilda possesses the garden only temporarily, but she claims the feelings and creative energies sparked by the garden for the remainder of her life. Near the end of the novel, readers gain a greater understanding of the garden's connection to Nilda's artistic gift—the garden and the gift become interchangeable symbols. Nilda's mother, Lydia, reserves her dying words to ask her daughter a thought-provoking question: "[I]f you have no money and little education, who will help you, Nilda?" The moment comes as an unexpected insight into Lydia Ramirez's broken dreams who, unlike her daughter, never found her own secret place, either real or imaginary. Lydia connects Nilda's privacy with her ability to draw: "Do you have that feeling honey? That you have something all yours . . . you must . . . like when I see you drawing sometimes, I know you have something all yours . . . Keep it . . . hold on, guard it. Never give it to nobody . . . not to your lover, not to your kids . . . it don't belong to them . . . and . . . they have no right . . . no right to take it" (277). Lydia's remarks are oddly similar to Mary's justifications for keeping her secret garden when she tells Dickon: "Nobody has any right to take it from me when I care about it and they don't. They're letting it die. . . . I've nothing to do. . . . Nothing belongs to me. I found it myself and I got into it myself. It's a secret garden, and I'm the only one in the world who wants it to be alive" (122). Both Lydia and Mary equate the cultivation of a private space with the right to ownership and control of access. Nilda's artistry allows her to have something her mother never had—namely, "a room of one's own."[32] It is also significant that the novel ends with a scene in which Nilda shows her drawings of the garden to her cousin, Claudia. Nilda emphasizes not only the garden, but the "special trail . . . see how it winds . . . well, that trail leads to the secret garden." Sanchez-Gonzalez writes that "the path leading to the garden suggests that Nilda has already found the tools she can use for demystifying an oppressive social order in the United States and successfully reconceptualizing herself as an integral and sovereign subject in the world" (131). However, more than finding the tools, I believe Mohr wishes for readers to see the path as an invitation. They, too, can develop the creative strategies necessary for surviving in a hostile environment. Nilda—as in the García Lorca poem that prefaces the novel, "Ballad of the Little Square" (1955)—has learned "the path of the poets," which, arguably, leads to a kind of preservation of the soul. In the Lorca poem, this soul is that of "a child, ripened with legends, with a feathered cap, and a wooden sword." Again, Mohr underlines the ability to maintain childlike innocence even within depressing conditions. Artistry and creativity outline this "path of the poets" that leads to survival. Survival is realized not by passively accepting social restrictions, but by carving out opportunities from what one is given. Even more important, perhaps, Nilda's drawing of the path also means that readers, like the girls at the camp, can follow Nilda into her secret garden, partaking in a cultural perspective radically different from their own. In fact, by the end of the novel, readers can get the sense that they have been standing in Nilda's secret garden all along, listening to her story of heartbreak and resistance.

Perhaps, this sense of gaining insider knowledge[33] into another culture, particularly subaltern cultures, is the most admirable, democratic promise of multicultural literature. Children's literature in particular, as Ann Gonzalez writes, seems to offer greater access into the consciousness and ideology of subaltern groups.[34] However, Mohr also offers a kind of cautionary tale against the uncritical, optimistic spirit of post-civil rights multiculturalism. I say this because her work has yet to receive the kind of critical attention of other "ethnic" writers. Instead, we have looked to Mohr as a kind of cultural guide and her texts as works testifying to "ghetto" life. Some of her original reviewers saw *Nilda* as "the story of the hardship and discrimination faced by a poor Puerto Rican girl" and "a beautiful expression of a young girl's coming of age in the ghetto."[35] However, it seems critics have done little more than celebrate Mohr as a voice of "hardship." Part of Roche-Rico's argument for the redirection of Mohr's critical appraisal includes looking to Mohr as a "naturally privileged—though not exclusive—authority on her own body of work." Roche-Rico writes that Mohr, like many female writers, has "combated the invisibility and silence of their positions—and the indifference, apathy, or antagonism of early reviewers—by devising their own polemics, their own language for assessing their literary output" (163). She points to Mohr's essays and her "partial memoir," *Growing Up in the Sanctuary of My Imagination* (1994), as the beginning for how to understand Mohr. It is easy to see Mohr's fiction as speaking to the importance of diversity and pluralism within the US. However, critics have turned a blind eye toward specificity in an optimistic vision of multiculturalism in which a Puerto Rican rose scattered in the US landscape is just another ethnic rose. Even in our current critiques about diversity and need for "own voices" authors, in which Mohr's novels often make the list for recommended books, the conversation rarely points to how US colonialism connects to racial paradigms and erasure in literature and literary study—stories about celebrating stories about immigrating to the US might receive preference over stories documenting US land seizure and contemporary colonialism. Critics have missed the specific ways in which Mohr holds US ideology accountable for its imperialism and its promises of democracy and pluralism to the colonized. The metaphor of the children's bookshelf, which has been so important in my study, demonstrates this desire for pluralism and inclusion; however, the organization of that bookshelf, and the children's literary world, continues to mirror a kind of separate, but equal ghettoization.

In this chapter, I have argued that Mohr's critical attention should shift away from her autobiography and toward her writing and art—toward the experimental and provocative portraits she creates in the imaginative worlds of *El Bronx Remembered* and *Nilda*. I have argued that we can begin assessing Mohr's critical, aesthetic practices by studying her appropriations of children's narratives, such as island folklore and Anglo children's literature. I have demonstrated that reading Mohr's work as children's literature should not limit our ability to study Mohr as an imposing force in US fiction, particularly since children's literature is a political medium. Moreover, considering youth literature a "reductive category" limits our ability to examine many writers who have used youth literature and culture as a means of experience and resistance.

Nicholasa Mohr is the child whom Belpré sought. She grew up in the same neighborhoods where Belpré planted island folklore as a way of harvesting Puerto Rican identity in diaspora children. Yet, Mohr did not recognize herself, her family, or her community in that folklore or in the Anglo children's stories available in the New York Public Library. Instead, Mohr, through her experimental fiction, asserts a new US identity by advocating a new folk culture and creating, for the first time, a diaspora heroine who resists the deficient paradigm by "stealing"[36] her own secret garden.

## Chapter Four

# THE LETTER OF THE DAY IS Ñ

## *Sesame Street,* a Girl Named Maria, and Performing Multilingualism in Children's Television

A wooden casita, built over an abandoned lot in East Harlem, foregrounds an icon of American children's lore: Big Bird. After greeting *Sesame Street's* child viewers by saying "Hola," Big Bird explains that a "casita is a special kind of house just like they have in Puerto Rico."[1] The casitas, rural island dwellings sandwiched by modern skyscrapers, exemplify a pattern in the art of the Puerto Rican diaspora: the building of a structure, whether imaginative, physical, or, in this chapter, linguistic, over a US given. Big Bird among the casitas also demonstrates how the diaspora's approach, and imposition, toward US culture imprints the dominant culture—an American icon speaking Spanish. "Hola" is a familiar word in the *Sesame Street* universe, particularly since the 1971 introduction of Sonia "Maria" Manzano, the Puerto Rican actress and writer for the Children's Television Workshop,[2] the production company that makes *Sesame Street.* Manzano, recently retired in 2014, began writing literature for young people in 2003 with her first picture book, *A Box Full of Kittens,* followed by *No Dogs Allowed!* (2007). Both celebrated the simple joys of young Latinxs growing up in New York. However, her turn to young adult audiences in *The Revolution of Evelyn Serrano* (2013) and *Becoming Maria* (2014) employs the kind of critical, creative lens she employed for years rendering Latinx lives and histories visible on *Sesame Street.* Manzano's revolutionary role of over forty years as performer and writer on *Sesame Street* as "Maria" gave a face and voice to a diaspora community that is significantly underrepresented in the children's literary world. Even with the work of Pura Belpré and Nicholasa Mohr, Puerto Ricans and Latinxs overall remain among the least represented groups in all youth literature and media.[3] As one of the "friendly neighbors" on one of the nation's most beloved television shows for young people, the celebrated presence and role of Maria/Manzano on *Sesame Street* forces a consideration of why children's television, as opposed to children's literature, offered such a prominent cultural address for this community.

What has been possible for Latinxs in children's television apart from children's literature? An irony exists when the erasure of people of color protagonists persists on the page, yet for fifty years *Sesame Street* has presented people of color as ordinary, friendly neighbors. Even in Latinx Studies, Sonia Manzano's performance and writing on *Sesame Street* is seldom discussed when considering Latinx representation and audience reception in media, as opposed to those happening in adult media around figures such as Jennifer Lopez, Rosario Dawson, and Selena Quintanilla (Baez 2019). Manzano belongs in conversations about how Latinxs as subjects and agents resist the rigid stereotypes of Latinas, ultimately owning and authoring representations in prominent venues. Youth media, television, film, and music, particularly during the 1980s and 1990s, should form part of our understanding of writing for young people and Latinx media more broadly. Angie Thomas, author of the breakout young adult novel *The Hate You Give* (2016), often credits Tupac Shakur and other rap artists as her writing role models when she was a young person struggling to find herself in the literary world. "Publishing did something pretty terrible. They made the assumption that black kids don't read" (*Telegraph*).[4] Thomas's references to television such as *It's a Different World* and artists like Shakur underline how literacy and reading function outside the dictates of literature, the canon, and school curriculum. Moreover, the notion in the 1970s and 1980s, when television was still blamed for "rotting minds," that the medium could transform and supplement learning, especially early literacy skills, was controversial and revolutionary.[5] From the late 1970s through the 1990s, while publishing dismissed generations of youth of color, television provided teachers and models of color such as Levar Burton in *Reading Rainbow* and Sonia Manzano in *Sesame Street* bridging the gap between audiences and books, echoing the kind of critical literacy practices modeled by Belpré and Schomburg decades before.

Manzano's performance and writing from the 1970s to the 2000s invites an examination of where generations of readers would turn when publishing remained silent, and what those audiences would learn about how multiple languages and cultures shape their worlds. The medium of television affords a playing with language which at times, registers as shallow ("Hola Means Hello"), but also revolutionary for its dedication to yielding to multilingual discourses. For example, although Nicholasa Mohr, the preeminent children's author of the Nuyorican era, injects Spanish words and phrases, she limits code-switching given her relationship to her audience: "[Poets] can read their work aloud and have close contact with their public. When I do use words in Spanish, I follow them up with English in a way that is clear" (Rodriquez, 93). Here, Mohr implies that speaking and performance transcend certain limits existing on the written page.

In this chapter, I focus on how the character of Maria functions in relationship to *Sesame Street*'s language pedagogy. During Manzano's tenure, the show emphasized language practices as a kind of performance, though problematically at times, such as through skits employing miming, music, theatre, and spoken word as a means of depicting language practices. However, as a character based in US and Puerto Rican cultures, Maria's role of teaching language through performance connects to Puerto Rican literacy traditions. Specifically, Manzano continues a trend of Puerto Ricans occupying spaces outside traditional literature as a means of critiquing literature, and encouraging self-education and critical literacy. Like the aesthetic of the casitas, *Sesame Street* presents Spanish as difficult to ignore since it has augmented the structure of official English. Bilingual characters like Maria and Luis collide with a variety of characters and cultures. On the show, Maria embodies bilingualism as a communicative gift which can benefit everyone on the *Street*. She is particularly intriguing in that, unlike Belpré and Mohr's creations, Maria is a combination of television producers' imaginings and Manzano's performative and literal authorship. While children's literature, as Clare Bradford writes, reflects the language-related power struggles of colonial societies,[6] such as naming and ordering territories, there is a lack of language experimentation and interaction in many books for youth (Bradford, 20–43). Despite growing interest in international and more diverse authors and stories in recent scholarship, outside of discussions on translation, children's literature scholars say little about the use and exchange of foreign languages, and even less about Spanish as a non-foreign part of US youth literature.[7] Yet, what happens when languages collide and break unspoken rules, such as when *Sesame Street* enables exchanges such as untranslated dialogue and segments completely in Spanish?

*Sesame Street* and Maria represent a paradox similar to how Jillian Baez describes the iconic *West Side Story* film and play, a cultural landmark that served as a filter for producers when creating *Sesame Street*'s Puerto Rican heroine. Baez writes about the ironies of problematic though useful portrayals: "On the one hand, *West Side Story* filled a gap in entertainment media, where Puerto Ricans were seldom represented. On the other hand, it served as a template through which non-Puerto Ricans made sense of Puerto Ricans, particularly in the 1960s and 1970s, when few cinematic representation of Puerto Ricans were in circulation" (1). *Sesame Street* circulates stories about Latinxs and language in a way unprecedented in print mediums, touting both the power of broadcast

media and its ability to intervene in communities disenfranchised by schooling situations. My analysis probes questions of access regarding racial justice
and historically disadvantaged children, among them African American and
Puerto Rican preschoolers, the two "at-risk" groups targeted by Sesame Street's
early research and self-esteem curriculum. Maria's creation marks television
producers' desire to reach a Puerto Rican community perceived as violent
and impoverished, a group of preschoolers that producers may have felt had
more access to television than literature. Yet, this is not a study in linguistics,
nor is it a comprehensive study on Sonia Manzano's role in television history,
although my analysis touches on these subjects.

Maria, a representation of Puerto Rican migrants in New York City—and,
specifically, Sonia Manzano's performance, embodiment, and later writing of
the Latinx content on the show—serves as an illustration in both sections of
this chapter since she embodies the show's language ideology. First, I analyze
the show's approach to presenting bilingual discourse as a give-and-take negotiation of power. What children's programs like Sesame Street compel us to see
is that languages do not always run parallel, as bilingual books often suggest.
"A bilingual," Ana Celia Zentella writes, "is not two monolinguals stuck at
the neck" (56). I highlight the historical and social issues underlying Maria's
creation as drawing on popular portrayals such as West Side Story while
still opposing stereotypes of migrants. Maria's character and performance
illustrates the show's approach to pacifying relations between rival languages,
English and Spanish. Second, I examine the role of performance in Sesame
Street's language instruction. Language and performance on Sesame Street are
interrelated to the point that the show presents performance as language, and
language as a performance. Maria, particularly in her performances as a mime,
illustrates the show's representation of language as a process of mimicking
sounds and/or gestures, like miming, singing, or dancing. In the show's pluralistic vision, Sesame Street portrays racial, cultural, and language difference
to preschool children as something akin to the theatrical concept of people
and languages as existing as an ensemble. For over fifty years, this concept of
ensemble has enabled Sesame Street to "do things with words"[8] that had not
been possible in youth literature.

## RUMBLE: LANGUAGE AS DUEL, BILINGUAL CHILDREN'S CULTURE, AND A GIRL NAMED MARIA

Throughout this book, I have asked us to consider how side-by-side relationships of close proximity often reflect deep colonial anxieties and colonial

violence in Puerto Rican/Latinx youth literature. I have also asked us to consider how narratives about childhood work to express ideas about coloniality, subjectivity, and citizenship—for example, how in the tradition of US children's books about colonized territories, the closer a territory was to the US, the more authors reflected a desire to manage the difference and potential threat of the inhabitants with close kinship ties, such as from cousin to brother in the case of Puerto Rico. Similarly, Cuban revolutionary and Latin American theorist José Martí, in "Nuestra America/Our America" (1891), invokes imagery of close neighborly relations to discuss the hemispheric tensions about the encroaching US empire. Belpré maintains that the Tiger and the Rabbit remained "ever the best of friends" in "The Tiger and the Rabbit" (1941), a tale about dysfunctional partnerships that form when colonizer and colonized live together "in the land." In this way, the strong Latinx contingent on *Sesame Street* is no accident nor is it simply an endearing way to manage inclusion for multicultural US audiences. Instead, though *Sesame Street* presents positive and uplifting depictions of Latinx neighborly lives, cultures, and languages, the way the show cast the bilingual, Puerto Rican Maria in the role of pacifier ties to a tradition of containing Puerto Rican difference while valuing youth as diplomats and bridge figures among competing cultures, and in this chapter, languages.

In "Bilingual Fruit Song" (1986) from Episode 1646 of *Sesame Street*, a pear, an apple, a banana, and a pineapple sing that "two names are better than one." The fruits chosen for the song symbolize the US Anglo (domestic apple and pear) and Hispanic cultures (the more tropical banana and pineapple acquired through trade and colonization) which, as in a fruit bowl, are forced to live together. However, the happy compromise between fruit does not come without a fight:

Apple: Hey, pear, this banana here says he is a platano and I'm a manzana.
Banana (to the pear): Si, Buenos días, pera.
Pear (to the banana): What did you call me?
Banana: Pera.
Pear (to the apple): Pera? I'm a pear.
Pineapple (to the apple and pear): But, pera is pear in Spanish.
Pear: It is? Hey, who are you anyway?
Pineapple: I'm piña.
Apple: Piña. You sure could pass for a pineapple.
Pineapple: That's right, I am a pineapple. Just like, platano is the Spanish word for banana . . .

Banana: ¿Yo soy un banana?
Pineapple: A-ha, and manzana is the Spanish word for apple.
Apple: Boy, well, I'm a big manzana.

The apple's final line cues the song, yet it is also a play on words for the Big Apple or New York City. The banana/platano symbolize the Latinx immigrant who, without knowledge of English, innocently begins speaking Spanish to his Anglo companions who react in fear at the notion of having Spanish names. The pineapple represents the bilingual who acts as an intermediary between the groups. Eventually, the "big" apple realizes that there is enough room for everyone in the fruit bowl: two names are better than one. The song illustrates a principle within *Sesame Street*'s pedagogy of language: the coexistence of languages leads to tension and compromise. To be bilingual is to participate—and, perhaps, pacify—in a battle between two languages.

Languages in bilingual cultures engage in a duel, according to Puerto Rican writer, Rosario Ferré.[9] "English and Spanish," Ferré writes, "have been at war since Queen Elizabeth sank King Felipe's Spanish Armada in 1588." In a bilingual book, Ferré suggests that languages face each other on opposite sides of the page as if on a battlefield. Here, placing languages side by side heightens a sense of rivalry rather than camaraderie, something often ignored when considering bilingual youth literature. For example, the parallel stories of a bilingual children's picture book are presented as conveying the same message through equal representation, but there is no consideration of the competition and collision between languages. Additionally, there is a presumption that languages never interact, instead remaining safely confined behind the border. The result leads to a mixed and misleading message, as illustrated in Monica Brown's *Side by Side: The Story of Dolores Huerta and Caesar Chavez / Lado a Lado: La Historia de Dolores Huerta y Caesar Chavez* (2009). The phrase "side by side" alludes to both the story's plot, the partnership between Dolores Huerta and Cesar Chavez for farm workers' rights, and the "side by side" Spanish and English narratives (separated by a black bar) telling the story. An illustration by Joe Cepeda, perhaps, attempts to unconsciously unite the narratives: Chavez and Huerta are pictured holding hands across the page division. Yet, considering Ferré's critique, "side by side" may precipitate the very issues this bilingual book seeks to inspire (e.g., partnership between cultures and languages), all the while leaving the reader in the thick of a duel. Readers must "side" with one or the other, at least initially, since no one can read both sides simultaneously.[10]

In illustrating "rules for justice and fair play,"[11] *Sesame Street* similarly admits the tension between rival languages. The skit "Vamos a Comer" (2006),

performed by Muppet characters Telly and Rosita, interprets the division
between languages as a space for dialogue. The skit begins with Telly standing
in a park, a narrator (human cast member Luis) says, "When Telly is hungry
he says . . ." Telly looks down at his stomach, saying, "Let's eat." Suddenly, the
screen splits, revealing Rosita at the beach with a picnic basket and sandwiches. The narrator says, "When Rosita eats, she says . . ." Rosita looks at
her sandwiches, announcing, "Vamos a comer." An astonished Telly looks at
Rosita's side of the screen, hearing her through the dividing blue line. As the
narrator continues repeating the prompts, the line between Telly (English)
and Rosita (Spanish) becomes inconsequential:

> Narrator: Telly says . . .
> Telly: Let's eat.
> Narrator: Rosita says . . .
> Rosita: Vamos a comer.
> Telly: (pointing to Rosita's side of the screen) Hey, Rosita, what did
> you just say.
> Rosita: (startled at first) Oh, I said, vamos a comer. That means let's
> eat in Spanish. Mmm, hmm.
> Telly: ¡Great! ¡Vamos a comer, Rosita!
> Rosita: ¡Si, Telly! ¡Vamos a comer!
> Telly: Oh, no. I can't eat. I didn't bring any food.
> Rosita: Ay, no hay problema, Telly. You can share some of mine.
> (pushing the sandwich to the Telly, across the blue line) Here you
> go . . .
> (Telly reaches over the blue line and grabs a sandwich. Rosita and
> Telly both laugh)
> Rosita and Telly (in unison): ¡Vamos a comer!

Ultimately, the skit illustrates the necessity of interaction, even between
languages, to bring about an expected end (i.e., eating). The division erodes
as the "English" side begins speaking Spanish, and the "Spanish" side begins
speaking English. It also suggests that while a division exists, either side
can easily cross the line. The notion of dueling languages enables us to see
language as a border, but also as a weapon, both defensive and offensive.

Maria's character, for over forty-years until the retirement of performer
Manzano in 2015, served as a kind of bilingual muse of communication on
*Sesame Street*, although notions of street rivalry and violent battles underlie
her creation. Indeed, Maria is a creation of the show's writers, but Manzano, since the 1980s, took the lead in writing scripts for the character and

ensemble. As a character, the 1970s-era, teenaged Maria provides a glimpse into how the CTW imagined the Puerto Rican and Latinx community within urban America. By the time Maria arrived at *Sesame Street*, the Puerto Rican diaspora had been fixed into US popular culture, mainly as a source of anxiety. Puerto Rican migrants dominated New York's Hispanic minority and established neighborhoods in El Barrio, El Bronx, and Loisaida (the Lower East Side), as Mohr affirms in her children's narratives. However, New York and island Puerto Rican educational officials, along with sociologists and psychologists, developed two popular labels for the diaspora: the "Puerto Rican problem"[12] and "the culture of poverty." As early as 1948, the New York Department of Education[13] began examining the "problem" of educating Puerto Rican migrants regarding economic progress and stability. The New York Public Library, under an initiative led by librarians Pura Belpré and Lillian Lopes called the South Bronx Project, identified the predominantly Puerto Rican South Bronx of the 1970–1980s as in need of special services due to the low education rates and poverty.[14] The consensus among psychologists and anthropologists like Dan Wakefield (1959),[15] Benjamin Malzberg (1965),[16] and Oscar Lewis (1966) was that Puerto Ricans' incorporation into US culture had been a catastrophic failure. "The culture of poverty," a phrase still in use in reference to cycles of dependency ascribed to the urban, racialized poor, emerged from Oscar Lewis's *La Vida* (1966),[17] a study on the lives of Puerto Rican migrants in New York. Researchers credited migration for every sort of malady, from overpopulation to mental illness.[18]

In *Sesame Street and the Reform of Children's Television* (2006), Robert W. Morrow writes that works such as Lewis's *La Vida* "shattered" postwar idealism about US prosperity and equality (33). National consciousness shifted toward targeting urban poverty and juvenile delinquency, both issues directly invoking the Puerto Rican migrant. Like *La Vida*, Leonard Bernstein's *West Side Story*, both the play and later the film version, immortalized the Puerto Rican migrant as trapped not only in a culture of poverty, but of gang violence and social unrest. During the late 1960s, educational reformers and those mobilizing the new "War on Poverty" emphasized poverty,[19] not race, as the source of social and educational inequality (Morrow, 37). Reformers, including President Lyndon Johnson, believed that early education would remedy the perceived correlation between poverty and social mobility. Eyes turned toward the preschool child or the preliterate child who would eventually enter the public school with considerable disadvantages in comparison to more affluent (mostly white) children. The Preschool Movement, the ideology that undergirded *Sesame Street*, focused on educating preschool children as an avenue for social mobility and equality. Joan Ganz Cooney, the founder of the Children's Television Workshop, seized the opportunity to unite children's educational programs with the newly approved medium of public television.[20] Yet, racial tensions and the reality of structural racism still shaped the way in which *Sesame Street* was imagined and engineered. These tensions remain in the duel of languages performed by characters such as Maria.

As Maria sits at her window during many a show opening in the early 1970s, she embodies the anxieties and hope for reform associated with the urban, bilingual Puerto Rican that led to programs like *Sesame Street*. Her character, as a product of the white imagination during the late twentieth century, connects to the Keats's renderings of Juanito in *My Dog is Lost*. Yet, what is fascinating about the story of Maria is how, at a moment when authorship was few and far between for Boricuas, a Puerto Rican woman is able to turn the tables on the writing and content of one of the most viewed broadcasts in modern television—from performing scripted lines to writing scripts in her own right. Manzano remembers producers telling her that they wanted "the kid on the Lower East Side to look at [her] and say, 'That's me.'" Producers also told her that they hoped to reach Latinx children through her presence.[21] Gerald S. Lesser and Joel Schneider (2001) confirm that the show's researchers targeted Puerto Rican children as representatives of the larger Latinx community while designing curriculum and content that raised self-esteem. Indeed, the book *"G" is for Growing: Thirty Years of Sesame Street Research* (2001) documents how show researchers found that Puerto Rican children were more likely to feel ashamed of the color of their skin rather than white, Asian, or African American children (Fisch and Truglio, 71). These children also had trouble identifying the color of their skin.

As Jillian Baez writes, *West Side Story*'s circulation meant that the larger culture used the musical as a means of assessing Puerto Rican culture. In the context of the history of Puerto Rican youth portrayals, what we see *Sesame Street* do through Maria's early creation is gather fragments of a formerly negative portrait of the Puerto Rican migrant and seek to transform it into a positive image of productivity and mobility. Although Manzano later exercised more control over her character, producers fashioned the early Maria by drawing on images of Puerto Rican culture engineered by white America. For this reason, Maria is partially drawn from "Maria" of *West Side Story*,[22] which, at the time, was ubiquitous as an icon of Puerto Rican youth and femininity. *West Side Story*'s influence is evident through Maria's position as a kind of beautiful peacemaker and intermediary, both roles that shape her task as language facilitator. For example, in the closing of 1974's Episode 666, the frame closes in on Maria, dressed in her nightgown, at her fire escape, tossing her hair, holding a book, and looking dreamily at the stars. The image mirrors a pivotal scene in *West Side Story* when Maria meets Tony on her fire escape, which, in turn, mimics Shakespeare's *Romeo and Juliet*.[23] In 1972's Episode 406, David asks Maria to "come down" from her fire escape. Maria proceeds to climb down and then walk down the street with David, arm in arm. Perhaps the most explicit homage to *West Side Story*'s Maria comes when the Spanish opera singer (and flamingo), Placido Flamingo, falls in love with Maria while visiting the Fix-It Shop. The Muppet bursts into song: "Maria, Maria, I love you, Maria . . ." Later, the love-struck Placido is seen standing outside Maria's fire escape at night where he again sings a tune that is almost identical to Bernstein's famous "Maria": "Maria, the sweetest one I know / Maria, the one that I love so / Maria, Maria."[24] The camera foregrounds Placido as Maria opens her window and tells him "this can't go on."

These allusions to *West Side Story* work in two ways regarding language instruction. First, they associate Maria with a strong femininity (beauty, love, and romance),[25] which can endear her to children as a motherly ideal of womanhood. In later years, Manzano made Maria's womanhood a central part of her writing content—marriage, pregnancy, delivery, and even breast-feeding.[26] Maria touts feminism, taking a position on a construction crew as a response to 1970s woman's liberation, while still possessing enough feminine charm to melt Oscar the Grouch who affectionately calls her "skinny." About Oscar, Maria's taming of this abrasive Muppet may suggest producers' hopes that she might also tame racial and linguistic prejudice since producers designed Oscar as a representation of the "conflicts arising from racial and ethnic diversity" (Morrow Figure, 10). Maria's femininity also reinforces her gender-appropriate role as a trustworthy teacher which she employs when instructing children in various subjects beyond Spanish (reading, hygiene, relationships, etc.). For example, in the skit "Captain Vegetable Rhymes," Maria cuddles two children (one white and one Latinx) on her lap while they listen to "superhero" Captain Vegetable offer recommendations on healthy eating. Maria hugs the children, examines the suggested vegetables, and gently encourages the children to listen ("We have to listen, now"). Her position as Spanish language instructor, however, places Maria in a culturally relevant role since, in Puerto Rican culture, women are often charged with conserving and teaching Spanish to Puerto Rican children.[27] Second, beyond under-scoring the "lovely" similarities between the two Marias (Puertorriqueñas singing, dancing, and "feeling pretty" in New York), invoking *West Side Story* also introduces the darker elements of gang rivalry from the play to *Sesame Street*. Both Marias are caught in a rumble: *West Side Story*'s Maria travails between rival white and Puerto Rican gangs, while *Sesame Street*'s Maria helps bridge together the rival "gangs" of Spanish and English. Considering Ferré's theory, the duel between Spanish and English is, perhaps, just another version of a knife fight. While *Sesame Street*'s pedagogy of language, as per the show's mission for equality, ultimately leads to a peaceful coexistence between languages, this coexistence requires a compromise between rivals. Maria's story will not end with a shootout in the streets, as in *West Side Story*, but she will cause rivals to drop their weapons.[28]

A Spanish-speaking Maria, presented as a model of instruction, disarms a major stereotype perpetuated by 1950–1960s-era educational studies that discriminated against Puerto Rican students. As Sonia Nieto has surveyed, such studies repeatedly label Puerto Rican children as "losers" and "outsiders."[29] *Sesame Street*, instead, develops the concept of bilingualism as an asset ("two names are better than one") to children's learning and not a deficiency. Migration because of colonialism seemingly shocked educators accustomed to a pattern of US immigration in which students forsook their native languages, such as Italian or Yiddish. Researchers studying children on the island and stateside insisted that school performance necessitated full assimilation (e.g., English-only) into US culture. Low scores and high dropout rates, according to researchers, resulted from children's exposure to Spanish. Later reports showed that tests and curriculum were, in some cases, deliberately discriminatory (Nieto, 16).[30] Manzano herself was a product of this derisive school environment. As a Bronx high school student, Manzano painted her nails in class, while teachers spent minimal time engaging with her class of Puerto Rican students. "Very little," Manzano says, "is expected of ghetto kids." One teacher, reminiscent of Mohr's character, Mrs. Langhorn, once told Manzano's class that the world was divided into "white people and black people."[31] A class member asked the teacher, "What about Brown people?" Manzano's teacher replied, "There is no such thing as Brown people."

Just as Belpré and Mohr believed their work addressed a void, Manzano underlines her performance as an intervention on behalf of a community she perceived as invisible in US culture: "As a kid, I asked, how can I contribute to a world that doesn't see me?" Manzano's position in television and drama as a means of shaping her community's portrayal highlights some key differences between her interventions and those of Belpré or Mohr. Manzano's statement about contributing to a world which "didn't see her" resonates with Belpré and Mohr's desire to testify to the community's existence. In Episode 4165, from 2008, cameras give audiences a glimpse of Maria and Luis's apartment, a set that displays objects celebrating the rural Puerto Rican past that was so dear to Belpré's generation: a painting of a rural casita and a jibraro farmer, a picture of flamboyan tree, and a vejigante mask. Because of Manzano's role as scriptwriter, we might infer that she had some say in the way sets and props emphasize Maria's culture. Each of these props also pay tribute to Puerto Rico's cultural and racial diversity and highlights a certain romanticization with island lore. However, perhaps as with Nicholasa Mohr, the traditional, folkloric narrative did not fulfill Manzano's desire for a place in US society. Maria's presence on *Sesame Street* speaks to the existence of an established community at home in the US. Perhaps due to the prominence of visual culture, Manzano has arguably been able to exercise a wider influence upon the image of Puerto Ricans and Latinxs projected toward US children than Mohr and Belpré combined. Indeed, Manzano's influence may expand beyond the children's realm considering she was one of the first, and remains one of the few, Latinx on television with the prominent roles of lead actor and writer for decades on an award-winning, globally recognized franchise.

Though *Sesame Street* producers originated the character of Maria, Manzano's interpretation of the role extended the character beyond stereotypical imaginings of Puerto Rican culture.[32] "Puerto Ricans," Manzano says, "are not just rice and beans." Manzano's location in children's educational television during its development allowed her to play the role of forerunner akin to Belpré's involvement at the NYPL during advancements in children's literature. Manzano, as a young actor on the set, began suggesting changes to the props such as adding plantains to the show's fruit cart. After discussing her desire to see more authentic pieces on culture (something "besides food and music") with CTW writers, one writer told Manzano, "The only way we are going to get this right is if you write it." *Sesame Street*'s writers handed Manzano the show's curriculum objectives, allowing her to write show segments if she stayed within that curriculum. Manzano points to her first written piece on the show during the 1980s as an example of transcending stereotypes. In the skit and bilingual song, Maria and Luis perform a la Fred Astaire and Ginger Rogers. For Manzano, Maria is "who I needed to see on television as a child."

In Maria, children see an example of bilingual culture presented as more than just a mish-mash of languages, but as a give-and-take negotiation of power. This illustration of bilingualism is much more in line with Ofelia Garcia's theory of translanguaging in which she explains that

> [T]ranslanguaging is not simply going from one language code to another. The notion of code-switching assumes that the two languages of bilinguals are two separate monolingual codes that could be used without reference to each other. Instead, translanguaging posits that bilinguals have one linguistic repertoire from which they select fea-

tures strategically to communicate effectively. That is, translanguaging takes as it's starting point the language practices of bilingual people as the norm, and not the language of monolinguals, as described by traditional usage books and grammars. (1)

*Sesame Street* presents Spanish words as a part of the community and culture of the show. Yet, ideas about language and power on the show depend much more on who says certain words rather than the words alone. Other characters like Luis, Grover, and even Big Bird introduce Spanish words to children on the show, but *Sesame Street* locates Maria within symbolic settings that hint at her strengths in communication, problem-solving, and literacy. Linking bilingualism with masterful communication and problem-solving skills coincides with the show's goal of presenting bilingualism as an asset. Even while sitting on her fire escape, the early Maria is often seen holding a book or reading. During her tenure on *Sesame Street*, Maria's jobs have always signaled ideas about skill and resourcefulness. Her first job as a teenager was in the show's bilingual lending library, a la Belpré. Maria then progressed to partnering with Luis at the Fix-It Shop, a hardware and repair store, which later Luis and Maria, as a married couple, converted into the Mail-It Shop (a post office). Other cast members often benefit from and rely on Maria's communication skills, such as in the *Sesame Street* film, *Follow that Bird* (1985). After Big Bird is adopted and leaves Sesame Street, it is Maria whom Big Bird entrusts with a letter for the cast. Maria calls the cast around her as she emphatically reads the letter aloud. In the letter, Big Bird seemingly praises his new family; however, Maria's keen sense for reading between the lines allows her to quickly sense his homesickness. She pauses and stares at the letter before reading his last line, "I should be happy here. What's wrong with me?" Maria, as the other cast members look on, also intercedes for Big Bird when his social worker demands that he return to his proper "bird" foster family: "He doesn't need another family. He has one right here. . . . We are all happy here on Sesame Street . . . we got all kinds . . . we got people and cows . . . and birds . . . and kids." Turning the social worker's attention to the similarities between neighbors ("We are all happy . . .") enables Maria to disarm the threat of difference that almost costs *Sesame Street* its most recognizable icon.

Maria's function as a bridge between Puerto Rican and US difference is exemplified in Episode 1316 from the 1979 season. This episode is also an example of what I suggest is truly bilingual children's culture (i.e., made for bilingual children). *Sesame Street*'s pedagogy of language from the 1970 and 1980s mainly incorporated Spanish through sight words (e.g., Luis writes "agua" on piece of paper next to a glass of water)[33] and untranslated dialogue by bilingual characters (e.g., Luis tells a young, African American girl that, "Si alguien llama, le dices que regreso en cinco minutes").[34] By including untranslated dialogue, producers presume and reward a multilingual audience. In Episode 1316, Maria travels to her homeland of Puerto Rico for her twenty-first birthday celebration. Maria and Olivia (her African American best friend) arrive in Puerto Rico and immediately take a bus that tours them through the island. The camera captures Puerto Rican landmarks such as San Juan del Morro and La Fortaleza, while a Spanish salsa-vamped version of *Sesame Street*'s theme song plays in the background: "Día de sol . . . si me dices como ir . . . como ir ha Sesame Street." The song implies that *Sesame Street*, this ideal community of cultures and languages, is not a fixed place in Manhattan, but a kind of state of mind that transcends geographic borders. Indeed, the CTW has taken its educational/cultural/linguistic philosophy around the globe by creating different *Sesame Streets* in countries ranging from Israel to Kosovo.

In this first scene between Maria and her island relatives, Maria continues her symbolic, almost ambassadorial role. As Maria and relatives embrace in a Spanish-style Plaza, the Puerto Rican and US flag fly "side by side"[35] in the distance. Maria and her family begin speaking entirely in Spanish without subtitles or translation, a gesture adding an element of authenticity and, once again, rewarding a US audience of Spanish-speakers. Maria hugs her cousin, Yamira, while stretching out her arm toward Olivia, introducing her to the family: "Quiero que conozcan a mi mejor amiga, Olivia." During each introduction, which she repeats in English, Maria holds onto Olivia's hand while also clasping the hand of one of her Puerto Rican relatives. At one point, Maria stands between her "primo," Ronaldo and Olivia, as she joins both their hands in hers. The scene prevents the viewer from seeing the monolingual Olivia as an outsider, but also avoids any awkwardness for native Spanish speakers by allowing Maria and her relatives to speak as they would without a monolingual present. The scene also familiarizes children with the linguistic format of the show, mainly crossing over from Spanish to English, and back. Following the scene in the plaza, a Spanish cartoon "commercial" introduces the letter "a." Children can see that "a," it turns out, is not just for "apple," but for "ancla" and "alfombra." Such alternating between languages suggests that, as in any diplomatic conversation, for one language to be heard, the other must fall silent.

*Sesame Street*'s pedagogy of language touts diplomacy;[36] however, the show's teaching of Spanish evidences the tensions and clinking of swords between rivals, even in the show's silences. In the 1990s and 2000s, *Sesame*

*Street* began presenting Spanish in more deliberately literary ways, perhaps because of a trend in pop culture spotlighting Latinx literature.[37] The "Spanish Word of the Day" took center stage as a regular skit on the show, representing time allotted for a segment dedicated only to the teaching of Spanish words and phrases. *Sesame Street* also introduced a bilingual Muppet, Rosita from Mexico. Maria and Luis continued as the show's lead Spanish teachers; however, other characters, such as the Count, Grover, and Mr. Snuffleupagus, began teaching Spanish counting and the "Spanish Word of the Day." This underscores Spanish as a practical language beyond a specific ethnic minority.

*Sesame Street*'s teaching of Spanish letters, however, arguably further highlights the borders of how far they are willing to demonstrate linguistic difference than, for example, the teaching of the American Sign Language Alphabet, which contains corresponding English letters for each sign. Teaching the corresponding letters and sounds for the letter "a" in Spanish and English highlights the similarities between English and Spanish as opposed to uncomfortable places where Spanish requires letters apart from the English language: "Ch," "LL," and "Ñ." The show's treatment of the letter "Ñ" particularly evidences the ruptures between languages. In a skit, "Professor" Grover, the lovable, absent-minded monster, introduces the words "niño" and "niña" as Episode 4040's "Spanish Word of the Day." A Latinx boy and girl listen as Grover announces that the word for "boy" and "girl" in Spanish is "spaghetti," giving the children a sense of agency as they correct the Muppet by announcing the proper "niño" and "niña." The words appear over the children's heads revealing the mysterious "ñ" required for each term. The letter "Ñ," with its unfamiliar tilde, presents a challenge as it is the one Spanish letter not found in the English language. Child viewers awkwardly receive the spelling and meaning to words requiring unfamiliar letters that are enunciated yet not introduced or taught. It is significant that this silence happens about letters—the building blocks of language. Preschoolers learn both letters and numbers as a basic code that helps them order their world. This silence signals that, regardless of Spanish words and phrases, *Sesame Street* positions the English alphabet as the clear victor in terms of the official US code. English is flavored and accented, though never ruled, by Spanish.

In a duel of languages, *Sesame Street* navigates between speech and silence, between cultural specificity and homogeneity, in its quest for peace. The show's emphasis on sameness means that sometimes language is, at times, presented in a superficial manner. Does knowing that "gato" means "cat" really make a native English-speaking preschooler suddenly bilingual? In Episode 3664 (1997), Rosita sings "No Matter What Your Language," which reinforces a desire for universalism: " . . . I say "me gustas" / that means

"I like you" / I say "Hola" / that means "Hello"/ . . . No matter what your language / no matter what your name / the things that you say can be the same." Though the message unifies, the performance relies heavily on ethnic stereotypes of Latinxs. For example, Rosita and her chorus of Muppets wear fruit hats and Mexican sombreros. The lyrics establish similarity between meanings, however, by the song's end, the subject shifts as Rosita transitions from "the things that we say can be the same" to "We're all the same." The show later revises this notion of words as inconsequential in Episode 3986 (2002) with a much more culturally specific lesson about the role of language as a site of history and place. The episode centers on Big Bird's rescue of a lost baby bird who only knows how to say one word: "Paraguay." Big Bird struggles with the word's meaning, thinking that, by shouting "Paraguay!" the baby bird is calling for help. He seeks guidance from various characters, each of whom interpret the mysterious word. Meanings change according to the character, suggesting the subjectivity of language and translation; for example, Snuffleupagus, a melancholy, elephant-like Muppet, interprets "Paraguay" as "I'm sick," while the ever-resourceful Alan, of Mr. Hopper's Store, immediately knows "Paraguay" is a country in Latin America. Alan and Big Bird eventually take the baby bird to the Mail-It Shop in the hope of using the internet for more information on Paraguay. Of course, entering the Mail-It Shop means encountering *Sesame Street*'s resident communication superstar, Maria. As Maria helps Alan and Big Bird with the computer, she asks the baby bird, "¿Eres de Paraguay?"[38] The baby bird's beak opens in awe upon hearing her native language.

Maria's bilingual skills enable her to assess the baby bird's true predicament. Through Maria, Big Bird, Allen, and the audience learn that the baby bird's name is Fatima and got separated from her parents on a trip. Mother and father bird arrive by the show's end. However, throughout this ordeal, the word "Paraguay" is repeated, each time with a new meaning. Children are exposed to the concept that one word can mean "help," "country," and "home." Words are defined according to meanings assigned by individuals with relationship to culture and family. Word meanings are also subject to individual expression or performance.

## PERFORMING LANGUAGE: MIMING, MUSIC, THEATRE, AND LANGUAGE ("RHYTHM IS GONNA GET YOU")

In my reading of *Sesame Street*'s portrayal of Spanish and the diaspora community, I underline two additional principles in the show's language pedagogy which support its staging of content like untranslated dialogue: performance is a type of language and language is a type of performance. The show's content resembles a televised musical theatre in which performance (e.g., puppetry, music, and dramatization) serves as the show's main "language." This "language" serves as the conduit for *Sesame Street*'s elementary and social curriculum. Performance also frames the show's representation of colonial relationships and colonial languages, such as Bob and Luis's performance of the song, "Bienvenido." The song consists of English and Spanish lyrics; the Spanish lyrics repeat only a key phrase in the English lyric. However, the musical arrangement blurs any audible division between languages by merging the lyrics in a way that makes it seem like Bob and Luis finish each other's sentences. Bob, a music teacher, and Luis meet at the Fix-It Shop, where Bob tells Luis, "Hello, Luis. Are you ready for the party?" Bob then turns to the camera and begins singing the lyrics, "I want to say, 'Welcome . . .'" Luis, also considering the camera, repeats "Bienvenido . . ." As Luis and Bob walk down Sesame Street singing ("Thanks for all the good things we'll share and come what may . . . pase lo que pase"), Bob leads the way while Luis walks slightly behind him. The scene suggests the interchangeability of English and Spanish. Yet, visually, the moment also invokes a subtle subordination of Spanish as an alternate but unofficial US language. In addition to framing the relationships between languages, performance also serves as the basis for communicating word meanings. For example, a typical "Spanish Word of the Day" segment features Maria walking by a flower pot. She sees, smells, and holds the flower to her face, enunciating, "F-ll-o-rrr. Flor is 'flower' in Spanish."

*Sesame Street*'s brand of educational entertainment is undergirded by how producers feel they will reach a perceived audience of preschool, preliterate children. The show attempts to include representatives of this child audience through child actors[39] and Muppet performers like Big Bird (who is six years old) and Elmo (three years old), all of whom depend on humans like Maria, Luis, and Bob.[40] Producers created the show as something of a television version of Head Start,[41] organizing production around a school readiness curriculum targeting disadvantaged, minority preschoolers. By 1969, television's accessibility meant that *Sesame Street* could reach children outside of Head Start.[42] I note that producers interpreted illiteracy in three-to-five-year-olds as a product of socioeconomic disadvantage, not simply youth. A key assumption, both for Head Start and the engineers of *Sesame Street*, is that low-income preschoolers (especially Black and Puerto Rican children) received inadequate literacy education both at home and in the community. However, the show's high viewership in this community seems to further suggest that Latinx children had greater access to television rather than literature in the form of books or home libraries.[43] *Sesame Street* actually testifies to a distinction between literacy education and literary education since it attempts to impart reading skills without using literature, something educators initially resisted and continue to resist.[44] Educators express concern over children's ability to process information through performance on television. However, the correlations between race, class, and access to literature suggest the importance of other mediums (e.g., musical theatre), aside from literature, when considering children of color and the texts they do (and do not) see themselves in.

Performance on *Sesame Street* presents children with a view of reading and literacy as a practical, everyday affair. Manzano's recollections during an oral history interview coincide with this notion of reading as a practical rather than academic, elite, skill: "[As a child] I thought you only read what the teacher told you to read. I didn't know that it was for reading a label or a traffic sign. What is reading good for except for reading what the teacher tells you [to read]? It never occurred to me that reading is everywhere. It is something everybody does." *Sesame Street*'s adoption of this anthropological concept of the world as a readable text[45] reinforces literature's importance while problematizing its institutional role. Performance enables the show to occupy a "safe space" outside of the academic literary establishment while empowering an audience of youngsters learning their letters and numbers with access to literary tools.

Communicating with children in the beginning stages of literacy requires *Sesame Street*'s language of performance (such as a comical skit introducing the letter "m") to convey meaning without relying on a child's preconceived knowledge of symbols or letters. This "performance language" allows the show to make some critical associations between colonial languages and performance arts such as miming, music, and theatre. Maria's performance also helps illustrate these alternative forms of communication. Throughout her years on *Sesame Street*, Manzano as Maria has performed the role of Charlie Chaplin in several pantomime skits.[46] In a 1974 skit about the topic of exits, Maria/Chaplin finds herself trapped in a room. She walks into walls, banging her head, seemingly ignorant of the "exit" sign above the two doors in the room. Children's voices[47] are heard yelling, "Exit!" as they direct Maria/Chaplin to the sign, thereby stressing the importance of reading. Yet, Maria/Chaplin, continuing to ignore the sign, opts for walking through the wall as her "exit." Her disregard for the sign, though perhaps meant to encourage reading, may have the opposite effect. The skit's charm derives from watching Maria/Chaplin walk through the wall, not the properly labeled door.

Considering Maria's position on the show as masterful communicator, I find it telling that she, rather than another *Sesame Street* character, should repeatedly perform Chaplin. Maria's performance of Chaplin works in two ways about language. First, merging Maria with Chaplin (an icon[48] for silent performance) reframes her multilingual skills, this time, by extending beyond merely speech, which, in turn, posits language as a performance. Second, by putting on the guise of Chaplin, Maria acts out the role of inventive "tramp" or outsider resisting the dominant culture, a theme resonating with the Puerto Rican diaspora's pattern of marginality and creativity. Yet, beyond the character's relevance to the diaspora, Maria/Chaplin continually subverts the scenarios (the "script") she encounters, highlighting the role of performance as a means of subverting traditional literacy and literary constructs.

As a mime, Maria/Chaplin illustrates a performer's capacity to embody an action, a story, or an object (animate or inanimate). The mime is a relevant image within language, childhood, and postcolonial theory. For example, Walter Benjamin writes that language is a manifestation of what he sees as one of humanity's greatest gifts, "the mimetic faculty."[49] Language emerges from the miming of sounds and utterances which creates an "archive" of "nonsensuous similarities, of nonsensuous correspondences" (333). Children, for Benjamin, employ "mimetic modes of behavior" naturally in play, yet their talent goes beyond imitating human behavior: "The child plays at being a shopkeeper or teacher but also a windmill and a train." However, Homi Bhaba emphasizes mimicry as an expression of resistance, in that, miming never produces an exact replica but always suggests a slight difference. In light of these theories, Maria/Chaplin's recurrent skits suggest the notion of a kind of inherent and symbolic language which may even mirror an illiterate child's "natural" language learning mode. This language, independent of sound or text, seems possible only in performance and allows for individual difference. However, as in Rosita's "No Matter What Your Language" song, the representation of this "pure" language teeters between universalism and specificity.

The Chaplinesque skit "Me" (1977)[50] simultaneously furthers the concept of a kind of embodied, universal language while promoting individuality. The skit helps children explore the complicated notion of identity represented by the word "Me."[51] Maria/Chaplin walks past a large mirror on an empty stage. Faced with her "reflection," she begins adjusting her mustache and suit, suddenly seeing a slight variation in the mirror. Her reflection is a fellow cast member, hearing-impaired actress Linda Bove (also "Linda" on the show). Like Maria, Linda demonstrated linguistic diversity on *Sesame Street* through her use of American Sign Language. Portraying Maria and Linda as reflections of each other highlights their common role as performers who regularly communicate with the audience using alternative linguistic symbols and embodiment. Together, Maria/Chaplin and Linda/Chaplin posit language as a system apart from the literal and the audible. Indeed, it is a system where the performer and the symbol are one. Interestingly, *Sesame Street* casts these two linguistic "tramps" as the duo most capable of imparting meaning without audible speech.[52] The pairing draws out the subversive qualities of mimicry, since from the beginning, we know this "mirroring" is performed by two nonconformists. After a few moments of mimicking each other, Maria/Chaplin turns to the camera and mouths the word, "Me?" For preschoolers, the skit seems to simplify the concept of "me" by attempting to answer questions such as, who does "me" refer to, or what does it mean to be "me"?

Maria/Chaplin and Linda/Chaplin circle the "mirror," each time trying to outdo the other in speed and precision. As Maria/Chaplin suddenly bows down, Linda/Chaplin's hat falls to the floor. The two Chaplins in the mirror project a powerful image which portrays identity as a process of exploration. Mimicking another's behavior aids in the discovery of one's uniqueness. In this illustration, the mimetic faculty works as a tool for learning one's subjectivity and place in the world, specifically, through interpretable silences. After Maria/Chaplin picks up Linda/Chaplin's hat, Linda/Chaplin accepts it back with a respectful bow and smile. All this "mirroring," it seems, forms part of a friendly competition fostering nonconformity where the objective is to usurp the mirror image through even the slightest difference, as in Bhaba's critique. The skit ends with both Chaplins standing arm in arm as they look into the camera, each pointing toward herself and confidently mouthing, "Me."

The skit "What Happens Next?" further explores the role of the mimetic faculty as a tool for resistance by challenging the concept of narrative sequences. "What Happens Next?"[53] is a lesson on narrative patterns and sequences, such as logical outcomes in a plot. The comedic performances of Gordon, the science teacher, playing the role of game show host, and Maria/Chaplin, playing the unsuspecting "fool" in each mystery scenario, frame the lesson. Child audiences must decide Maria/Chaplin's fate as she encounters what seems like one disastrous circumstance after another. To prompt the audience's decision, Gordon sings the show's theme song, "Do you know what's going to happen next? / Do you think that you can tell? / If you know what's going to happen next / then tell me before I ring this bell." A spilt screen separates Gordon and Maria/Chaplin. He is seemingly safe in his game show studio while Maria/Chaplin, walking in a park with a stack of newspapers, seems unaware of her position as a character governed by an audience or script. In the first scenario, Maria/Chaplin walks through the park as she tucks her newspapers and cane under her arms. Yet, as Gordon begins to sing the theme song, she suddenly freezes with one foot suspended off the floor, unaware of the banana peel directly below. "Well, what do you think?" asks Gordon. "Do you think that our friend here is going to slip on the banana peel and fall down?" The unseen audience[54] bursts with delight, exclaiming, "Yes!" The audience claps as Maria/Chaplin slips and falls backward, her facial expressions revealing a sense of suspicion. She stands up slowly, still hurting from the fall, as Gordon introduces the second scenario: "Our friend here is about to sit on that park bench . . . but you will notice that the bench has only one-two-three legs." Gordon's introduction dictates Maria/Chaplin's action; she "mirrors" his directions by walking toward the flimsy bench, doomed by the scripted scenario. As she begins preparing to sit and read her newspapers, Gordon begins swaying and smiling as the ominous theme song begins playing. In mid-squat, Maria/Chaplin once again seems suspended in action as the audience contemplates her fate. "What's that?" Gordon says. "You think that our friend here is going to sit on the bench and that the bench is going to fall. Well, let's find out." Instantly, the bench comes apart as Maria/Chaplin falls with her stack of newspapers to the delight of Gordon and the audience. This time, she remains on the floor, looking into the camera and gathering her newspapers. "Our friend here is now getting ready to read a newspaper. But, and this is our last and final mystery situation . . . will our friend be able to read it?" Gordon asks. A cloud suddenly appears over Maria/Chaplin's head, with sounds of thunder audible in the distance. She freezes as Gordon begins swaying to the tune. However, as Gordon asks the audience ("What happens next?"), unlike in the other scenarios, Maria/Chaplin quickly unfreezes and begins rising from the ground, discerning the joke and Gordon's questions to the audience: "What's that, you said? You think our friend here is going to get all wet?" Maria/Chaplin looks into the camera and shakes her head at the audience. She is a character in rebellion about to usurp the plot of her "story." As Gordon laughs, anticipating the imminent rainstorm, Maria/Chaplin lassoes the cloud with her cane and pushes it into Gordon's side of the screen. Interestingly, it is only when Gordon says "rain" that rain, as per the script, begins pouring into his game show studio.

"What Happens Next" highlights the distinctions between literature and performance. Literature (the script), represented by Gordon as the host, is portrayed as a source of predictable, stifling control, while performance (the mime), represented by Maria/Chaplin, wins the ultimate favor of the audience through its playfully subversive ability to change the story, the scenario, and even fate. Gordon's annunciation ("rain") brought about the storm, suggesting the power of audible and written language for creating and ordering circumstances.[55] In this skit, power was initially assigned to Gordon; it was his use of language that allowed him control of the script, the narrative, the audience, and the character. However, mimicry and silent performance allow Maria/Chaplin[56] to thrive using a language discernible only to the audience, though not to the literature-reliant Gordon. Like Belpré's storytelling at the New York Public Library, performance enables Maria/Chaplin to gain power by outsmarting the stagnant rules of literature. The script continues, affecting only Gordon, even when the character has managed to perform her way out of the plot, resulting in shouts of victory from the audience. In the end, Maria/Chaplin clicks her heels together and dances out of the shot. Regarding the diaspora, I see Maria/Chaplin's ability to transcend the script as commenting on the place of the multilingual within a monolingual society. To speak Spanish in a predominately English language society, to enunciate Spanish words and letters where there have only ever been English ones, to switch from English to Spanish and back—this constitutes Maria's breaking of the standardized dialogue in the US, both within and without[57] *Sesame Street*.

*Sesame Street* further illustrates the mimetic faculty's role regarding language through the show's linking of miming to music. Several episodes unite the concept of miming audible language as analogous to singing a song, dancing with a rhythm, or playing an instrument. Episode 4046 (2003) and Episode 3901 (2000) emphasize the musicality of speech by presenting speech as an activity like singing. They also suggest musical sounds and rhythms as infectious. In a musical theatre format, Episode 4046 features the intermingling of speech and song. These musical intonations arise from cast members due to an infectious though imperceptible quality "in the air." In the show's opening, Bob and Alan announce, in song, that "there is something in the air today / that makes you want to sing /. . . . it's not a smell / it's not a sound / it's nowhere, yet it is all around." Big Bird arrives and tells Bob and Alan that, though he does not know why, he also has a sudden urge to sing. Gabi, Maria and Luis's daughter, enters the scene with Miles, Gordon and Susan's adopted son. Gabi repeats Bob and Alan's melody about this sense of "nothing, yet it's something" that has overtaken the street's residents. Even a group of sheep chime in by contributing their "bah" sounds to the chorus. Episode 3901 unites singing and speaking as one and the same by introducing children to the mechanics of opera. Big Bird persuades residents to completely forgo speaking in exchange for "singing everything [we] say." Bob tells Big Bird, "You know, that's a lot like opera." Big Bird then initiates "Opera Day" on Sesame Street. Bob sings his shopping list (" . . . I need to buy socks and dennntal, dennntal, dennntal floss"), Alan sings the contents of his menu, and Gordon sings an operetta with the number "o." As Elmo sings about "Opera Day" with a group of child actors, Oscar the Grouch protests the annoying habit of singing instead of speaking. Yet, Elmo responds to Oscar in song: "The I Don't Want to Sing Song." Before long, and much to his outrage, Oscar unwillingly begins mimicking the notes in the song even as he enunciates his protests. Elmo leaves with the children while a dumbfounded Oscar remains unable to speak without singing. In both examples, singing involves the verbal copying of another's intonations. Also, anyone can sing because sounds and rhythms are transmittable even to those who may resist.

Maria and Luis, in the skit "Firefly Song,"[58] help illustrate how *Sesame Street* blends the musicality of speech, music, and language instruction. At dusk, Maria and Luis sit on the famous Sesame Street stoop with a group of multiracial children. Muppets Telly and Baby Bear enter the scene in search of a firefly. "Have you seen a firefly?" Telly asks Luis. "No, but I know a song about a firefly," Luis responds. Luis sings his "firefly song" with the chorus, "Fly / little firefly / fly," which Maria and the children repeat. Suddenly, Maria asks the children, "Do you know what the Spanish word for 'firefly' is? It's luciernaga. Can you say that? Luccc-ie-rrrr-naga." She repeats the words several times, asking each of the children to repeat the word. One of the boys, deciphering Maria's way of rolling her "r"s, mimics the sound. Luis then looks into the camera and asks, "Can you say 'luciernaga?'" He pauses, waiting for the child audience's reply. "Good," Luis says in affirmation of the audiences' possible attempt at copying the sound at home. Continuing the theme of music as infectious, Telly asks Baby Bear if he wants to leave so they can continue looking for the firefly, but a mesmerized Baby Bear replies, "No, I want to listen to the rest of the song." Referring to Maria and the children, Luis strikes his guitar, saying, "Let's sing it [the firefly song] again . . . en Español." The children, Luis, and Maria repeat the chorus, this time exchanging the word "luciernaga" for "firefly": "Fly / luciernaga / fly." The children seamlessly sing the Spanish word (rolling their "r"s) along with the English. Baby Bear then tells Telly, "Let's go find that luciernaga." Through music and repetition, Baby Bear learns the proper pronunciation and meaning of the word.

Maria and Luis also illustrate the show's connecting of musical rhythm and speech within Episode 3917 (2001). The episode features, among other things, a salsa-dancing letter "e" and the notion of the "salsa-bet," implying the ways in which Spanish has impressed the rhythms and codes of English on *Sesame Street*. The show opens with Elmo walking down Sesame Street in pursuit of a catchy rhythm he hears but is unable to identify. The audible trail leads him to Maria and Luis, who are teaching Gaby and Miles to dance salsa. "What's salsa?" Elmo asks, prompting Maria to reply, "It's an old dance that I learned to dance when I was a little girl in Puerto Rico." Elmo insists on learning the new dance, so Maria begins her lesson by instructing him on the salsa's 1–2–3 rhythm. As a means of learning the dance, Elmo both repeats the counts ("1–2–3, 1–2–3") and dances the beat, suggesting the transferability of this new rhythm through mimicking speech (i.e., sound of the beat) and movement (i.e., silent performance). Once he has mastered some of the steps, Elmo begins his search for a salsa partner for Sesame Street's salsa party. One of his prospects for a partner: the letter "e." The letter "e" tells Elmo that he loves the salsa because "it's *e*xciting, *e*ntertaining, and *e*nticing" (emphasis mine). "E" begins dancing the 1–2–3 rhythm and recommends that Elmo track the beat by inserting the letter "e" into the salsa counts ("e-e-e"). Elmo dances the salsa with "e" to the modified counts of e-e-e. A salsa dancing letter illustrates how Spanish can and has modified the English language, in this case, with Puerto Rican intonations and rhythms. Moreover, this example portrays English letters as musical notes that have been augmented to the extent that they have been incorporated into another cadence. Equating letters with musical notes, again, links the concept of language with performance, particularly language as performance. As in a song or dance, language requires the mimicking of sounds (or notes) and gestures. Mimicking movements and sounds is presented as something anyone can do (i.e., inherent), as by the show's end, the entire cast dances the salsa on Sesame Street. Elmo invites the viewer to dance the salsa with him, "Try it. 1–2–3, 1–2–3. Or like the letter 'e' told us, e-e-e, e-e-e."

## ENSEMBLE: "THERE'S A PLACE FOR US"[59]

The interrelationships of performance, language, miming, speech, sound, and music promoted on *Sesame Street* has implications in terms of the incorporation of foreign languages into US society. These interrelationships underline the battles involved when interacting in a multilingual society. The notion of language as music frames linguistic diversity within a theatrical metaphor. Languages, like instruments, form an ensemble which reinforces the way the show fosters US and global diversity. However, in these interrelationships, I emphasize the program's pattern of depicting music (particularly rhythms associated with Puerto Rico like salsa)[60] as infectious or, as the letter "e" tells Elmo, "enticing." The theme of enticement also coincides with *Sesame Street's* early casting of Maria as a beautiful and perhaps, beguiling, arbitrator between Puerto Rican and US culture.

Tito Puente's 1993 appearances on *Sesame Street* further demonstrate the show's strong association of language, mimicry, music, and enticement. Puente, a legendary Puerto Rican drum (timbalon) soloist, plays his "catchy" rhythms in at least two *Sesame Street* episodes. On the show, Puente acts as type of Puerto Rican pied piper; his beats enrapture the cast and the child extras as they all dance and sing (in English and Spanish): "Play the Timbalon, Tito / Play the Timbalon / Suena el Timbalon, Tito / Suena el Timbalon." However, like Elmo's "singing" with Oscar the Grouch, Puente's interaction with Oscar (again, a character symbolic of prejudice) emphasizes music, and in turn language, as charming even the most resistant bigot:

> Oscar: Whoa, hold it. Who are you and what are you doing?
> Puente: My name is T. P. Tito Puente. And I was about to start my band and play a number.
> Oscar: Oh, yeah. Well, my name is Oscar the Grouch and I was about to start a Grouchketeer meeting here. So, I suggest you and your little band here go play somewhere else.
> Other Grouches: You tell 'em, Oscar.
> Puente: Hey, what's the matter? Don't you guys like my music?
> Oscar: Is your music lively and does it have a nice catchy rhythm that people love to dance to?
> Puente: It sure does.
> Oscar: Well, then we don't like it.
> Puente: Hey, wait a minute, Mr. Oscar. I have a feeling we could get even Grouches like you to dance to our kind of music?
> Oscar: Oh, yeah!
> Puente: (defiantly) Si. Yeah.
> Oscar: I'd like to see you try. . . . You'll just be wasting your time. (sarcastically, to the camera) You know, I think this might be fun to watch.
> Puente (to the band): ¡Arriba muchachos!

As Puente begins playing, the Grouchketeers (children dressed like Oscar)[61] are the first group to start dancing, perhaps suggesting the malleability of children when it comes to culture. Slowly, the other "grouches" begin moving to the rhythm, something they are ashamed to do in front of their supremely grouchy leader. For shame, each grouch ducks into their respective trash can. The camera later catches them swaying behind Puente. Losing his resistance, Oscar begins unconsciously tapping his fingers to the beat. The tapping turns into full dancing and swaying, and Oscar also hides in his trash can.

Puente continues playing the drums as the children gather around him. His music ultimately makes the reclusive Oscar leave the safety of his trash can, a notable circumstance for regular viewers. Oscar dances frenetically in front of the drums; his movements are depicted as uncontrollable. When the music ends, Puente asks, "Well, Oscar, what do you say now? I got you to dance." Oscar responds, "What do I say now? Don't ever do that to me again!" However, the rhythm rules over Oscar, something Puente exploits by, once again, banging on his seductive drum, saying "Do what? . . . This."

Oscar's frenetic dance, though comical, posits both democratic and problematic notions about sound and rhythm about language. In terms of the democratic, pluralistic nature of *Sesame Street*, Oscar's exposure to the music melted his harsh exterior, and he not only listened but took part in its performance. This coincides with the show's offering of new experiences and languages that enrich the metaphorical fruit bowl such as in "Bilingual Fruit Song." As Maria advises the Muppet Lu Lu, who refuses to sing with others unless they sing her favorite song, "Well, Lu Lu, maybe it's time to sing a new song."[62] Maria's words, like Puente's drums, also gesture towards the notion of US children's culture "singing a new song" through the incorporation of Spanish as an accessible, practical, and performable language for US preschoolers. Oscar's dancing, as with the salsa dancing letters, illustrates the fluidity of language and culture. Language and culture are moldable, performable aspects of everyday life. Anyone, even a grouch, can incorporate the sounds and cadences found in Puerto Rican culture. However, emphasizing linguistic/musical rhythms as uncontrollable and seductive suggests a problematic exoticization of Puerto Rican culture.

However, regardless of *Sesame Street*'s exoticism, the show boldly accepts the messy task of representing bilingual discourse and culture. Particularly in the show's early days, *Sesame Street* displays a raw, experimental quality (in the ensemble of performances, writing, and producing featuring people from diverse cultural and linguistic backgrounds) that keeps the show from "getting it all right." The tension *Sesame Street* displays in managing rivals (such as sameness and difference and English and Spanish) and switching codes (such as silence and speech) does not compromise its holistic vision of peace. The show's employment of theatrical concepts such as embodied performance and ensemble challenges the children's literary world in terms of access as well as racial and linguistic representation.

First, children who may never read books like *The Secret Garden*, *Perez and Martina*, or *Nilda* watch *Sesame Street*. Many children and adults, Puerto Rican or otherwise, will never meet Mohr's Felita, but they will know *Sesame Street*'s Maria. The case of *Sesame Street* is one that highlights the gap between literature and marginalized communities constructed either through ambiguity, scarcity, or indifference projected from both sides. As much as authors like Belpré and Mohr contribute to an ongoing narrative about Puerto Rican history and culture in youth literature and culture, these authors' out-of-print and undersold titles, and lack of academic and publisher support, tells another story. Although Belpré is the namesake of a literary award, the literary world has historically been ambivalent to Puerto Rican writers, regardless of how prominently her face sits on the Belpré Medal. As creative artists, Belpré, Mohr, and Manzano are united by a common project to represent Puerto Rican culture as rich and varied. These women writers and artists all underline the importance of building figurative "casitas," in this case, educational and creative outlets outside of the US given (e.g., the education system and literary establishment) which foster cultural pride. Librarian and storyteller Belpré began a pattern of going outside the schools and texts by implementing storytelling programs and puppet shows within the Puerto Rican community around New York. Likewise, Mohr highlights the importance of the library and art as a means of filling in the gaps left by the New York City school system. Mohr also creates characters that draw and build over the racist and stifling environments they encounter by transforming marginalized spaces into thriving, creative training grounds. Manzano, through her performance as Maria, illustrates the Puerto Rican community's restructuring and augmenting of US English through her breaking of established linguistic codes. She emphasizes the role of educating children about cultural and linguistic differences before they even enter the school system. Manzano also highlights how language and language pedagogy can alter children's perspectives of the world, perhaps, as in Mohr's *Nilda*, even creating a world outside the lines. *Sesame Street*'s Maria, as a personification and embodiment of bilingualism, maneuvers in and out of languages, rules, and artistic forms. Second, I have suggested that the Puerto Rican and Latinx population's adherence to Spanish has complicated their representation in the predominantly monolingual literary market. However, *Sesame Street*'s preschool audience means that the show communicates to a group of children who have not yet been coached on the limitations of traditional US dialogical relationships (e.g., English-only). Remaining just outside the literary and inhabiting a world constructed through performance supports the show's presentation of Spanish within such radical[63] contexts as untranslated dialogue. Spanish is not treated as a foreign language to children who are still learning the basics of communication and literacy, such as letters and numbers. Third, performance on *Sesame Street* portrays English and Spanish as colliding and mixing much in the same way that children might experience in their communities. English and Spanish are not presented as equals, but as languages vying for children's attention. Fourth, performances introduce children to the concept of language as a performance, much like miming someone's gestures or mimicking sounds like music. Presenting language as a mimicking of sounds and gestures removes language from the realm of inherent linguistic codes and into the realm of transferring and molding language, perhaps even creating new, unofficial languages.

Finally, the notion of ensemble—that is, several characters and languages simultaneously performing audibly and visibly for an audience—posits perhaps the greatest challenge to a literary world. In the *Sesame Street* universe, since languages are presented as a product of the people who speak them, individuals are also presented in the context of ensemble. Episode 1056 (1977) illustrates this notion of people as an ensemble in its "One of These is not Like the Other" portion of the show. The song focuses on the concept of matching patterns and prompts children to choose the out-of-place object or picture in the pattern: "One of these things is not like the other / one of these things just doesn't belong." The skit features Maria, David, Gordon, Susan, Mr. Hooper, Luis, Olivia, and Bob surrounded by a group of children and Gladys (a cow Muppet). The song begins and the camera pans over the group, prompting the viewer's choice. David says, "Hey, I know, it Gladys because, you see, we [pointing to cast and the children] are all people and Gladys is not." The idealist vision ("we are all people") perhaps captures the dreams of racial equality that were so prominent during the civil and post-Civil Rights movements. The 1960s–1970s ideals of Martin Luther King's revolutionary "beloved community" and Lyndon Johnson's public service-driven "Great Society" seem safely stored within the *Sesame Street* universe. Faith in these ideologies, and in the malleability of children, may contribute to why the show has been central on children's television for more than fifty years, and why audiences and sponsors continue rallying around the show, even during its recent move to HBO.

In terms of the comparisons I have made in this chapter between literature and television, some may object to my critiques by pointing out that "one of these things is not like the other." Few, however, can deny the tendency in children's literature to organize books, librarians, and awards by ethnicity. A world constructed by children's books is a highly segregated world. I have said that this ghettoization has contributed to the sense that a type of child, culture, or language can register as nonexistent without a properly labeled national or ethnic identity. What *Sesame Street* has done—something that children's books arguably have yet to do—is present children, visually and linguistically, in the context of a group of players all playing a part on the same "stage." I underline the importance of studying children's and youth media in conversations about diversity, particularly since communities of color, as a history of Latinx and Black feminist thought has shown, have often had to invent ways to survive outside of the established literary norms of the American canon (Moraga and Anzaldua, 1). Latinxs have argued for the incorporation of salsa and corridos into literary conversations. I suggest we do the same for children's television, especially when Latinxs have participated in the writing of Latinx characters in cultural milestones such as *Sesame Street.*

As a performer and script writer, Manzano believes her presence on *Sesame Street* helps counteract the stereotypical portrayals of Puerto Rican and Latinxs in US society. According to Manzano, outside of *Sesame Street,* she was offered roles where producers directed her to perform with an accent, something she said, "wasn't me." Her auditions before *Sesame Street* were for "the prostitute . . . the drug addict . . . the maid." She describes that, even recently, when she auditioned for roles outside *Sesame Street,* she still gets offered the part of "the maid," never the "soccer mom." She jokingly suggests that she gets offered "the Latina soccer mom that now has a catering business because she used to be a maid." Her role on *Sesame Street,* according to Manzano, is the only place that allows her "to be a real person," which, in turn, invites child viewers to see themselves as "real people, they don't have to be a black person or a Latin person, they can just be a person." Manzano objects to those who would present Puerto Rican and Latinx culture as stagnant, something she also desired to remedy through her writing of the show's scripts: "I got tired of the Hispanic culture bits always being presented as the same . . . food and music . . . like cultures don't grow. Like all Puerto Ricans are food and music and we don't change." My study of *Sesame Street*'s pedagogy of language has examined the show's portrayal of Spanish as well as the role of historic, bilingual characters like Maria. My analysis provides a context in which we can examine how the complexities of language and culture are presented in Latinx youth media as moldable facets in a young person's life.

Manzano, ultimately, challenged producers on the show to see beyond rigid stereotypes about ethnic cultures as represented through specific kinds of iconography. Culture, in the form of language and literature, shifts and changes according to the needs and creative expression of the community, something my next chapter engages with through a discussion of contemporary writers in Puerto Rico since the 1990s. In this new era, including the current economic and environmental crisis, Puerto Rican writers continue to play an important part in the formation of new, interactive ways in which youth might imagine alternatives to solving persistent community problems, such as disaster capitalism, displacement, and disenfranchisement. I examine how contemporary Puerto Rican authors on the archipelago, in the face of man-made and natural disasters, have embraced the diaspora as a means of reclaiming public spaces and as a symbol for resistance and political consciousness.

## Chapter Five

# HOW TO SURVIVE THE
# END OF THE WORLD

**Founding Fathers, Super-heroines, and Writing
and Performing When the Lights Go Out**

Aparicio Distributors is a two-story bookstore in Bayamon, Puerto Rico, on Avenida Lomas Verdes. Hurricanes Maria and Irma left the store damaged and faded; for example, its popular storytelling theatre was left "en pedazos/ in pieces," owner Hector Aparicio says, during a tour of the facility. Inside the store, the neat bookshelves organize award-winning titles from Latin American and Caribbean writers and illustrators US readers may never see. As the only independent children's bookstore in Puerto Rico, Aparicio's, as a site, testifies to how US and European colonialism affects the publishing and distribution of youth literature in the Caribbean, a situation further exacerbated by the hurricanes, as well as the general conversation on rebuilding and recovery for Puerto Rico (Edwards 2018). In July 2018, Aparicio's also served as a meeting space for a collective of women writers and storytellers, Tere Marichal, Wanda de Jesus and Ada Haiman, who organize around the barriers and advancements they have experienced in the world of literatura infantil and juvenil. Currently, the collective stresses the importance of seeing youth literature as an artistic rather than didactic medium. Puerto Rico's lack of publishing and distribution opportunities beyond its own shores highlights how US colonialism, and Puerto Rican assimilationist governments, employ institutions such as its school system and printing presses as a means of sustaining status quo narratives.

Reimagining Puerto Rico as a government enterprise, and even in creative projects, has often meant forgoing the interests of its most vulnerable populations, including Afro-Boricuas, women, and youth. After centuries of colonialism, the Puerto Rican government's descent into bankruptcy beginning in 2006, the congressional appointment of the non-Puerto Rican elected fiscal board (the Financial Oversight and Management Board of Puerto Rico)[1] in 2016, and financial and environmental crises have made

Puerto Rico a test case for disaster capitalism,[2] as journalist and researcher Naomi Klein emphasizes in *The Battle for Paradise: Puerto Rico Takes on the Disaster Capitalists* (2018). Klein's work is especially helpful for seeing how natural disasters, such as those that occur in racially segregated areas like New Orleans during Hurricane Katrina, open the door for policies which create havoc for communities of color. Economic, legal, and political analysts have provided countless reports and data on the economic crisis, and in the months after the hurricanes, public and private research institutes attempted to access the damages of man-made and natural disasters. Even the death counts in Puerto Rico after the storm became a political battle for numbers and fodder for social media debate, including President Donald Trump.

Hurricane Maria's aftermath exposed, once again, the general lack of knowledge about Puerto Rico's relationship to the US, underlining the need for critical Caribbean and Puerto Rican Studies, especially stories helping provide a human context beyond the numbers. The story of Puerto Rican youth literature and culture bridges the importance of qualitative and quantitative knowledge for scholars hoping to "humanize research" (Paris 2017). In *Side by Side*, I have argued that youth literature and culture provide a literal stage for the Puerto Rican story, who gets to tell it, and how. Here, I analyze how youth texts provide a window into how contemporary Puerto Rican writers resist cultural nationalism—something central to Puerto Rican and US assimilationist ideology—and signal it as a failed ideology for sustaining social change. The lack of scholarship on contemporary Puerto Rican youth literature within Puerto Rico veils our ability to see how writers converge and disagree in terms of political status, and how they unite in projects across generations. In fact, youth texts in Puerto Rico have been subject to censorship by the Puerto Rican Department of Education, particularly during civil rights struggles in the US and third-world movements during the late 1960s. Apart from censoring books deemed subversive to the US government, since the 1990s, books upholding a kind of Puerto Rican national ideology, such as those published by the autora-cátedras, were removed from schools in favor of translated books more in line with US traditions. Indeed, many of the writers and educators I spoke with during my research for this book discussed how the closing of school and public libraries in Puerto Rico since the 1990s has suppressed Puerto Ricans' ability to critique the institutions governing the archipelago's economic and cultural production and independent creative expression.

However, women writers, in particular since the generation of the autora-cátedras, have found ways to resist the assimilationist politics of Puerto Rican and US governments by resisting cultural nationalism and its tendency

to portray nature and national flora and fauna as politically neutral—and
national culture as containable. The little to no scholarship on this group of
writers maintains a sense that these were sweet women who simply wrote
books for young people that have since been out-of-print. Even today, in
works which I refer to as "frontline kid lit," how have Puerto Rican writers,
mainly women, been preparing young people for the inevitability of both
man-made and environmental disasters? This chapter also looks at how the
inability to create, distribute, and sell content for young people in Puerto Rico
damages both cultural and economic capital. I intertwine three examples of
how youth culture illustrates the complications with so-called rebuilding and
reinventing Puerto Rico and reflect on what it means to "restore power" to
the archipelago, a phrase used in relationship to the loss of electricity after
Hurricanes Irma and Maria, and more recently, during the earthquakes. First,
I analyze the work of children's author and poet Georgina Lázaro, a literary
figure who emerged in the 1990s and whose picture books bring together
former and current generations of women writers and speak to Puerto Rico's
constant uncertainties in the face of economic and environmental crisis. Second, in the context of rebuilding Puerto Rico after the hurricanes, I consider
and contrast the art and activism of entertainment superstar Lin-Manuel
Miranda and popular comics artist Edgardo Miranda-Rodriguez for how
each asks young people to identify in two contrasting revolutionary mythologies based on the elevating of heroes as a means of empowerment. Third, I
consider the collective work of Tere Marichal, Wanda de Jesus, Ada Haiman,
and Laura Rexach Olivencia, each of whom provide new stories using traditional and nontraditional literacy practices in the face of uncertainty, school
privatization, and closures. Actually, in contemporary Puerto Rico, Pura
Belpré's work in oral culture and storytelling is seen as a way forward from
disaster. Ultimately, this is the story of how contemporary youth literature
and culture in Puerto Rico breaks from a tradition of depending on official
Puerto Rican and US pedagogy and education administration and embraces
the diaspora as a symbol of resilience and solidarity like never before.

## BEYOND CULTURAL NATIONALISM: CONFRONTING A LEGACY OF SILENCE

Researchers in Puerto Rican youth literature and literacy traveling to Puerto
Rico quickly learn that the story of our field is entrenched and often unwrit-
ten, making field research in the form of interviews with local librarians,
booksellers, searching research collections, and visiting educational and

mainstream bookstores invaluable. I underline the University of Puerto Rico Colleción Puertorriqueña, the Center for Puerto Rican Studies at Hunter College, CUNY, Norberto Booksellers, and Aparicio Distributors as public spaces that testify to the formation and continuing history of youth literature. Little if any critical assessments analyze the work of contemporary Puerto Rican writers for youth beyond 1980 and into the 1990s; in particular, there is a paucity of scholarship on how past generations of Puerto Rican writers converge and contrast, particularly on political ideals. As addressed by writers such as Tere Marichal and Georgina Lázaro, few books by Puerto Rican writers travel beyond the archipelago, hindering the opportunities for critical inquiry and reviewers of children's and young adult books outside Puerto Rico. In Puerto Rico, academic inquiry focusing on literature for youth as literature is also sparse, with few courses, if any, offered in undergraduate and graduate education, particularly as part of a literary foundation. Flor Piñeiro de Rivera's definitive resource, *Un Siglo de Literatura Infantil Puertorriqueña / A Century of Puerto Rican Children's Literature* (1987), is often cited and guides the discussion of the field. Although de Rivera's book outlines the bibliography of writers and details the history, her work ends at 1987, which time-capsules how current researchers learn about Puerto Rican children's literature. By this, I mean that writers in the evolving diaspora beyond the 1980s lose visibility in critical discussions for researchers and teachers, simultaneously contemporary writers lose a kind of official designation as to what is considered Puerto Rican on the island, particularly when, at this point, we know the diaspora continues in both directions.

The big five (Scholastic, Penguin, Random House, HarperCollins, Simon and Schuster) in the children's publishing-industrial complex—by which I mean the influence these companies exert over school book orders and teacher curriculum fairs—and literary agents seem indifferent to prospective authors and illustrators on the island. Indeed, the bulk of these publishers' contributions to young people's literature in Puerto Rico comes through selling translations of North American books rather than investing in Puerto Rican writers and illustrators. Youth literature as an industry and economy, as with any other economy in Puerto Rico, demonstrates how wealth is extracted rather than retained on the island (Edwards 2019). Yet, the publishing of Puerto Rican youth literature has always existed in economic, and to some extent, creative dependence on government initiatives, whether Spanish colonial, US colonial, or Puerto Rican commonwealth. The medium's ties to school curriculum, and the lack of independent publishers publishing Puerto Rican books, made it especially vulnerable to the growing economic crisis, starting in the early 2000s.

Budget cuts to cultural institutions resulted in the paralysis of three of the main publishers of children's books in Puerto Rico, el Departamento de Educación (formerly El Departamento de Instrucción, which closed its operations in 1990), El Editorial de la Universidad de Puerto Rico, and Instituto de Cultura Puertorriqueña. Certainly, other publishers have existed beyond these three, such as Ediciones Huracán, which also closed during the early 2000s, but the amount of titles generated and distributed by public institutions accounted for a large portion of all books published in Puerto Rico. According to Consuelo Figueras, the loss of Editorial, the imprint of the Department of Education, accounted for a decrease of 18 percent of Puerto Rican books published. In her analysis, Figueras suggests a kind of self-determination for Puerto Rican authors and artists through children's literature. She surveys the 1990s as a kind of renaissance period for Puerto Rican children's literature, citing a greater awareness among writers and publishers for the medium as an art form and the work of award-winning authors such as Georgina Lázaro's *El Flamboyan Amarillo* (1996) and Fernando Picó's *La Pieneta Colorada* (1991).[3] Figueras then casts a long view of what she hopes will guide the future of Puerto Rican children's literature in the twenty-first century, and what she lists as the purpose of such literature:

> To attract and keep children as life-long readers, authors and publishers are connected to providing books with higher quality of illustration and design and making books in a variety of genres available to children. Important Puerto Rican figures, historical events, natural environment, festivities, clothing, values, and aspirations will be more strongly evident in future books, so that the identity of Puerto Rican children's literature as distinct from that of the US will be further assured. (27)

However, the qualities that Figueras praises here as authentic to Puerto Rican children's literature, such as "figures, historical events, natural environment, clothing, and values," suggests her adherence to cultural nationalism, an ideology closely associated with the rise of Puerto Rican intellectual life in the 1930s that reemerges with the forming of the commonwealth. As Raquel Z. Rivera writes, in the face of US colonialism, cultural nationalism serves to portray a distinct Puerto Ricanness, though it varies depending on those utilizing it for the purposes of political ideology whether independentista in which it serves to sustain "a strong and distinct Puerto Rican culture theorized as unassimilable to US culture" or whether it serves a pro-statehood or

-commonwealth status. Rivera suggests that at the service of assimilationist politics cultural nationalism becomes a force which shapes and restricts political, creative, gendered expressions in maintaining state power:

> Cultural nationalism has also been championed by sectors that do not favor independence, including the Puerto Rican government itself (in both its pro-statehood and pro-commonwealth manifestations). Incidentally, the local colonial government has at times been the most influential promoter of the dominant strand of cultural nationalism, with all its racist, classist, xenophobic, patriarchal, and homophobic shortcomings. In these cases where cultural nationalism is not linked to the project of political independence, the "defense" of Puerto Rican culture is an end unto itself and serves a multiplicity of interests and institutions. (218)

For example, one of the ways we have seen cultural nationalism operate in children's texts as a means to condone a separate culture but not a separate government is through Manuel Fernandez Juncos's adaptations of Puerto Rican readers for colonial schools. Juncos idealized poetry and stories upholding seemingly neutral symbols which build community such as the love of the land, language, and jíbaro mythology, but steered clear of Puerto Rican revolutionary thinkers like Hostos or Betances. The love of land and nature as a kind of predictable and dependable symbol of Puerto Rico also served as a means of reiterating much of the patriarchal deficient, insular imagery which sustains dependency on the US; hence, women revolutionaries' (such as de Burgos) emphasis on waterways as a symbol of liberation and transnationalism (Perez-Rosario 2014). Figueras's assertion that adhering to this specific Puerto Rican iconography would "assure" a distinct literature from the US underlines an interrelationship between pro-statehood and commonwealth cultural nationalism and stagnant forms of culture.

However, I argue that articles such as Figueras's, and the lack of critique of children's and young adult texts, veils the aesthetic and political legacies of youth literature in Puerto Rico. Through my comparative and literary analysis in this book, for example, I hope to shift scholarly attention beyond cultural nationalism as a sole organizing factor. Using cultural nationalism as a guide tends to limit conversations to how the authenticity of book should be judged based on a specific set of cultural markers, such as a coquí frog for example. Yet, the transnational story of Puerto Rican youth literature emphasizes the importance of subverting rigid monoliths of culture, whether US or Puerto

Rican. Instead, I highlight, for example, the distinctness of Puerto Rican youth culture for its employment of Afro-Boricua epistemologies of literacy, storytelling, and Indigenous survivance.

A richness of critique would allow writers and scholars to observe how current and former generations of writers often credited with maintaining a kind of cultural nationalism—such as Georgina Lázaro and even Ángeles Pastor in Figueras's article—actually resist this paradigm in both subtle and outright ways. In particular, writers reflect on the unpredictable and un-containable aspects of nature. For example, as I analyzed in my first chapter, autora-cátedras such as Ángeles Pastor, following in the tradition of poet Juan Ramon Jiménez, who set a standard for children's literature in the mid-1930s, align with a style of avant-garde poetry and transnationalism which resisted Treintista writers' adherence to cultural nationalism. Pastor and autora-cátedras such as Carmen Gomez-Tejera actually created a generation of school readers which always connected Puerto Rican children to a kind of global landscape, celebrating advances in technology and travel even in relationship to Puerto Rican circular migration to the US as in *Amigos de Aqui y de Alla*.

Authors working in Puerto Rico in the 1990s and beyond reflect a deep concern about breaking from essentialist identities and official colonial pedagogies. The desire to create a self-governing body of work and repre-sentation remains, even as authors in Puerto Rico maneuver the creative and publishing process without access to the mainstays of publishing in the US, such as literary agents and independent presses. Contemporary authors strive to create literary works without the agenda of government-dependent public institutions that wax and wane depending on political party. The paucity of literary and sociocultural analysis given to children's literature in Puerto Rico leads educators and scholars to accept these texts as forming a kind of neutral, yet distinctive tradition. Few linger on the ruptures between generations of writers and, indeed, schools of political thought on the colo-nial status of Puerto Rico, gender, race, and class—even in the face of legal policy favoring the censoring and criminalization of independence. How did authors supporting independence, among them Isabel Freire de Matos, maneuver a children's reading tradition and a government-dependent pub-lishing apparatus, which favored colonial status and schooling? The Puerto Rican government, through the Department of Education, has certainly not viewed children's reading materials as neutral, banning the circulation of materials deemed "anti-American" and "subversive." For example, the work of Manuel Fernandez Juncos unites with Freire de Matos in the search for preserving a Puerto Rican worldview for young people, yet Juncos's work in folklore was never banned while Ruben del Rosario and Freire de Matos's *ABC de Puerto Rico*, celebrated as a hallmark of Puerto Rican letters by Flor Piñeiro de Rivera's *Un Siglo de Literature Infantil Puertorriqueña*, was pulled from classrooms and libraries by a pro-statehood administration in 1968. Furthermore, toward the end of the 1990s, the school reader tradition ala Ángeles Pastor—upholding ideals of a Puerto Rican national literary tradition to youth—was retired from classrooms in favor of books in translation and, as in the US, texts centered on standardized testing standards. Yet, I draw attention to a parallel here between the decline of children's reading materials published and supported by the Puerto Rican government and the economic, environmental, and political crisis that ensues by the early twenty-first century.

## UNEXPECTED FRUIT: GEORGINA LÁZARO, ANTONIO MARTORELL AND ANSWERING THE UNANSWERABLE IN LATE TWENTIETH- TO TWENTY-FIRST-CENTURY PUERTO RICO

Award-winning author and poet Georgina Lázaro-Leon demonstrates the progression among generations perhaps more than other writers in the archipelago. I analyze this progression through Lázaro-Leon's first, renowned picture book, *El Flamboyan Amarillo* (1996), illustrated by Lula Delacre, and her latest *¿Y Por Qué?* (2016), illustrated by Antonio Martorell. Martorell and Delacre also serve as examples of bridging generations. Delacre's artwork has rendered visible the lives of past and present figures such as Sonia Sotomayor and Pura Belpré in children's books. Martorell's work spans from illustrating the first renowned picture book in Puerto Rico, Ruben del Rosario and Isabel Freire de Matos's *ABC de Puerto Rico* (1966)—banned by the Department of Education as "subversive"—and Pura Belpré's *The Rainbow Colored Horse* (1978).

 *El Flamboyan Amarillo* and *¿Y Por Qué?* represent Lázaro-Leon's revision and resistance of totalizing standards of children's reading and her yearning for literature "sin edad/without age." Lázaro-Leon sees herself as bridging the former and new generation of Puerto Rican poets for young people (interview). When asked how she would define Puerto Rican children's literature, Lázaro-Leon reveals deep reflection on the medium's history:

> Empezó como un literatura para la escuela, para los libros de texto [al servicio del Departamento de Instrucción] y una literatura comprometida de una manera obvia con la cultura, la naturaleza, una litera-

tura romántica, de añoranza de la patria—porque en un momento no
se podia decir patria—del terruño, de la tierra, de la naturaleza—pero
eso a cambiado mucho.

It began as a literature for schools, for textbooks and at the service of
the Department of Education and a kind of literature which was invested in obvious ways in depicting culture, nature—a kind of romantic literature about yearning for your patria (homeland)—although
at one moment you couldn't say patria [about Puerto Rico]—a literature about the landscape, the land, and the environment—but this
has changed a lot.

Lázaro-Leon's reference to a "yearning for your patria" during a moment
when one "couldn't say patria" highlights the unsettling political context of
the auto-cátedras—charged with writing books that would instill national
pride without being able to mention political sovereignty. From the 1940s to
the 1960s, Ángeles Pastor, Isabel Freire de Matos, and Ester Feliciano Mendoza created countless texts that guided the formation of the commonwealth,
yet these women writers found ways to subvert the insularity of cultural
nationalism by celebrating transnationalism and technological advancements. They wrote in the context of the Puerto Rican and US government
creating laws and policies that eradicated ideals for independence, such
as the Puerto Rican legislature's Ley de la Moradaza or Gag Law in 1948,
making the flying of the Puerto Rican flag, the singing of patriotic music,
and the meeting together of independence supporters criminal activities
worthy of imprisonment. The doctrine of cultural nationalism, disassociated
from political independence, allowed for the creation of a Puerto Rican
children's tradition which was "obvious," as Lázaro-Leon says, in its manner of celebrating the land and environment. However, writers from the
feminist school of the auto-cátedras, such as Lázaro-Leon, actually continue
a legacy of celebrating nature as a means of warning youth about the unpredictable and uncontainable aspects of nature. This decision to dwell on
the unpredictable, and even unanswerable, resists the status quo of cultural
nationalism doctrine in colonial schooling. Indeed, what these authors do
instead is draw young readers' attention to the creative unpredictability and
possibilities beyond the stagnant "mirrors" and even "windows" provided
by US and Puerto Rican official pedagogies. Lázaro-Leon's *El Flamboyan
Amarillo*, the story of a little boy who sows what he least expected, demonstrates this feminist tradition of Puerto Rican school poetry, acting as an ode

to national flora and fauna while dwelling on the uncontainable aspects of nature. In chapter one, I analyzed the feminist tradition as a responding to the male-dominated treintista-style of school readers proscribing to ideals of Puerto Rican docility and insularity. For example, in *Conozcamos a Puerto Rico* (1972), a literary anthology that showcases the geography, environment, and communities throughout the island, Pastor includes her homage to the Loiza River, in a poem which alludes to revolutionary writers of the diaspora, Julia de Burgos's "Rio Grande de Loiza." Pastor's "Rio Grande de Loiza" is less sexualized, with no allusions to the female body, which may connote a standard for what was deemed appropriate for young readers. Yet, Pastor continues de Burgos's images of the formidable, unyielding river—images aligned with notions of Indigenous survivance as the river testifies to the stories of an Indigenous past: "The river remembers these sad things and without warning its waters surge and grow. The water runs with great force through valleys and neighborhoods and levels everything it finds in its path" (105). The river is capable of destroying man-made structures, which include, in my reading, colonialism.

Lázaro-Leon's affinity with the auto-cátedras is clear through her preference for poetry as a means of storytelling. However, she distinguishes her style as separate from the textbook tradition in her use of poetic narration as opposed to poems written for young readers' recitation and memorization (interview). Indeed, the romantic, idyllic world of *El Flamboyán Amarillo* draws in readers raised on the textbook tradition with familiar scenes in Puerto Rican children's literature—a boy and his mother, peaceful, rural hillside, and a story centered on a tree often celebrated in Puerto Rican cultural lore, the flamboyán or royal poinciana tree. Actually, it is the same tree that Belpré's Inés sought to plant among the green of El Yunque, that Mohr's Nilda remembers as she steps toward her "secret garden," and that adorns Luis and Maria's apartment on *Sesame Street* in a framed portrait. However, the imagined flamboyán at the center of Lázaro-Leon's story is one which grows yellow flowers, in contrast to the red, fiery ones Inés admired. The voice of the poetic narrator belongs to the boy, an aspect which esteems young people as storytellers. I mark this as a break from past traditions such as Juan Ramon Jiménez and the auto-cátedras who usually assumed the role of adult narrator through the lens of an observer or teacher, while young people were expected to act out the lessons. Lázaro-Leon's tale begins,

Hace tiempo y no hace tanto, / unos años nada más, / fui a un paseo por el campo / de la mano de mamá.

> A long time ago and not that long ago / a few years only / I went for a
> stroll around the country / holding my mother's hand.

The mother and boy become enthralled with the tree's "gold" leaves, which
seem to glow even from far away (2–3). The tree's attractive glow seems to
make the rest of the scene even more beautiful and accessible: "El monte
se hizo más monte, el camino más estrecho, y el paisaje más hermoso . . . /
The mountains become more like mountains, the path shorter, and the view
more beautiful" (2–3). After spending time basking in the tree's shade, the
boy decides to save a seed from the tree that he can plant for himself and his
mother, whom he observes as "falling in love" with the tree (4–5). He picks
up the seed, which he describes as "el comienzo de un flamboyán amarillo/
the beginning of a yellow flamboyán." The boy then recounts his steps in
planting, watering, and caring for his tree. His use of the phrase "mi" or "my"
connotes his desire for ownership. Lázaro-Leon uses the boy's exertion of
ownership and repetition of the phrase "mi flamboyán amarillo" to create a
sense of expectation in readers. As the first few leaves begin sprouting, the
boy describes his feelings of joy and fulfillment in creation and the land:

> *Fue como abrazar la tierra.*
> *Fue como el cielo besar.*
> *Me acerqué a la eternidad*
> *con un gesto tan sencillo;*
> *ayudé en la creación*
> *de un flamboyán amarillo. (14)*

> *It was like hugging the land.*
> *It was like kissing the sky.*
> *I reached for eternity*
> *And with this simple gesture;*
> *I aided the creation*
> *Of a yellow flamboyan.*

The imagery in this passage ascribes to the boy an almost divine power. The
planting of the tree is likened to "reaching for eternity." He is a cocreator
along with the Creator—a master of the land and nature. Yet, it is also nature
who holds back a secret from this little master. As the boy grows, he is visited
by a small grasshopper / grillo who tells him that "Tiene un secreto tu árbol
/ Your tree has a secret" (18). The tree continues to grow, and eventually the
boy, older now, can sit in its branches, yet the familiar leaves of the colorful,

yellow tree have yet to bloom. Then one morning the older boy passes his bedroom window, but he sees something that leaves him surprised. Delacre's illustrations ensure that readers see the expression of bewilderment on the boy's face, even as a yellow glow, perhaps from the sun, shines through the window. The boy and his mother walk outside the house to confirm the secret:

*No había oro entre sus ramas. Había coral, fuego, sangre*
*como el amor que mi tierra*
*me enseño a darle a mi madre.*
*Y entonces supe el secreto,*
*aquel del que me habló el grillo: ¡Había florecido rojo/ mi flamboyán*
*amarillo!*

*There was no gold between its branches. There was coral, fire, blood*
*Like the love my land*
*Taught me to have for my mother*
*And then I knew the secret,*
*That the grasshopper had spoken to me: It had bloomed red / my yellow flamboyán. (23)*

The allusions of gold, fire, and blood in reference to the tree leaves suggest to readers the consequences of colonial violence. The young boy, in his attempts to subjugate and reproduce nature for the beauty and benefits of the gold in its leaves—a reference underlining financial and aesthetic value—fails to yield the supposedly predictable results of planting a specific seed. The value assigned to nature in cultural nationalism comes from its benign predictability and beauty, from the idea of it as neutral and available to be claimed as a resource at the service of the colonizer. Nature, symbolized through the seed, breaks from the predictable code it is expected to reproduce. Instead of gold, Lázaro-Leon asks readers to contemplate the color red through the image of "coral, fire, and blood," which resonates with Puerto Rico's history: exploited land, people, and waterways, genocide, and land seizure.

The red flamboyán in Lázaro-Leon's tale causes a similar commotion as Inés's trees did for the personified El Yunque and El Torro in Belpré's story—it causes a rupture for the inhabitants, particularly males. In *Inés*, El Torro and El Yunqué believed the trees were a raging fire. They warned Inés to "save herself," but Inés simply laughed at the thought of such danger. Something to consider here is the way in which Inés's tale serves to show a female child seeking knowledge and permission from nature in order to gain its benefits, as opposed to the manner in which males are depicted as attempting to possess it. Lázaro-Leon depicts the boy as playfully going off on his own and picking up the seed and later sharing his conquest with his mother on the return home:

> Cuando venia de regreso
> yo le conté mi ocurrencia y mi "primera maestra"
> me dio una clase de ciencias.
> Pero yo no podía oírla; tenía en el alma un tordillo
> que me cantaba canciones
> del flamboyán amarillo.

> When I was coming back home
> I told my "first teacher"
> and she gave me a science class.
> But I couldn't hear her because my soul was wrapped up
> And it was singing songs about the yellow flamboyan. (8)

Perhaps, during her science lesson, his mother revealed the curiosity of how a yellow flamboyán may still yield a red one from its seed. A yellow one is quite rare, which is perhaps why it grabs such attention. The boy, however, says he was unable to hear because he was so enraptured with the thought of his tree. I mark the significance in terms of the way Lázaro-Leon and Belpré both suggest the importance of listening to Boricua women and, nature, when it comes to a yielding crop and for what purpose. In her author's note, Lázaro-Leon emphasizes the history of the flamboyán as "originating in Madagascar . . . and growing in other areas" such as Cuba and Mexico. She also lists the various names of the tree in different languages, reflecting the geography in which it grows including French and English: guacamayo, flame tree, flamboyant. Through this history, Lázaro-Leon resists a monolithic approach to culture by revealing that this iconic tree—which has become synonymous with Puerto Rican flora and fauna—hails from off the coast of Africa. This detail implies the exchange of goods and crops through conquest and colonization, making it possible for the flamboyán to adorn parts of the Caribbean and North America. As the author, she also removes herself as one who would define the experiences of young readers, telling readers that the story of the flamboyán "no termina con mi cuento / doesn't end with my story." Her story is one which she hopes will "awaken" young readers to protect and "know the land better." Yet, in relationship to a history of Puerto Rican women's writers for young people, Lázaro-Leon's El Flamboyán

*Amarillo* builds a sense of wonder but also a formidable respect for nature. *El Flamboyán Amarillo* also suggests that those who wish to subjugate the land may receive, as illustrator Delacre says "fruto inesperado/unexpected fruit." The flamboyán, ultimately, serves to tie together images of fire and blood among the generations, and this awareness of struggle and violence is what teaches young people to love their families and communities. The land, instead of turning young people onto themselves, reaches outward and ultimately ties Puerto Ricans to other histories, countries, and peoples, as opposed to a closed landscape which might be contained.

One legacy of the Puerto Rican children's literature I highlight here is that—behind the idyllic scenery immortalized in the texts of the autora-cátedras—there is a lesson about surviving disasters, whether natural or man-made. Pastor's message of a river that overflows and breaks the boundaries of its banks, destroying "anything its is path," speaks to a kind of cycle of violence and renewal. In this context, natural events such as floods and, perhaps, hurricanes may even act as a form higher justice. In the world of *El Flamboyán Amarillo*, readers enter a familiar, romantic landscape yet ultimately Lázaro-Leon underlines the unpredictability of nature, resisting, as her feminist predecessors did before her, the notion that national culture should rely on specific cultural iconography as culturally "pure" and dependable. Like Pastor and Belpré, Lázaro-Leon emphasizes flora and fauna as politically non-neutral and as carriers of historical memory and trauma. I mark the timing of this message of uncontainable nature and unexpected fruit as coinciding with key events in Puerto Rico's history by 2004. By then, the economic crisis in Puerto Rico was already in its early stages, many would contend, among other colonial economic policies, triggered by the congressional passage of Section 936. This bill, signed under President Bill Clinton, removed many of the tax breaks and incentives making Puerto Rico the land of commerce and industry during Operation Bootstrap (celebrated in texts like *Amigos de Aqui y Alla* [1960]). Lázaro-Leon's contemporary legacy is one that lingers on the uncertainty of the material world and the human experience, through the eyes of a child.

In 2016, in the aftermath of the economic crisis, and the Puerto Rican government's official declaration of bankruptcy, Lázaro-Leon released a book she believes breaks from many of the traditions in Latin American and the Caribbean about what a children's book should be. Lázaro-Leon's newest picture book—*¿Y Por Qué?*—centered on the relationship between a grandfather and his grandson, and the author intended it as a book meant for all ages. "La buena literatura no tiene edad / good literature has no age," Lázaro-Leon emphasizes, mentioning that the picture book's launch was at the Museo de Las Americas in San Juan, with a room full of adults. "There was not even one child" (interview). She describes her frustrations with publishers and bookstores who ask her, "What is the reading level for this book?" When she asserts that "hay que romper con todo eso / we have to break away from all that," she underlines the problems with youth literature's deep ties to the schooling system and didacticism, as well as the need to consider the medium an art form for all in its own right. *¿Y Por Qué?* is also Lázaro-Leon's first project with the publication company SM, a Spanish publisher with branches throughout Latin American and the Caribbean, establishing an office in Puerto Rico since 2004 just after many publishers had closed their doors, including Ediciones Huracán, a Caribbean publisher, and Lecturum, a US publisher, both of which published Lázaro-Leon in the past. One of the head editors at SM, Elsa Aquier, reflected, in a 2014 blog post, on rigid definitions of literature for young people, wanting to separate it from didacticism and focusing instead on what she says this literature "is not":

> Literatura infantil y juvenil no es lo mismo que pedagogía. Y esto es importante, porque, a pesar de que, de palabra, todos—autores, editores, mediadores . . . —lo tenemos más o menos claro, lo de la "literatura" con intención (moralizante, educativa . . . ), parece que nos tienta más de la cuenta. En palabras de una de las grandes autoras de la literatura infantil: La literatura infantil no es una píldora pedagógica envuelta en papel de letras, sino literatura, es decir, mundo transformado en lenguaje. (Christine Nöstlinger)

> Literature for children and young adults is not the same thing as pedagogy. And this is important because, even though by word of mouth everyone—authors, editors, agents—we have this concept pretty clear, the issue of "literature" with an intention (morally, educationally . . . ) seems to test us more than anything. In the words of a great author of literature for young people: Literature for youth is not a pill box of pedagogy wrapped in a lettered paper, instead literature, is a world transformed by language.

Aquier, like Lázaro-Leon, emphasizes the value of literature for young people as a literary art form in much the same way that W. E. B. Du Bois and other writers of color exhibit during the formation of the field in the US (Capshaw Smith 2004). Aquier seeks no separation between the child and adult reader in this "world transformed by language." Yet, Lázaro-Leon believes that Puerto Rico is behind in terms of the collective elevation of literature for youth as an art form. The government's policing of the kinds of stories young Boricuas would read in school, along with supporting a problematic notion that printed stories and reading happens in schools, reveals a self-consciousness about how political ideals for this shifting colony would and would not arise. Maintaining a colonial status quo in Puerto Rico seems to have meant censoring and restricting the interrelated aesthetic and political ideals of youth literature, though my reading has shown ways in which these ideals continued to survive through clever negotiating by female educators. Considering the amount of time the medium has spent in the realm of government institutions, one can't help but wonder if it isn't a blessing that less governmental support also results in more creative expression and new pathways, even for the exploration of what children's literature is rather than what children's literature has been in the archipelago.[4]

My work in bringing a comparative analysis of past and present youth literature in Puerto Rico helps scholars go beyond generalized tropes into how contemporary authors build on a foundation of resistance and trans-nationalism across the Americas. For example, Lázaro-Leon describes her writing as influenced by the "resto de America como Ruben Dario, José Martí/the rest of America such as Ruben Dario and José Martí," which she credits as the poetry of her youth: "Cogí algo de la literatura que había leído de Estado Unidos y de otros países de Hispanoamérica y luego me lanze al ortro lado / I took inspiration from literature I read from the United States and other countries in Hispanoamérica, and then I leaped to the other side." The other side, or "otro lado," which Lázaro-Leon speaks of is the place in which contemporary Puerto Rican literature finds itself today, on the other side of the 1940s–1970s generation of those writing textbooks, and the post-boom of the 1990s, when more independent presses published Puerto Rican authors living on the island.

Moreover, through Martorell's paintings and Lázaro-Leon's narration, we see that one of the things that makes Puerto Rican youth literature distinctive—rather than flora and fauna or specific cultural iconography—is the longstanding tradition of casting young people as knowledge bearers and producers. The exchanges between adult and child, and the hope for the future this relationship represents, reappears and reaches into the despair of the contemporary economic decline in a book celebrating the reality of uncertainty. Martorell's beautiful artwork creates scenes which could be any-where in the world through emphasizing both urban and country landscapes. Martorell's emphasis on the windows and mirrors, many of which show a child looking into and past, connects with Rudine Sims Bishop's metaphor for children's literature: "Books are sometimes windows, offering views of worlds that may be real or imagined, familiar or strange. These windows are also sliding glass doors, and readers have only to walk through in imagination to be become part of whatever world has been created by the author" (1). Early in the picture book, Lázaro-Leon has the boy, painted by Martorell, staring into a mirror as if almost to walk through it, asking:

> *Y ese que me mira*
> *Ahi desde el espejo,*
> *¿piensa que el es el niño*
> *Y yo soy su reflejo?*

> *And that boy looking at me*
> *There in the mirror,*
> *Does he think he is the boy*
> *And I am his reflection?*

This scene with the mirror is symbolic of the literary world, and a child's ability to see himself, critically, but the reflections represent a child imagining another's subjectivity. I read this moment as representative of a shift in how Puerto Rican children might see themselves reflected in literature, as well as the kind of literature which should sustain their lives. As with Sims Bishop, the mirror should allow children to see themselves but should not consume them to the point of falling in love with their reflection.

*¿Y Por Qué?* explores the worlds a child's imagination could reach as opposed to containing that imagination in a recognizable Puerto Rican space or on an individual. Yet, the visual universe Martorell creates still contains markers of Puerto Rican culture. Martorell's history, as one of the only censored artists and children's book illustrators in Puerto Rico, resonates with his work in *¿Y Por Qué?* For example, *ABC de Puerto Rico* featured Martorell's prints of images such as Tainos, Lareños (the historical site of Puerto Ricans' revolt against the Spanish), and ruiseñor fighting against an eagle as part of a primer; in 1968, these might have been deemed too subversive for Luis Ferré's administration during the time, the first proponents of statehood in the governor's seat in history (Diaz-Royo). Yet *¿Y Por Qué?* locates this book as coming from a Puerto Rican imagination, yet does so subtly with the story's message existing independently from such political and cultural markers. For example, as the boy asks "¿Quién inventó las letras?" Martorell paints the boy and his grandfather as standing on dictionary pages with the word "bregar" beneath their feet, a distinctive way Puerto Ricans refer to work (46–47). In another frame, Martorell lightly sketches the famous tower

at the University of Puerto Rico, Rio Piedras, in the distance, as the boy asks, "Antes de los relojes, ¿cómo existía el tiempo? ¿Era como es ahora? ¿Mas rápido o mas lento? / Before clocks, how did time exist? Was it the way it is now? Was it faster or slower?" (52–53)

This image of the UPR clock tower is placed across from the image of the boy as if he were standing inside a clock, his arms signaling the time (9:05). Martorell seems to suggest the passage of time, the uncertainty that such important national landmarks might remain, and the boy's place in enacting future events. It is an image that speaks to the sense of urgency for Puerto Rico's future, particularly as it pertains to public education and public repositories. Yet, the boy's question, through Lázaro-Leon's narration, generates a sense of hope that, even without this historic clock, time cannot be contained or even lost. This moment connects to the work of Belpré and Schomburg, who underlined the importance of community-based education and taking ownership of knowledge and documenting the past, as opposed to relying on the recognition of institutions which were often subject to imperial control. The resurgence of such foundational ideas about Puerto Rican intellectual and creative resources coincides with the 2016 economic crisis, which, since 2006, has meant the closing of over 40 percent of the island's schools through privatization (Martinez and Lee 2018). The managing of the debt, through the congressionally appointed PROMESA board, has meant severe cuts for public education. Indeed, the future of the University of Puerto Rico, after the crisis and subsequent hurricanes, has been left in jeopardy.

Another way of reading this text as a response to the 2016 economic crisis is by observing the shift in the child narrator's perspective in ¿Y Por Qué? from that in El Flamboyán Amarillo. Though he might represent a younger child than in El Flamboyán, ¿Y Por Qué?'s child narrator seems less interested in taking ownership of the material world around him. His desire for knowledge is what keeps him motivated to ask questions, and specifically his desire to learn the boundaries of his and his grandfather's existence. If the child in El Flamboyán Amarillo saw himself as a little master, the child in ¿Y Por Qué? is a little philosopher who decenters the grandfather's dependence on expertise and wisdom gained through years. He finds amusement in his grandfather's inability to answer his questions:

¿Por qué soy yo, y no otro?
¿Seré siempre así mismo?
¿Seré otro, diferente
Cuando no sea un niño?

*Why am I me and not some other child?*
*Will I always be the same?*
*Or will I be different*
*When I am no longer a child? (10)*

Gone, to a certain extent, is the sense that the adult is the teacher while the child is the student, as was the case in *Flamboyan* for the boy and his mother. Instead, Lázaro-Leon centers the grandfather and child as learning from each other. Even further, the grandfather is depicted as sort of returning to the same stage of learning as the child through the series of questions. In the backmatter of the book, Martorell removes himself from the position of expert in terms of providing answers for children:

> ¡Cuán difícil es contestar lo que no se sabe! La curiosidad es la llave del conocimiento y los niños la poseen. Si a algo aspiran las ilustra-ciones de estos ¿por qués? Es alentar el cuestionamiento, conservar su poesía original y hacer de todo el libro un signo de interrogación.

> How difficult it is to answer what one does know! Curiosity is the key to understanding and children possess that key. If my illustrations aspire to anything stemming from all these "whys" it is to encourage questions, and conserve the original poetry of these questions and to make the entire book a question mark.

Readers never hear the grandfather speak through Lázaro-Leon's narration. Martorell's paintings depict a demonstrative, affectionate grandfather showing the boy his old pictures, and reaching for the boy as they enter into a sea of question marks. Again, Lázaro-Leon plays with reader's expectations that a wise man should provide answers. However, the grandfather remains silent, only offering an embrace to the child as they sit in the last frame. The boy asks:

*Algún día existiremos*
*En el <<había una vez>>>*
*Y entones abuelito . . .*
*y después y después?*

*Will we exist, someday,*
*In [a story] as "once upon a time"?*
*And then grandfather . . .*
*Then what? Then what?*

The genius of this moment comes through how Lázaro-Leon uses tropes from youth literature, and even media when we consider shows such as *Sesame Street*'s segment, "What Happens Next?" As an author, she plays with what we expect as the "natural" rhythm and sequence. For example, it would seem that what might happen next is that the grandfather answers one of the questions, or that the boy is rewarded or reassured through some kind of diversion from the sense of dread of not knowing what happens next. The boy's awareness of his life as a possible story demonstrates how he attempts to bring order to the chaos of uncertainty through narrative. In this case, trying to figure out whether his story is a fairy tale ("once upon a time"). Yet, as we have come to expect in Boricua women's writing for young people, "once upon a time" signifies more than a yearning for a happy ending, the sort of ending that certain children, especially children of colonialism, may not expect. Lázaro-Leon ends the tale at this moment, leaving the reader engaged in the questions. Of course, in the summer of 2017, beyond the economic crisis and government bankruptcy, what would happen next is two back-to-back hurricanes that together would literally render Puerto Rico silent and off the satellite and communication grid for several days. And children's writers would be there to think of new ways to tell stories when the lights went out.

## FRONTLINE KID LIT: FOUNDING FATHERS, HEROES, AND STORIES FOR WHEN THE LIGHTS GO OUT

A particularly traumatizing aspect of Hurricane Maria for the Puerto Rican diaspora—an aspect talked about by many in the hours after the hurricanes impact—was the silence in communication. The electrical grid and satellite technologies were rendered useless; basic modern conveniences such as cellular phones and internet access were lost for a number of weeks. In the coming days, cars on the major highways in metropolitan areas such as San Juan and Bayamon would be lined up with *ciudadanos*, eager to access the intermittent cell phone signal available in the zone. During this period, it was common for family members—both stateside and on the archipelago—to have no information about the whereabouts of loved ones even months after the storm. In contemporary Puerto Rico, a year and half since Hurricanes Maria and Irma, the reality that electrical power has yet to be restored to the entire grid is unsettling. Moreover, the number of lives lost during the storm remains a controversial topic, with Governor Ricardo Rossello and his pro-statehood administration initially reporting sixty-four deaths during

President Donald Trump's initial visit while later raising the toll to 2,975 (George Washington University). The words "rebuild," "recover," and "restore" reoccur in the rhetoric centered on aiding Puerto Rico; for example, the Center for Puerto Rican Studies, Hunter College began a database and studies, even before the hurricanes, "Rebuild Puerto Rico" based on researching recovery efforts. Since 2016, Centro has organized symposiums and conferences around the topic. Puerto Rico faces its newest, and perhaps most critical, reinterpretation since colonization and the forming of the ELA. Additionally, the number of Puerto Ricans migrating to the US since 2006 exceeds what historians refer to as the First (1917–1930s) and Second (1940–1950s) Great Migrations. Particularly, as young Boricuas enter the classrooms across the US in primary through higher ed, how will academic institutions respond? These are institutions that, to a certain extent, have yet to respond even to the prior waves of migration.

I spend the next portion of this chapter contemplating the idea of restoring power, and restoring communication, with regards to youth literature and culture by contrasting two kinds of projects that have emerged since the economic decline in Puerto Rico: the hero-based, prominent recovery projects of two male writers of the diaspora, Lin Manuel-Miranda and Edgardo Miranda-Rodriquez, and the collective history-based projects of women writers in Puerto Rico, such as Tere Marichal and Ada Haiman. In both cases, I note the distinctiveness of twenty-first-century Puerto Rican culture through its embrace of the diaspora and the reality of what Juan Flores wrote, "The Diaspora Strikes Back"—meaning how the diaspora has shaped culture on the island as opposed to simply the reverse. However, I still note the reality of visibility given those in the diaspora versus those in the archipelago by the US publishing industry. This is particularly important because this book has analyzed the notion of "restorying" as a means of marginalized communities taking ownership of narratives, yet also highlights the complications that come with an effort to reimagine Puerto Rico—for example, the exclusion of poor communities of color, many of which were the hardest hit by Hurricane Maria and the recent earthquakes, often referred to as frontline communities in environmental justice circles (Adichie, Thomas, Klein). Even before the economic crisis, Puerto Rican authors such as Tere Marichal, Wanda de Jesus, Ada Haiman, and Laura Rexach Olivencia continued a legacy of feminist and Afro and Indigenous pedagogies through engaging audiences in stories about self-determination and community solidarity as opposed to individual heroism. I also note a turn toward recognizing the contributions of diaspora writers such as Pura Belpré and refiguring the work she did for disenfranchised communities of color in New York as a means of defending public literacy and libraries in Puerto Rico.

Moreover, as educators and grassroots organizers in Puerto Rico such as Federación de Maestros de Puerto Rico (FMPR) emphasize, I make the case that the natural disaster of the hurricane functions as a platform for a man-made disaster, widely known as policies of disaster capitalism (Martinez and Lee 2017). Indeed, much of the declining federal support for public education and libraries, and the push toward privatization of schools, began in 2006—around the time when the Puerto Rican government turned to hedge funds to finance public spending. In this chapter, I argue that Puerto Rican authors have been undergirding a project for political self-determination and transnational cooperation with the diaspora that emphasizes the return to community education and storytelling.

## WHOSE REVOLUTION? FOUNDING FATHERS AND SUPERHERO MYTHOLOGIES RISE UP

Actor and playwright Lin-Manuel Miranda has taken the stage, literally, in the public as a champion of Puerto Rico's rebuilding. Making his Broadway debut in 2008 with *In the Heights*, which he also authored and starred in, Miranda became the first Nuyorican writer since Miguel Piñero and his *Short Eyes* (1974) to have a play open at the Joseph Papp Public Theatre. His work and role in Puerto Rican letters, and his adoption of youth culture roots in hip hop and slam poetry, requires much more research and critique than I can give in one chapter let alone one section. However, I want to touch on the questions Miranda's work raises, particularly through his incorporation of hero mythology as a means of inspiration for "revolution" in Puerto Rico. His work also contrasts with the arguably more collective approach of Miranda-Rodriguez. Unlike Piñero, Miranda has secured the mainstream spotlight like few writers of color before him, Puerto Rican or otherwise. Miranda's blockbuster *Hamilton*, perhaps more than any other work, illustrates what I mean by the concept of "side by side." *Hamilton*, at once, speaks to the prominence of Puerto Rican culture shaping what the US public recognizes as pop culture, while also speaking to the erasure of Puerto Ricans from discourses of revolution and political independence. Miranda rewrote the history of Alexander Hamilton as a means of reframing the value of immigrants to the US. Broadway audiences embraced the hip hop based musical full of actors of color playing prominent US figures such as George Washington and Thomas Jefferson.

Yet, Miranda's ongoing legacy is not without its critique from communities of color and grassroots activists, particularly those who believe he gained white normative audiences at the expense of Indigenous and African American history, including his omission of Indigenous land displacement and Alexander Hamilton as a slaveholder (Jiménez Garcia, "Teaching about *Hamilton*," *Caribbean Connections*, 2019). Indeed, it is Miranda off-stage that I want to focus on in this section—more specifically, the kinds of performances of liberation and "rising up" activism encouraged through the iconography of *Hamilton: An American Musical*. I call attention to what seem to be irreconcilable differences between the January 2019 staging of the play in Puerto Rico, inspiring the social media hashtag such as #RiseUp, and the #RickyRenuncia protests in July 2019, during which hundreds of thousands of Puerto Ricans filled the streets of San Juan to oust Governor Ricardo Rossello. Miranda has adopted the role of Hamilton to advocate for Puerto Rico, particularly since Puerto Rico's public debt crisis and in the days following Hurricane Maria. In 2015, Miranda's op-ed in the *New York Times* advocated for Congress's passing of the Promesa Bill, which assigned a congressionally appointed financial oversight board to financially mange the public debt (2015). Miranda's support of this bill placed him at odds with grassroots activists who believe the bill, like the debt itself, continues the history of colonial oppression against the Puerto Rican people—who had no role in the creation of the debt, nor in the appointment of the board, yet whose public funds and benefits function as the means to pay. In the 2016 op-ed, Miranda quotes the words of the central "founding father" for which he named his blockbuster musical, *Hamilton*:

O ye, who revel in affluence, see the afflictions of humanity and bestow your superfluity to ease them. Say not, we have suffered also, and thence withhold your compassion. What are your sufferings compared to those? Ye have still more than enough left. Act wisely. Succour the miserable and lay up a treasure in Heaven. (NYT)

Miranda tells readers that the quote was written by a teenaged Alexander Hamilton in a plea for his birthplace of St. Croix, which was also devastated by a hurricane, but that "I'm invoking Hamilton's words today, in this plea for relief for Puerto Rico." The Latinx argument in the musical is often missed by the affluent white Broadway-goers frequenting Miranda's shows. For one, that immigrants built the US from the ground up and should be seen as heroic pillars of the republic as opposed to outsiders and weights on the society. However, even with people of color as prominent players on the stage, the universality (i.e., whiteness) of *Hamilton* often means the racial, ethnic, and social specificity in the history of immigration, US imperialism, and conquest—and how these histories play out in government policy for Latinx and Black immigrant and citizens through branches such as the Immigration and Naturalization Service and Immigration (INS) and its newer iteration, Immigration Crime Engagement (ICE)—is lost.

Miranda as Hamilton, however, perhaps like no other artist or figure, brings the history of colonialism into the front streets of American life and culture. In early 2019, Miranda brought *Hamilton* to Puerto Rico as a means of raising funds for hurricane recovery. The production's sudden and controversial move from the University of Puerto Rico's theatre—after students protested the musical's run and the actor's lack of political engagement with issues draining funds from public education, including policies like PROMESA—to the more commercial Centro de Bellas Artes was largely ignored by the mainstream media. Yet, some noted the irony of bringing a musical about US independence and revolution to the world's oldest colony (Bonilla 2018)—moreover, "the colony of a democracy," as scholar and founder of the Caribbean Cultural Arts Center, Marta Moreno-Vega has said (Education Anew 2018). In many ways, *Hamilton* in Puerto Rico is the utmost performance of the "tropical yankees" ideology (Navarro 2002).

As a scholar of Puerto Rican youth literature history, one image really struck me of the photos shared online through the #HamiltonPR and #RiseUp hashtags. Even with regard to tag phrases for young audiences, such as "rise up," who was really being invited to "rise up" and in what ways? In a way that enacts a similar critique of colonial oppression in Puerto Rico? The photo is of a young girl, her fist raised to the sky, standing on a wall in Old San Juan, dressed in US colonial garb, slacks, and a Yankee overcoat. She smiles while the caption written by @CaptainNelee reads, "Thank you @LinManuel for bringing @HamiltonMusical to Puerto Rico."[5] Whether the young girl is of Puerto Rican descent is unclear, but the image connects to the tradition of US colonial readers in which white children adventure in Puerto Rico and take ownership of the land. The images also harkens to how young Puerto Ricans were depicted in colonial readers as performing during patriotic celebrations for Americans. This picture is a stark contrast from the picture of a young Puerto Rican boy, pictured in traditional jíbaro dress, holding a machete and kneeling before police barricades in front of La Fortaleza in July 2019, just six months after Miranda's opening.[6] Apart from the contrast in patriotic dress, the young Boricua boy performs a sense of restriction in his role as a Puerto Rican kneeling in front of government oppression, though holding his machete in tandem with jíbaro dress, while the young girl with her first raised smiles as she celebrates the US revolution. Miranda's staging of *Hamilton* in Puerto Rico invites a strong comparison between the performance of American revolutionary heroes by Puerto Rican actors and the scene in *Greater America: Our Latest Insular Possessions* (1899) in which a group of US soldiers assemble Puerto Rican performers to celebrate the Fourth of July. At one point, the soldiers ask a young Boricua boy to sound a "rebel yell"—they are then taken aback at his capacity to "shout" as loudly as his "American brother." Yet, this boy and the Boricua actors who performed in Miranda's Puerto Rico run, and Miranda himself to an extent, are only able to hold the attention of members of Congress, former presidents, and other government officials through a rehearsing and celebration of US patriotic rhetoric. In view of US policies such as the 1948 Gag Law, US revolution is the only story of independence that they are able to publicly perform in their embodiments as Puerto Ricans that will not bring about their death, arrest, or imprisonment.

Indeed, the "rebel yells" of Puerto Rican revolutionary thinkers, among them Ramon Emeterio Betances, Eugenio Maria de Hostos, and Lola Rodríquez de Tío, were censored from the school textbook tradition and even from the Puerto Rican national anthem. Furthermore, the rebel yells of hundreds of thousands of Puerto Ricans, with their fists held high protesting austerity, high rates of femicide, and government corruption, were met with rubber bullets and tear gas in the streets of San Juan during el Verano del 2019. The stark contrast between Puerto Ricans dancing on stage about the US revolution in January 2019 and those dancing in front of El Catedral de San Juan, directing their calls to oust Governor Rossello in June 2019, is almost deafening. Miranda as Hamilton, whom the young girl in the picture models, with his fist held high in the iconic *Hamilton* poster—a gesture traditionally read as a sign of Black power and solitary for communities of color and radical movements—is only able to perform a Boricua liberation that is consistent with US assimilation. In other words, Miranda aligns with a benign form of cultural nationalism—the very sort of cultural nationalism that many Boricua writers, particularly women, have countered throughout their writings. Actually, I suggest it is Miranda's adherence to assimilationist cultural nationalism ideology that allows him to gain such visibility and acceptance in mainstream markets.

Miranda's *Hamilton*, both through his personal and stage performance, is one prominent example of a hero or individual based mythology emerging in post-Hurricane Maria conversations about Puerto Rico. The other is a more radical project by another Miranda, Edgardo Miranda-Rodriquez, author of the popular independent comic series *La Borinqueña*. Since 2016, through

"Marisol" *La Borinqueña*, Miranda-Rodriguez has centered an Afro-Boricua woman as the embodiment of leadership and heroism, Puerto Rican morale, and renewal. In the video segment, "The First Latina Superhero," produced by the Latinx media platform *Mitú*, Miranda-Rodriguez, who publishes the series through his own Brooklyn-based studio Somos Arte, Inc., comments on *La Borinqueña*'s intersectional symbolism for Puerto Rican activism as AfroLatina artist Imani Nuñez performs the role:

> A hero is there to inspire. A hero is there to remind us of ourselves and remind us that we as a people have the potential and the power to rise up. La Borinqueña was always going to be a woman. And she needed to be negra. There was no other way around it. Her complexion, hair, her costume, were all intentional. They were created to empower . . . to remind us of our own power . . . to remind us of our heritage . . . to remind us what makes us beautiful. And that is embracing our diversity.

Centering Marisol's Blackness allows Miranda-Rodriquez to disrupt the symbols of racial democracy present in such celebrated institutions as El Instituto de Cultural Puertorriqueña, whose emblem featuring the three races—African-Spaniard-Taino—has been criticized by scholars for its problematic erasure of colonial violence and racial hierarchies. Even in Puerto Rican comics culture, Marisol's Blackness is especially important given that El Instituto began a comic series for young readers in 2004 featuring three child protagonists who coincide with the three-race emblem, Ines (representative of the Taino), Ceci (representative of the African), and Pepe (representative of the Spaniard). In other words, Miranda resists the othering of African heritage, and even the idea that it is just one of the many. In his comic, we must access Marisol through her Blackness, and embrace her Blackness, which is more than a color but also an epistemological register and history which literally empowers her (Llorens 2018).

Miranda-Rodriguez is also keen on representing Taino heritage, in tandem with Puerto Rico's revolutionary past, as the means to which Marisol gains her superpowers. Marisol is a graduate student at Columbia University, demonstrating how the Puerto Rican diaspora has created inroads into academic spaces through avenues such as Ethnic Studies and Puerto Rican Studies. For example, from one page to another, we see Marisol make the commute from her Williamsburg neighborhood, known as Los Sures to the Puerto Rican community, to Columbia and then enter Professor Robles' office. Professor Robles, the study-abroad liaison for Marisol's field research trip to

Puerto Rico, has a poster of Atabex, a Taino goddess in his office. This places Taino traditions and customs within scholarly circles, not as just ephemeral heroes, legends, and myths, but as knowledge producers young people like Marisol might study in college. Robles tells Marisol that it has been "twenty years" since he went to Puerto Rico, which suggests Miranda-Rodriguez's critique of academic institutions as distant from the actual communities they claim to serve and study, even for Latinx/Puerto Rican Studies academics (12). Miranda-Rodriguez suggests a return to the roots of community-based education and revisiting of decolonial histories through Marisol's interests and journey to Puerto Rico. Miranda-Rodriguez also suggests honoring legacies of intellectual mothers through Mami's gift to Marisol before leaving. Mami tells Marisol that the Lares flag ribbon she gives her "has been in the family for generations. Abuela gave it to Mami when we first moved to Los Sures, Mami gave it to me when I started medical school. Now I'm giving it to you" (14). The ribbon consists of a piece of "fabric left over from the fabric that Mariana Bracetti used to sew the flag of Lares"—a significant detail in that it speaks to a tradition of oral collective histories needed for such a detail to survive. It also speaks to the role of women in teaching and archiving for revolutionary movements to persist under extreme surveillance. The Lares flag—in light blue and red, in solidarity with the Antillean Federation for liberation so often censured in US and Puerto Rican history books—is centered in Miranda-Rodriguez's super-heroine origin story in tandem with Taino ways of knowing.

The image of the superhero in itself empowers literally through the notion of physical strength and supernatural ability to counter injustice. Yet, drawing on a feminist retelling to craft his super-heroine's transformation, Miranda-Rodriguez has publicly credited his own set of intellectual mothers such as Dr. Marta Moreno-Vega and Dr. Iris Morales, both scholars and activists of, and for, Puerto Rican feminism, in his journey to becoming an artist and the author of La Borinqueña (Miranda-Rodriquez 2017). One might argue Marisol is already super before she gains supernatural abilities. Indeed, Miranda-Rodriguez has said he decided to have the character and others in the community refer to her as Marisol rather than La Borinqueña to suggest a distinction away from alter egos of superheroes. Miranda-Rodriguez's super-heroine relies on her knowledge of her history and culture and her further research into Puerto Rico's environmental issues as a strength. Again, Marisol is deeply rooted in Afro and Indigenous Puerto Rican narratives, as she gains her powers through an encounter with the Taino deity Atabex. The figure who had once been on posters in her professor's office appears to Marisol when Marisol finds "La Estrella del Camino," a relic of Taino past: "I am the

Mother of Boriken. I am the Ancient Spirit of your deep past. I am the water that flows through your consciousness. I am the love of my people. Mar y Sol, My Sea and Sun. I am Atabex." Atabex reorders Marisol's life around Taino knowledge, expressing the importance of how these principles command all life, not just her own. This image joins with Belpré and the auto-cátedras lessons of how Puerto Rico's land remembers and contains memories of the Indigenous past that survive oppression and, to an extent, the oppressor.

Miranda-Rodriguez is also one of the few authors to picture the Taino people fighting against Spanish conquistadors, as Atabex tells Marisol: "My island has been suffering for hundreds of years. And when my children suffer . . . they need a champion." Marisol is able to witness Taino men and women warriors, up in arms against the Spanish, as opposed to the symbols of silent resistance offered by previous authors—something which again speaks to alternate ways Puerto Rican youth have been taught to resist oppression. In contrast with Miranda's *Hamilton*, Miranda-Rodriguez suggests an actual rather than figurative revolution against colonizing forces in this image. It is in this moment that the ribbon pinned on Marisol by Mami begins to unravel into La Borinqueña's costume, a symbol of the 1868 anti-Spanish, anti-colonial Puerto Rican battle, El Grito de Lares. This moment in the graphic novel transforms into an homage to Puerto Rican revolutionaries when they declared their independence. The image of the flag changing into a suit of clothes for a new super-heroine signals how such a flag invites more than just symbolic performances but everyday actions for empowerment and self-determination.

The teaching of El Grito de Lares in Puerto Rican and American history is almost nonexistent, even when we consider the early texts by US authors which referenced heroes of this cause, such as Betances, as exiled "long before" the US arrival. Marisol's wearing of the Lares flag is also a powerful symbol when considering that Martorell's illustrations of "L es de Lareño" was part of what made *ABC de Puerto Rico* subversive in the eyes of the assimilationist Puerto Rican government administration in 1968. Miranda's position in the diaspora and place as an independent publisher perhaps enables him to create such a deliberately political heroine. *La Borinqueña's* story was embraced by the diaspora especially as a symbol of solidarity and Puerto Rican resilience, making appearances at the 2016 National Puerto Rican Day Parade in New York City, and garnering support from such visible Puerto Rican women leaders such as Congresswoman Nydia Velasquez and Supreme Court Justice Sonia Sotomayor.

Marisol represents a decolonial, anti-patriarchal turn in the Puerto Rican imagination, though I would specify that she seems most prominently celebrated and displayed in the diaspora. As a woman, rooted in Afro-Boricua, feminist ideologies, Marisol is also seen throughout the comic conferring with the Puerto Rican community, members of whom rally around her as she comes to their aid. Miranda spotlights the leadership of women in activist movements for Puerto Rican liberation, from Mariana Bracetti to Lola Rodriquez de Tio to Julia de Burgos to Lolita Lebron, all of whom appear on the cover of *La Borinqueña*'s first issue, along with Arturo Schomburg, Jesus Colon, and Pedro Albizu Campos. The crowd of Boricua independentistas smile as they look up to see the flying Marisol; they are members of the community that Marisol has risen up to protect. Absent from *La Borinqueña*'s story is also the traditional villain, popular in stories where traditional masculinity also shapes the character arc of a superhero. Instead, the villains, as Miranda-Rodriguez has stated in his speeches across college campuses, are climate change, inequity, and colonialism (Miranda 2018).

Miranda-Rodriguez talks about how even two years before Hurricanes Maria and Irma, his study into the Puerto Rico's vulnerabilities to environmental crisis and receiving aid caused him to include a blackout in the first comic. Little did he, or those reading the comic in 2016, know how prophetic the images of Marisol flying over a Puerto Rico gone completely dark and ciudadanos at the mercy of flooded roads would be. Yet, beyond prophecy, Miranda-Rodriguez simply states that he "paid attention to science" in order to create a story whose inevitability ultimately came to pass, with the exception of a flying, super heroine to guide the days (Miranda-Rodriguez 2017). Contrasting Lin-Manuel Miranda and Edgardo Miranda-Rodriquez, we see how they invite young Boricuas to identify in two different kinds of revolutions. Miranda invites young Boricuas to perform in the American Revolution—an event which ultimately led to the occupation of Puerto Rico. Only as soldiers sway the flag of Old Glory can young Boricuas rise up. For Miranda-Rodriguez, the flag of Lares sways as a symbol for coalitional-feminist, revolutionary thinking—embracing that kind of thinking leads to the epic transformation tied to Afro and Indigenous ways of knowing and outward demonstrations for sovereignty. The revival of past revolutionary figures from Puerto Rican history arguably presents a way forward, especially in a kind of post-apocalyptic Puerto Rico.

## LESSONS FROM WOMEN WRITERS ON THE FRONTLINES:
## LA LECTURA ES MÁS QUE EL LIBRO

Contemporary Puerto Rican literature for youth is deeply invested in a project of strategies for educational and political liberation through its incorporation of the diaspora. For example, in a current collective of Puerto Rican
women storytellers seeking to inspire young readers through storytelling
performances and access to books, Ada Haiman was born in Puerto Rico and
migrated to New York City as a child. Returning to Puerto Rico as a university student, Haiman pursued her doctorate and became a professor in the
UPR English department. Haiman's series, *Tulipán: La Girafa Puertorriqueña*,
speaks to an emergent group of Puerto Ricans returning to contemporary
Puerto Rico. Her work resists the kind of time capsuled nostalgia of former
generations, even of those in the diaspora such as Mohr who write from the
perspective of a Nuyorican childhood and a second-generation memory of
1940s–1950s-era Puerto Rico. In contemporary Puerto Rico, Ada Haiman
wants youth literature to go beyond traditional Puerto Rican cultural typology, challenging her readers to see that a giraffe is just as acceptable for
Puerto Rican storytelling as a coqui frog. Haiman's dedication at the beginning of *Tulipán* recounts an incident which sparked her writing for young
people: "Written for my daughter, whose giraffe prints were not accepted at
the gift shop of the Puerto Rican Museum of Contemporary Art in 2004
because 'giraffes were not Puerto Rican'; they unabashedly recommended she
paint coquis. Dedicated to all those who have come from all over the word
to settle, live, breathe, grow, and work productively in Puerto Rico."

In Haiman's *Tulipan*, Tulipan seamlessly maneuvers between the worlds of
Aibonito and the Bronx. Haiman stories speak to both parents and children
growing up in both places, and how the diaspora's vaivén has imprinted
US and island culture. In an early illustration, Atabey Sanchez-Haiman,
Haiman's daughter, depicts the happy giraffe in a diverse neighborhood of
red-outlined houses with figures representing different kinds of families and
neighbors, including single parent homes, same-sex families, and persons
with disabilities. It is on this same page that Sanchez-Haiman also draws an
enormous index finger pointing to Tulipan's smiling face in the foreground:
"Some people, when they met her for the first time, would say: 'You don't look
Puerto Rican'" (3). The juxtaposition of illustrations with the text suggest the
multiplicity of Puerto Rican young people and families, and the absurdity
of emphasizing one image as a definitive and even "typical." Surrounded by
images of cultural iconography such as a coqui, plantains, and the island of
Puerto Rico, Tulipan contemplates the "strange statement" and questions the

reader, "What does it mean to be Puerto Rican?" (11) As an author, Haiman emphasizes lived experience and family knowledge as foundational rather than visual cues in terms of cultural authenticity. Haiman connects with Sonia Manzano's work on *Sesame Street* since both emphasize a turn from static portrayals of culture, making an argument for the fluidity of culture and language. For example, Tulipan revels in how the words she knows mark her Puerto Rican experience, words that evidence the interaction between English and Spanish which Haiman and Atabey-Haiman depict in a sequences of pages:

> El Rufo: That's the roof of the building.
> La Marketa: That's where Tulipan and her family would shop for all
>    kinds of stuff cheaper than at the mall.
> Pegao: That's the crispy rice that's stuck to the bottom of the pot;
>    Revolú: That was how her mother described the mess in Tulipan's
>    room.
> Guagua: Her friend from Chile would correct her: Autobús, Tuli,
>    autobus. But Tulipan loved the unique and familiar sound of the
>    word guagua. (23–26)

This short series of words allows Haiman to demonstrate the nuances of the Puerto Rican experience as a US colony with a large diaspora and as a Latin American and Caribbean commonwealth with a particular set of Ibero, Indigenous, and African influences. Yet, what is revolutionary in the case of *Tulipan* is how it embraces the diaspora and cultural remittances as normative and additive. As Tulipan says at the end of the book, "And the best word of all: Nuyorican. It simply means there can be more than one you" (37). The book's prominence and acceptance in the University of Puerto Rico collections, Aparicio Distributors, La Casa Del Libro, and Casa Norberto Liberia—hallmarks of Puerto Rican public and academic literary arts—demonstrates the indelible impression of circular migration on the Puerto Rican imagination. From the rise of the ELA and school texts such as Pastor and Tejara's *Amigos de Aqui y Allá*, which reflected the vaivén migration of Puerto Ricans to and from New York, I emphasize a shift in representing migration to young readers from necessary evil to exciting inevitability to, finally, an asset for creative and political freedom.

Literature for youth, as opposed to a general Puerto Rican literary canon, demonstrates an incorporation of the diaspora in ways scholars such as Flor Piñeiro de Rivera likely never anticipated. For example, the sala infantil in the Library School at the University of Puerto Rico, Rio Piedras was renamed

Colleción Pura Belpré, a space for those training in library sciences that also honored the legacy of a woman who demonstrated how to preserve literacy and literary legacies, even without paper or books. As early as 1987, Piñeiro de Rivera incorporated Belpré and Mohr into *Cien Años de Literatura Infantil Puertoriqueña* as part of the list of books cataloged as a national tradition of Puerto Rican children's literature. Piñeiro de Rivera admits that "a change in sovereignty initiated a tide of Puerto Rican migrants to the United States, and the possession of American citizenship encouraged this population flow, which increased after the Second World War" (42). She outlines what she saw as "two approaches" coming from what at that point were first- and second-generation writers:

> The first generation . . . found its inspiration in the memories of the folklore, the scenery, the history and personal experiences of Puerto Rico of its childhood. This generation now bases its writings on memories not of the island, but of the Hispanic areas where its life is rooted. This present generation is interested in social problems, searching for new structures to replace the depressing conditions of the Barrio. (42)

Piñeiro de Rivera goes on to say that Belpré and Mohr represent these two approaches. One of the interventions resulting from *Side by Side* has been my call for scholars to rethink how these generations of writers for young people work not "to replace" or to deny social problems but to reinvent and subvert the oppressive systems around them. To imply that Belpré's work, or that of members of her generation, is less interested in social problems than Mohr is simply untrue. Belpré used folklore in ways that recentered Afro and Indigenous cultures, framing her work as a portal for transcending deeply rooted in histories of violence that young people could subvert through the lessons of folk culture. Simultaneously, Mohr created stories representing the everyday Puerto Rican in New York as a new folk culture that emerged out of the power of imagination, asking us to consider the ways previous generations romanticized the past and even present. Additionally, one could argue that the lack of books published independently in Puerto Rico results in a scarcity that made embracing the wide distribution of Belpré and Mohr's titles more acceptable than they were in adult literary circles. Yet, beyond matters of distribution and even literary aesthetics, contemporary authors use Belpré's position and embodiment of the role of storyteller as a model for storytelling and librarianship today, particularly in the time of economic and natural disasters. In contemporary Puerto Rico, Belpré represents the possibilities of cultivating literacy and literary safe havens and working around oppressive institutions. Yet, perhaps even Belpré would have never imagined that the work she did in cultivating spaces for young Boricuas in New York City during the height of two Great Migrations would be what authors, librarians, and educators would turn to in order to cultivate and defend such spaces in Puerto Rico today. For example, Isamar Abreu Gomez, a librarian at the University of Puerto Rico School of Education and a storyteller cites Belpré as an inspiration when she began telling stories to schoolchildren after the hurricanes with her "Maleta Cuentera" or "Suitcase of Stories" (Lugo 2017). Like Belpré's traveling puppet theatre, Abreau underlines the need to take stories where children are: "The idea came of that blend of a travel bag as a medium to carry and transport artifacts, but also to travel and migrate to other places, like started happening after María." However, in her use of the suitcase, she decided to take an object that was causing anxiety for children—suitcases of family members leaving—and transform it into a space for storytelling and possibility.

A return to, and affirmation of, storytelling seems a pressing need in contemporary Puerto Rico as a direct response to economic and environmental uncertainty. In San Juan on February 2, 2019, Tere Marichal, Wanda de Jesus-Arevelo, and Ada Haiman among others convened the Día Nacional de Narración Oral/National Day of Oral Narration, which was dedicated in honor to Pura Belpré. The poster for the event features a smiling Belpré holding an open book, as characters from her stories surround her: La Cucarachita Martina and Ratoncito Perez, the Rainbow Colored Horse, and Nangato. As with Edgardo Miranda-Rodriguez's Marisol, this poster invites us to embrace Belpré's Blackness, as she is rendered beautifully Black in the portrait, as opposed to a gold face on the Belpré Medal. The event was staged by this collective of women writers as an intervention for the lack of public support for literacies spaces, such as public, research, and school libraries in Puerto Rico, and as a means of reclaiming those spaces that were designated as such—for example, the Biblioteca Nacional, which has a small children's reading room, but has been without a staff of professional librarians since 2006.

The lack of a national Puerto Rican library system is such that the local library is a distant reality for the average Puerto Rican citizen. The University of Puerto Rico, the largest public library system, with libraries in each branch, draws attention to how the public must access libraries mostly through overlapping systems of government and academic allocations, something coinciding with the problematic history of literature for youth and the Puerto Rican government. The economic crisis and post-Hurricane Maria budget cuts and move towards privatization of schools means over one-third of Puerto Rico's schools have closed (Lee and Martinez 2018). In an article in *El Nuevo Dia*, Tere Marichal said, "They have closed so many public and school libraries that children have really lost space"—a comment which underlines importance of material spaces dedicated to young people's literacy which cultivate a community outside of the classroom and home, something very much in line with the work of Rafael and Celestina Cordero, Arturo Schomburg, and Pura Belpré. Marichal, along with de Jesus and Haiman, are among a group of authors and storytellers who travel the island, hosting mobile libraries—what Marichal calls a Lotobiblio—on beaches. Along with read-alouds and storytelling activities, through a partnership with Aparicio Distributors bookstore, children also have access to the books to read on their own. What I find fascinating is how Belpré's experiences in the diaspora have become a model for an island in recovery, and how these woman authors position themselves as existing inside and outside printed books always in relationship to performed storytelling.

Tere Marichal is a writer and cuentera or storyteller, a tradition she believes to be essential in the recovery process in Puerto Rico. In a project that connects to Sonia Manzano's work on public access television in the US, Marichal made a name for herself in the 1990s and 2000s on the island as a cuentera on PBS. Her show, *La Casa de Maria Chucena*, cemented her character "Maria Chucena" as a feminist heroine for young woman on the island for twenty-two years. Marichal was also the illustrator of the Center for Puerto Rican Studies' 2013 documentary on Belpré; she created the illustrations of *Perez and Martina* which audiences see as Belpré reads the tale. Marichal credits this moment as introducing her to Belpré's work:

> Me prugunté como es posible que una mujer que había hecho tanto por este país, aquí era prácticamente desconocida, y en Estados Unidos tan conocida. Así que me preguntaba cómo era posible que eso pasara.

> I asked myself, how is it possible that a woman who did so much for our country was practically unknown here, yet in the United States she is so well-known. I kept asking myself how this was possible. (*El Nuevo Dia*, February 2, 2019)

Though Belpré's literary contributions have gained more recognition in the US, Marichal underlines how Belpré's position in the diaspora made her somewhat of an outsider to Puerto Rican literary arts—yet how she has become a point of visibility and inspiration in recent years. For example, the Dia of Narración Oral activity was sponsored by REFORMA, the historically Hispanic-serving association for library services, in partnership with the American Library Association, which eventually created the Belpré Medal in 1996. Something to ponder here is how island-based writers who feel invisibilized by public institutions and publishing industries reach out to the memory of a marginalized figure in literary history. More work remains to be done on how Belpré models defeating marginalization and working with while also resisting institutional politics and how this will play out in Puerto Rico in the mid-twenty-first century. However, I want to conclude this chapter by looking at the contemporary works which these authors, specifically Marichal, de Jesus, and Laura Rexach Olivencia, offer young Puerto Rican readers in the age of disaster and disaster capitalism. I also want to offer some potential questions and lessons that these stories spark for the work of scholars and public audiences looking to continue researching Puerto Rican youth literature and culture.

Again, contemporary Puerto Rican authors have been providing strategies for young readers to cope with the unexpected realities of man-made and environmental disasters before the hurricanes—I argue as a response to the impending financial and material crisis that Puerto Rico has undergone in the last two decades. The recent hurricanes and earthquakes simply provide an opportunity to reflect on how authors arrived at this point and how their work connects back to previous generations who survived the ongoing effects of colonialism and racial capitalism, including endless rebuilding and reinventions of their homeland(s). As early as 2006, again the time most economists say the financial crisis begins, Tere Marichal published *Una Terrible Tormenta* through an independent publisher in Columbia, Camara Mundi, with offices in Puerto Rico. The story of a horrible storm that threatens the safety of all the animals might be read as a political animal allegory similar to Belpré's "The Tiger and the Rabbit." However, what we see in comparing "The Tiger in the Rabbit" is how, through the progression of time, the oppressive colonial politics represented by the hierarchy of predator and prey animals has turned to a more post-apocalyptic vision in Marichal's *Una Terrible Tormenta*. For example, instead of strategies for outsmarting and outlasting the colonizer, Marchial's tale features predatory animals such as snakes and birds who must work together with the small insects, all of whom face the same storm. Marichal creates a kind of animal solitary in which the animals may only survive the hurricane if they take shelter together in a cave.

Particularly when we consider projects of rebuilding and restoring power to Puerto Rico, Marichal's main character, "Maria Chucena," a feminist heroine, offers the power of self-determination in difficult times for young readers in *María Chucena techaba su choza (Maria Chucena fixes her roof)* (2011). The cover art designed by Marichal prominently displays a Puerto Rican woman, walking up a ladder, with a hammer raised and yellow hard hat ready to take on the task of fixing her leaky roof, while large white rain-drops fall in the foreground under a grey sky. Marichal dedicates the book to Belpré, and a drawing of "Cucarachita Martina" seemingly welcomes young readers into the story of "Maria Chucena." This framing of the tale allows us to see a kind of circular migration in contemporary writing, whereas Belpré's US-based writing claimed that she continued in the traditions of Puerto Rican folklorists on the island, island storytellers and folklorists now claim to continue the traditions of Belpré in the diaspora. *Maria Chucena* begins with the main character reading a book, specifically a book about carpentry: "María Chucena leía un libro sobre carpintería porque quería apreder a con-truír un anaquel / Maria Chucena read a book about carpentry because she wanted to construct a book shelf." The scene immediately aligns reading and literacy with self-reliance and self-education even as it also presents reading as a pleasurable and aesthetic activity. Marichal illustrates Maria Chucena's stack of books as alongside a Taino symbol necklace and a vejigante mask, affirming Black and Indigenous legacies.

The story centers on Maria Chucena's managing of a home library, em-phasizing the importance of books and home literacy, and specifically of books as valuable possessions. Although the book was written in 2013, Maria Chucema's leaking roof speaks to everyday vulnerabilities of homes in the Caribbean subject to tropical storms and hurricanes. "Tengo que encontrar un lugar seguro para proteger mis libros / I have to find a secure place to protect my books," Maria Chucena says as, holding a stack of books, she watches with wide eyes as the large raindrops fall on others stacks around the house (18–19). One of the most Boricua feminist scenes occurs when Maria Chucena stores her books in the kitchen, literally reframing a domestic female's space as a location for literacy, learning, and rebuilding. After build-ing her study in the kitchen, Maria Chucena "immediately" finds a hammer, a saw, nails, and wood, armed with the necessary tools to fix the roof herself. Marichal writes, "Maria Chucena martillaba con fuerza. / Maria Chucena hammered with force" (28–29). Young readers are invited to act out the sound of Maria Chucena's hammer, "Tun! Tun! Tun!" Maria Chucena fixes her roof and constructs library worthy shelves for her books. At the end of the story, we see Maria Chucena happily sitting on her couch with her favorite book, Belpré's *Perez and Martina* (1931)—raindrops visibly falling through the window. Marichal suggests that though Maria Chucena may never change the inevitably of storms, she can educate herself and learn how to prepare and fix her dwelling in an emergency. Marichal inserts Belpré's *Perez and Martina*, a tale that might also be read, as I have previously argued, as an anticolonial allegory about a fancy Spanish mouse (Perez) who was unprepared for island life and Boricua women, ultimately giving into the greedy desires of a colonizer by eating too much of a hot dessert, to the point that he falls into the pot. Maria Chucena tells readers in the books' finale that she is learning to cook the same recipe which Martina made for Perez, a recipe which, in my analysis, has the power to destroy a colonizer (Jiménez Garcia 2014). Marichal, in kinship with Belpré, creates a world which encourages young Boricuas to think and learn for themselves and look for resources which might help them survive. As Maria Chucena says at the end, "Todo lo aprende leyendo / Learning everything by reading."

In the same vein of cultivating a love of *lectura* and learning through stories of diaspora women, Wanda de Jesus-Arevelo published in 2016 a picture book about a young Julia de Burgos, *Julia, Corazón de Un Poeta*. The book was a partnership between the National Endowment of the Arts, Museo de Carolina, and the Fundación Puertorriqueña de Las Humanidades (an organization currently closed due to financial crisis). *Júlia, Corazón de Una Poeta* introduces young readers to de Burgos's revolutionary life and writing. The celebration of a feminist, revolutionary writer for younger audiences, and specifically how young readers might identify with de Burgos's early love for words and stories, underlines a project in this new generation of revisiting revolutionary thought—which had remained veiled in a tradition of school texts—through women in the diaspora such as Belpré and de Burgos. For example, de Jesus highlights de Burgos's education, both at home and in formal schooling, as one which taught the young writer "que siempre hay que luchar, que siempre hay que intentar, que siempre hay que sequir/ that you always have to fight / that you always have to try/that you always have to continue" (10). De Jesus does not shield young readers from de Burgos's life of extreme poverty and hunger in Puerto Rico during the Great Depression. Readers see how de Burgos's educational journey is also nonlinear in that although she is an excellent student and graduates with honors from the University of Puerto Rico, at graduation the Puerto Rican economy makes it impossible for her to find work as a teacher. Yet, de Jesus underscores the strong families ties of Boricua women as what ultimately empowers them: "pero la fortaleza de la mamá de Julia / era más grande que toda la pobreza y el hambre / both strength of Julia's mother was greater than all of the poverty and hunger" (10). Like Marichal, de Jesus emphasizes the values of self-education and self-determination. De Burgos continues reading an ecelctic collection of revolutionary thinkers, including Neruda, Lorca, Nietzsche, and Kant. De Jesus also mentions de Burgos's reading of "Albizu" or Pedro Albizu Campos, the leader of the nationalist party in Puerto Rico. Albizu's radical ideas placed him at the top of lists maintained by the Federal Bureau of Investigation and the Central Intelligence Agency. His death, many believed, was caused by his time in questioning by the US agencies and exposure to radioactive materials. On the same page, de Jesus reflects on the state violence enacted on Puerto Rican nationalists during de Burgos's time—events which inspired her poems. De Jesus suggests how de Burgos's self-education in revolutionary thought shapes her gaze, and her ability to witness Puerto Rico's history of oppression, particularly the criminalization of independentismo, or Puerto Rican independence:

> Con su independencia de criterio,
> Comienza a ver, a pensar, a escribir.
> . . . Ve la Masacre de Ponce
> Y escribe "Viva la Republica."
> . . . Ve la encarcelacion de los nacionalistas
> Y escribe "Responso de ocho partidas."
> Ve a los obreros en huelga
> Y escribe "Somos puños cerrados."
> ¡De su ver y su pensar nace su poesía revolucionaria!
>
> From the independence of her critique,
> She begins to see, to think, to write.
> . . . She sees the Ponce Massacre
> And she writes "Long Live the Republic."
> . . . She see the jailing of the nationalists
> And she writes "Responsory of Eight Departures."
> She sees the workers on strike
> Años she writes "We are Closed Fists."
> From her vision and her thought is born her revolutionary poetry! (28)

Here, de Jesus allows young readers to contemplate a list of state-sanctioned death and incarceration targeting Puerto Rican revolutionaries—along with a list of the poems de Burgos wrote in response. De Jesus suggests to readers how essential the cause for Puerto Rican independence and anti-imperialist thinking was in shaping de Burgos's work. It is an aspect of the poet which young readers are invited to perhaps see as their own legacy for activism. For example, de Jesus includes a question-and-answer section in the back

214 How to Survive the End of the World

of the book on the main topics of *Julia Corazón de Un Poeta*, including the poet's bravery, her migration to the US, and her struggle for women to be respected as political thinkers. In this section, a black box asks young readers to consider the de Burgos fight for human rights, specifically how de Burgos defended "la justicia y la libertad." The prompt asks readers, "How do you use your words? What would you like to use them for?" (45).

## CONCLUSION: WE DON'T NEED A ANOTHER HERO: TEACHING COLLECTIVE HISTORY

The diaspora in contemporary youth literature represents a revival of Puerto Rican revolutionary thinking from the perspective of those often left out of traditional revolutionary rhetoric, including Indigenous communities, Afro-Latinas, and children. The diaspora, as a symbol, also represents transnational community solidarity. In light of disasters, stories from the frontlines repeat a message of community solidarity and collective heroism as opposed to the advancing of one dynamic leader who will help organize relief. If there is a word which comes through at this moment, it is "collective"—in particular through the work of authors and writers banding together to tell stories and provide spaces to the real-life news stories of ciudadanos who cleared the roads and fed entire neighborhoods when government agencies and FEMA aid seemed absent. *Por Ahí Viene el Huracán*, by Laura Rexach Olivencia and illustrated by Mya Pagán, perhaps like no other book in this period, provides a snapshot of what life was like for young people and their families in the days after Hurricane Maria and beyond. Olivencia's book was the only children's book read at the frontline of protests during the Verano del 2019. Olivencia herself was pictured, standing by as hosts of Puerto Ricans, young and old, read aloud the tale just in front of the governor's mansion, La Fortaleza. The everyday struggles of a Puerto Rican girl and her family surviving the storm transformed into a literal protest of government suppression, injustice, and a call for new pathways for self-governance. Olivencia opens the book with Isa the young protagonist standing in her classroom on September 18, 2017, one day before Hurricane Maria would strike Puerto Rico:

En el salon, los compañeros de primer grado andaban emocionadi-simos porque mañana no habrá clases. Llevan más de una semana hablando de huracanes y los más que le llama la atención a Isa es su forma circular, que le recuerda la de un torbellino. Ahora ve torbelli-

nos en todas partes. Hasta en la bañera, cuando los restos del aqua ba-
jan por el boquete negra del desagüe con su GRLOP GRLOP GRLOP.

In the classroom, Isa's first grade classmates are very excited because
there will be no classes tomorrow. They have been talking for more
than a week now about hurricanes and what draws Isa's attention
the most is how hurricanes seem to go around and around like a
whirlwind. Now she seems to see whirlwinds everywhere. Even in the
bathtub when the water goes down the drain with its GRLOP GRLOP
GRLOP. (4)

Olivencia invites readers to follow Isa as she experiences the travesties of the
hurricane, including the closing of her school, the long lines for supplies, and
the moving away of her best friend Nico—whose family home is destroyed
by the hurricane. Readers may also note the long passage of time without
electricity: "Llega el mes de noviembre y la escuela del pueblo sigue cerrada
porque aun no llega la electricidad / November arrives and the neighborhood
school is still closed because electricity has yet to be restored" (30). Isa lives
the experiences of many Puerto Ricans without electrical power; she relies
on neighbors cooking for the entire block and planting their own vegetables.
The ending of *Por Ahi Viene El Huracán*, much like reality itself for Puerto
Rico, remains unresolved in that Isa doesn't regain the things—including
friends—which the natural and man-made disasters took. The lessons of
Puerto Rican youth literature, particularly through the legacies of women
writers, come through in the upholding of family and community legacies, as
opposed to one single hero or even superhero/ine who will come to save the
day. Ultimately, even *La Borinqueña* will not come flying in to lift the years
of colonial oppression that would suddenly render an entire community
"powerless." Yet, the legacies of Puerto Rican youth literature and culture lies
in its strength to survive without institutional power—without paper, without
presses, without classrooms, and without libraries—and comes through in
the elevating of what cannot be taken away: a legacy of survivance, orature,
imagination, and the desire to create stories which seemingly can survive
the end of the world.
     Para Carlos Daniel

# NOTES

## INTRODUCTION

1. Valdes wrote on her Twitter account, @valdes23: "#Afrolatinidad all up in the National Book Awards!!! Thank you, @AcevedoWrites, for writing US into the canon!!!!! #BlackLatinaGirls #TheReaderWriterTypes," Twitter, November 15, 2018, 8:20 a.m., twitter.com/valdes23/status/1063074284019638272.

2. Meg Medina, "Writing the American Familia," talk at Bank Street College of Education, March 2018.

3. Some scholars may still use "Latina/o" and "Latin@" in different contexts; however, "Latinx" was adopted around 2015 as a means of challenging the gender normative aspects of Spanish. It should not be assumed that all scholars adhere to this term. Please see Scharrón-del Río and Aja.

## CHAPTER ONE

1. The program was called programa "normalista," or normal schools, for teacher training. Oral history with Matilde Jiménez, June 29, 2017.

## CHAPTER TWO

1. Bank Street School of Education, Mini-Conference on Bilingual Children's Literature, March 3, 2018. Quotes from Velasquez in this book come from an interview I conducted with him, March 3, 2018.

2. Nuñez also suggests that activities such the poetry and art gatherings at the 115th Street Branch "beg[an] to play a role in the Spanish-speaking community similar to that being played by the 135th Street Branch in the Black community" (67).

3. New York State Archives, "Pura Belpré Papers," http://iarchives.nysed.gov/dmsBlue/viewImageData.jsp?id=169445.

4. Pedro Juan Hernandez, archivist at the Centro de Estudios Puertorriqueños, Hunter College, CUNY, discussed this with me during one of my visits to the archives. He says that, during the time it was common for displaced, college-educated exiles from Spain to work for publishing houses editing Spanish-language content. Many were also language teachers in public schools and universities in New York City.

**CHAPTER THREE**

1. Elliot uses the term "wayfinding" to describe Afro-urban folk culture developed from African American migration around the US.

2. Pura Belpré, *Santiago* (1969). This is Belpré's only original publication, and I review this book in the previous chapter.

3. See "Nicholasa Mohr," "Meet Our Authors and Illustrators," www.scholastic.com.

4. I use the term "diaspora children" here to denote Puerto Rican children. I have three reasons for using this term. One, to challenge the geographical terminology (Puerto Rican, Nuyorican, Neorican, and diasporican) that dominates discussions of the Puerto Rican diaspora). Geographic locations shape our discussion, but I want to consider the idea of how diaspora children have been imagined beyond physical space. Second, I think the term opens up my study to other immigrant, diaspora, and migrant cultures. Third, to break away from using the perpetually universalized term "the child," which I find problematic in children's literature and children's studies. More specific terminology is needed when discussing children and children's literature or media.

5. Marah Gubar discusses the "the child of nature" paradigm in her study, *Artful Dodgers: Reconceiving the Golden Age of Children's Literature* (2009). Popular notions of children as innocents, perhaps, can be traced to the Romantic movement and Romantic poets such as William Wordsworth. "Child of nature" is actually a line from Wordsworth's "Immortality Ode." There are also those who believe the so-called "cult of the child," a movement in nineteenth-century England continued and perhaps even cemented childhood as a cultural construction. However, stemming from this, within critical Children's Literature Studies, Jacqueline Rose's *The Case of Peter Pan* began a dialogue about children as "colonized" and children's literature as a kind of apparatus of adult desire designed to "colonize" children. Gubar, through her discussion of the "child of nature" paradigm, contests the model as providing little room for child agency. The displaced child that I underline and the child of nature share similarities, in that both feature children within a construct of an idealized, rural past. However, the biggest difference between Anglo constructs of children and Puerto Rican constructs of children is that Puerto Ricans narrate children as containing the stories/histories and ideal form of literature within them. That is, authors are on a search to draw out the narratives that are already within children, as opposed to filling them with literature. Also, the displaced child model I identify contains the tools to resist colonial ideologies, but often must do so in a way that always leads him/her back to the homeland.

6. Barbara Roche-Rico, "'Rituals of Survival': A Critical Reassessment of the Work of Nicholasa Mohr" *Frontiers* 28, no. 3 (2007): 160–78.

7. Such interviews include Leonard S. Marcus, "Song of Myself: Talking with Authors" (2000), in the *School Library Journal*, in which he interviews Mohr along with Lawrence Yep and Bruce Brooks. He also published "Talking with Authors" (2000) in *Publisher's Weekly*. Roni Natov and Geraldine DeLuca also published "Interview with Nicholasa Mohr" in the *Lion and the Unicorn* 11, no. 1 (June 1987). See also Myra Zarnowski, "An Interview with Nicholasa Mohr," *Reading Teacher* 45, no.2 (October 1991). Additionally, Mohr has published a variety of essays on the autobiographical connections in her writing, however, she often reminds us that the works are still fiction. See Mohr's "Puerto Rican Writers in the United States, Puerto

Rican Writers on the Island: A Separation Beyond Language" (1987) and "Journey Toward a Common Ground: Struggle and Identity of Hispanics in the US" (1990), both published in the *Americas Review.*

8. I purposely draw a reference here to Piri Thomas since Mohr herself has said that publishers were initially disappointed with her stories, hoping for more "shock-effect." Flores writes that publishers probably were looking for a "female Piri Thomas" (53).

9. My use of the term "postcolonial," when referring to the US-Puerto Rico relationship, by no means implies that Puerto Rico is post-colony, since the island remains a colony of the United States. Rather, I employ it to denote the relationship and consequences after colonization. Puerto Rico has always never been a sovereign nation.

10. From *The Secret Garden.*

11. El Editorial has been a key player within some of the debates about representing Puerto Rican culture, both in the US and on the island. For example, the press recently accepted English manuscripts for publication, a controversial decision given their strict adherence to only Spanish-language texts as representative of the Island. See Frances R. Aparicio's "Writing Migrations: The Place(s) of US Puerto Rican Literature" in *Beyond Borders: American Literature and Postcolonial Theory* (2003).

12. The exclusion of diaspora voices from the US and island canons is an important argument in Puerto Rican Studies scholarship, and one that I do not want to dedicate the chapter to, however, I believe this situation has influenced the trope of orphanhood in Mohr's texts. My book adopts a transnational stand.

13. The problems with placing Puerto Rican literature in both island and US canons is a long-standing dilemma in Puerto Rican Studies (see Juan Flores, Efraín Barradas, and Lisa Sanchez-Gonzalez).

14. Nicholasa Mohr, *Growing up in the Sanctuary of My Imagination* (1994).

15. Juan Flores writes, in his influential essay "Puerto Rican Literature in the United States: Stages and Perspectives" (1988), that "[n]ot until the late 1960s, when distinctly Nuyorican voices emerged on the literary landscape, did it occur to anyone to speak of a Puerto Rican literature emanating from life in this country" (143). The emergence of the Nuyorican movement in the 1960s and 1970s was a result of a long history of Puerto Rican literature in the US, both in English and Spanish.

16. Sanchez-Gonzalez writes that Mohr and Thomas's use of migrant speech is significant in that "all first-person direct or indirect discourse and third-person narration" is presented in "so-called idiomatic speech" (107). It is interesting to note that children's book reviewers have actually criticized Mohr's decision to incorporate the speech patterns and colloquialisms of the diaspora community within her fiction, citing it as improper grammar and usage.

17. As mentioned in the previous chapter, within the nineteenth century, fairy tales and folklore increasingly became part of library catalogs in Europe and Latin America as a reflection of nationalism. After two subsequent World Wars, twentieth-century trends in fairy and folklore and nationalism took on another level of patriotism. Twentieth-century cultural institutions such as the New York Public Library and the children's room projects of Anne Carroll Moore reflect this connection between national character and folklore (see Jack Zipes's chapter, "Storytelling as Spectacle," in *Relentless Progress: The Reconfiguration of Children's Literature, Fairy Tales, and Storytelling* [2009]).

18. Eugene Mohr, in *The Nuyorican Experience* (1982), believes that "the underplaying of sensationalism in her work" has led to problematic assumptions that her texts are somehow innocent or not as gritty as her male contemporaries such as Piri Thomas. Approaching works like *El Bronx* as "innocent" children's texts gives readers "the misleading impression of their seriousness and has encouraged the quality of criticism they deserve." Mohr writes that readers neglect "the adult looking out through the children's points of view is clearly writing for people as adult as she" (74). Again, as with Roche-Rico's critique of Mohr's juvenile label, I maintain that comparing Mohr's texts to children's literature, or examining how Mohr employs tropes from children's narratives, should not mean undermining her complexity as a writer. If it has, it is because of the prejudices that have surrounded children's literature within the academy—for one, that children's texts make no considerable impact on societal culture.

19. *Songs of Innocence and Experience* (1789). Blake chose to depict children within the two sides of life which he referred to as innocence and experience. Images of innocence in these poems depicted children within more rural, spiritual settings, while experience portrayed children suffering from the decays of society such as poverty and abandonment. I believe, Blake, perhaps more than other Romantic writers, demonstrates innocence and experience, light and darkness, as sort of two halves of the same coin.

20. Nathaniel Cordova, "In His Image and Likeness: The Puerto Rican Jibaro as Political Icon" (2005). The emblem for the party features the silhouette of the jíbaro.

21. *Juan Bobo and The Queen's Necklace* (1962).

22. Pura Belpré, *Santiago* (1969).

23. Homi Bhadha writes in his chapter, "Of Mimicry and Man," in *The Location of Culture* (1994) about the how subjugated cultures incorporate elements of a dominant culture within their practices and ritual. This "mimicry" or appropriation "repeats rather than *re-presents*"; in other words, mimicry repeats with a difference and that difference is the location of contention (125).

24. This is really the only moment in which Carpenter discusses *The Secret Garden*, although the entire critical work is named after Burnett's novel. The Arcadian movement, for Carpenter, refers to an unprecedented celebration of agrarian lifestyles and childhood innocence in nineteenth-century English literature which gave rise to the classics of children's literature (*Peter Pan and Wendy*, *Alice's Adventures in Wonderland*, *The Secret Garden*, *Winnie the Pooh*, etc.).

25. In "Puerto Ricans in New York: Cultural Evolution and Identity," Mohr has actually defended graffiti artists saying that it an expression of "children of color—mostly Hispanic and Black." Mohr sees this example of graffiti as a cry demanding recognition: "I exist" (157–58). I underline that this coincides with her presentation of the diaspora child's imagination as a process of drawing around or over the US given.

26. See Carroll; C. S. Lewis, *The Chronicles of Narnia*.

27. Separation between the adult and the child is an important point of contention within Children's Literature Studies.

28. In terms of the nineteenth-century rise of childhood and the notion of children having a separate world from adults. Children in Anglo stories are often depicted as having their "spaces of childhood," connoting how race and class privilege shapes such ideals.

29. In Humphrey Carpenter's "The Road to Arcadia," his introduction to *Secret Gardens*, he implies that a desire to escape the childhood death rates, uncertain political conditions, and overly religious instruction of children may have sparked a Golden Age of children's narratives and children's text, specifically as a proliferation of literature tending toward "introspection" and the security of childhood. Gubar (2010) has recently challenged this with a much more nuanced view of the "cult of the child" and cultists like Carroll and Burnett, mainly by claiming that Golden Age authors did not separate children from the adult world.

30. Mohr's illustrations are perhaps the least-mentioned elements of her creative work in children's fiction, which is ironic since she began as a graphic artist.

31. In an interview in 2015, Mohr told me her original inspiration for the secret garden was Central Park, although the novel locates this moment of solace in upstate New York.

32. Virginia Woolf.

33. Lawrence Sipe, "Children's Response to Literature: Author, Text, Reader, Context," *Theory into Practice* 38 (3): 120–29. In this article, Sipes describes what he calls "insider" and "outsider knowledge" referring to an author's knowledge of a culture. For example, a writer narrating experiences from his/her culture of origin would possess "insider knowledge" of that culture.

34. Citing Gayatri Spivak and John Beverly, respectively, Gonzalez notes that critics have argued that "the subaltern cannot speak" and that "the subaltern cannot speak in a way that really matters, 'a way that would carry any sort of authority or meaning for us without altering the relations of power/knowledge that constitute it as a subaltern in the first place' children's literature offers a different opportunity. She writes, 'Clearly, peripheral groups find it difficult, if not impossible to speak to the metropolis, to "us," but even they can and do speak to each other and to their children (who are even more marginalized than they are), often through oral storytelling, myths, and legends'" (4–5).

35. The first quote, from the *School Library Journal*, and the second, from the *Amsterdam News* (1973), are both cited on the cover on the first edition of *Nilda*.

36. Mary Lennox says, "I've stolen a garden" (105).

## CHAPTER FOUR

1. "Big Bird Visits a Casita," Sesame Street.com, http://www.sesamestreet.org/video_player/-/pgpv/videoplayer/0/07ee9f76-1562-11dd-a62f-919b98326687/big_bird_visits_a_casita.

2. The Children's Television Workshop changed their name to the Sesame Street Workshop. They have productions in at least eleven countries around their world, including Israel, Palestine, and Germany. However, I will refer to it as the CTW since many of the historical sources on *Sesame Street* refer to the group as CTW.

3. Denise Agosto et al, "The All White World of Middle School Genre Fiction" (2003); and Sonia Nieto (1992).

4. "Meet Angie Thomas," https://www.telegraph.co.uk/books/authors/meet-angie-thomas-author-new-ya-sensation-inspired-black-lives/.

5. Levar Burton, National Museum of African American History, panel, December 15, 2018.

6. In *Unsettling Narratives* (2007), Clare Bradford dedicates a chapter to language and the notion of languages "collid[ing]." She examines books like the *Papunya School Book of*

*Country and History* (2001), a picture book from Australia depicting Aboriginals. Bradford examines "narrative modes" and some bilingual books such as *Caribou Song: Atihko Nikamon* (2001). In terms of the *Caribou* book, she writes about how words are "glossed" by providing readers enough information about a certain word to decipher meaning, and then use the word multiple times to engage a reader's memory. I would say these examples still enforce monolingual discourse. (25, 55)

7. Emer O'Sullivan, *Comparative Children's Literature* (2005).

8. J. L. Austin's title.

9. See Rosario Ferré's bilingual poetry anthology, *Duelo de Lenguage / Language Duel* (2002).

10. The use of interlinear books, such as the interlinear Bible translations, may help remedy this situation, although I would say one still needs to make a choice over which language to read.

11. This phrase is part of *Sesame Street*'s goals/learning objectives from its first season. We should remember that the show is made up from what is called the CTW model: independent researchers who test the content's effects on preschool children, curriculum supervisors, or educators who suggest learning objectives to production, and content producers who write the scripts (Fisch and Truglio, xvii).

12. This phrase is taken from a special 1955 commission by the New York Department of Education that was formed to investigate the educational patterns of Puerto Rican migrants in New York (Nieto 2000).

13. The New York Department of Education had an island official on its board, and studies were conducted on the island as well.

14. Oral History with Pura Belpré, Columbia University Oral History Project, 1979, NYPL files.

15. *Island in the City: Puerto Ricans in New York* (New York: Corinth), 1959.

16. Benjamin Malzberg, *Mental Disease among the Puerto Rican Population in New York State, 1960–1961* (Albany, NY: Research Foundation of Mental Hygiene), 1961.

17. *La Vida: A Puerto Rican Family Living in the Culture of Poverty-San Juan and New York* (New York: Random House), 1966.

18. *Mental Disease among the Puerto Rican Population in New York State, 1960–1961.*

19. Morrow emphasizes that this line of thinking was problematic as it critiqued poverty itself as opposed to the economic system.

20. The Killian Commission recommended public television in 1967.

21. Manzano, "Speech at the Television Board."

22. Charles Rosen, the set designer for *Sesame Street*, conceived of the show's set as a hodgepodge of New York's ethnic areas, including Harlem and the Upper West Side neighborhood memorialized in the Leonard Bernstein musical (Murphy, 1).

23. Playwright Andrew Laurents based *West Side Story* on Shakespeare's *Romeo and Juliet*.

24. Bernstein's lyrics read: "Maria, the most beautiful name. . . . Maria, I just met a girl named Maria."

25. Maria has played the love interest of both David, the lovable, African American neighbor and employee of Mr. Hopper's Store, and Luis, the charming Latinx neighbor and manager of the Fix-It Shop.

26. "Maria and Luis are in Love," baby video.

27. *Growing Up Bilingual* (1997), by Ana Celia Zentella.

28. The scene with Maria where the gang members drop their guns in *West Side Story*.

29. Nieto.

30. Nieto also writes that some New York City teachers went so far as to design curriculum and classroom activities ridiculing Puerto Rican culture and language (16–17). Nieto references a case study she did on "Miss Dwight," who, among other things, taught a lesson on nutrition "in which no Puerto Rican foods were included."

31. Oral history with Sonia Manzano, Archive of American Television, http://www.em mytvlegends.org/interviews/people/sonia-manzano. Many of the quotes I have attributed to Manzano are taken from this oral history.

32. Interestingly, in later years, although Maria and characters like Luis are still featured, they are not as prominent as newer characters like Leela, representing the Indian American community. Maria was one of the first Hispanic characters on television. Maria and Luis were the first Hispanic married couple on television, remaining one of the few until Manzano's retirement. Manzano won fifteen Emmys for her writing on *Sesame Street*.

33. Episode 536 (1972). "Sight words" refers to a phrase used in literacy research that indicates words which children should recognize during preschool age. The words are usually presented in flashcards or, often on *Sesame Street* itself, through the appearance of a word on the screen. Also, as per the curriculum, *Sesame Street* began incorporating Spanish sight words in 1972–1973 season (Fisch, 31). The show was accused of stereotyping Latinx and Spanish by a group in New Mexico, according to Morrow, which led to their casting of bilingual characters like Maria and Luis (Morrow, 155).

34. "If anybody calls, tell them I will be back in five minutes."

35. Pun intended. Side by side, as we have seen, can reveal anxiety about difference rather than a spirit of cooperation.

36. The 2009 annual report lists diplomacy as one of the goals within *Sesame Street* education objectives. The official term is "Muppet diplomacy."

37. This would be around the time of the so-called Latinx boom, when the publishing mainstream took notice of Latinx readership and writership in unprecedented ways. Flores writes about the proliferation of Latinx narratives after *The Mambo Kings*, by Oscar Hijuelos, won a Pulitzer Prize in 1990 (167). This award made the literary world take more notice of Latinxs readership.

38. Are you from Paraguay?

39. *Sesame Street* originally solicited regular children (non-actors) to assist on the show. Producer/cocreator Jon Stone discusses the use of Muppets representing the child audience (*40 Years of Sunny Days*, DVD).

40. Maria, in particular, is the object of Zoe's song "Read Me a Story," which depicts how children need to ask an adult for assistance with reading.

41. Fisch and Truglio write that "compensatory education was part of the first proposal for Sesame Street."

42. 98 percent of people had a television (*"G" is for Growing*).

43. Statistics show that children who are not read to at home are less likely to watch *Sesame Street* than children who receive reading instruction at home. However, low-income children were more likely to watch *Sesame Street* than more affluent children (89, 134, 135)

44. Cooney's introduction to *"G" is for Growing*. Also, some researchers spoke out against television as an interference to literacy (134).

45. Paul Ricoeur, "Meaningful Action as a Text."

46. "Exit" is from Episode 666, "What Happens Next?"

47. Morrow writes that *Sesame Street* uses children's voiceovers in at least sixty-three segments of the show. As a way of testing the show's educational outcomes, researchers would tape children as they watched the show and then use these voices for production. The voiceovers were another way of representing the child viewer as part of the show (102–3).

48. Benjamin calls Chaplin, with his black top hat, tailcoat, cane, and signature walk, a "walking trademark."

49. Benjamin writes that the script also incorporates mimetic modes of behavior, although in less ephemeral ways.

50. Episode 1032.

51. Many theorists, among them Michel Foucault, Mikhail Bakhtin, and Jacques Lacan, analyze the formation of human subjectivity as predicated on language and dialogical relationships.

52. Maria and Linda are also featured in the "Chaplin" skits, "The Picnic," where Linda plays the love interest to Maria/Chaplin; and "The Museum," where she plays a woman in a painting that comes alive during Maria/Chaplin's visit. I find it telling that both these actresses are always paired in the Chaplinesque skits.

53. Episode 2407.

54. Again, these voices could come from *Sesame Street* researchers' recording of viewer's responses to the show. This is an interesting notion because it would suggest that viewers delighted in the character's misfortune and rebellion.

55. J. L. Austin, "speech acts."

56. Maria (Manzano) is also featured in another skit that demonstrates this kind of "script breaking": "The Cursed Prince." Grover, dressed as a fairytale character, reads the story of a "beautiful princess [Maria] and a handsome prince." The prince has been cursed by a witch; the spell can only be broken by three kisses from a beautiful princess. Grover reads the story which dictates the action of the actors, though they sometimes forget to do as Grover says, which angers Grover tremendously. In the end, the actors "break character" when they are unhappy with the result of the story and walk out of the shot, leaving Grover alone with his book.

57. Derrida including the performer in the "speech act" process.

58. Episode 4165.

59. "Somewhere," lyrics by Stephen Sondheim, from *West Side Story*.

60. Salsa has its origins in Puerto Rico and Cuba, although it is traditionally considered a dance from Puerto Rico.

61. Since Oscar lives in his life in a trash can, the Grouchketeers don tin, trash can lids on their heads, and green T-shirts.

62. Episode 3920.

63. Lourdes Torres, in "In the Contact Zone: Code-Switching Strategies by Latina/o Writers," writes about something she calls "radical bilingualism," a concept she illustrates through Giannina Braschi's novel *Yo-Yo Boing*, which contains passages completely in Spanish,

without any translation. I believe that children's literature tends to support notions of child socialization and enforces the language of the state. This is why I think we don't see a truly bilingual children's book—that is, a book made for a bilingual audience and not a monolingual one.

**CHAPTER FIVE**

1. https://juntasupervision.pr.gov.

2. Klein, in *The Shock Doctrine: The Rise of Disaster Capitalism* (2007), analyzes the phenomena of how governments under neoliberalism exploit natural disasters when citizens are under distress economically and emotionally in order to further policies, such as privatization, which might received more public recognition and resistance otherwise. Some cases where activists and community members have discussed the effects of disaster capitalism include New Orleans after Hurricane Katrina, where lawmakers lobbied to privatize schools after the hurricane, and Puerto Rico after Hurricane Maria.

3. I note a parallel here between what many Latinx scholars identify as the Latino boom of the 1990s. However, this boom is characterized by the sudden awareness of mainstream publishers and the white public of Latinx writing.

4. The arrival of independent publishers from Spain such as SM, however, has brought new challenges to the historicizing and analysis of youth literature. Fundación SM has also taken on the project of historicizing youth literature in the countries where they publish through publications such as the *Gran Dicionario de Autores de Latinamericanos de Literatura Infantil y Juvenil*, an index of transnational authors and their works, and *Anuarios de Literatura Infantil y Juvenil*, a yearbook providing an essay summary of the books published in each country, trends, awards, and collective themes. Although SM has brought financial support and renewed visibility in Latin America and the Caribbean to Puerto Rican texts, its summaries of books published in Puerto Rico tend to rely too often on those published in-house (i.e., authors working with SM). For example, the annual often overlooks self-published authors and books published by Aparicio Distributors. This is a critical exclusion considering the number of self-published authors and how the rest of the Latin American and Caribbean book world learns about books published in Puerto Rico.

5. The tweet can be found at: https://twitter.com/milkdrunkbaby_/status/10897110830 89285120?s=20.

6. The picture circulated on Twitter, including in my own tweets during the protests: https://twitter.com/MarilisaJimenez/status/1151539186689859590?s=20.

# BIBLIOGRAPHY

Acosta-Belen, Edna, and Judith Ortíz-Cofer. "A MELUS Interview: Judith Ortíz-Cofer." *MELUS* 18.3 (Autumn 1993): 83–97.

Acosta-Belen, Edna, Judith Ortíz-Cofer, and Carlos E. Santiago. *Puerto Ricans in the United States: A Contemporary Portrait*. Boulder: Lynne Rienner Publishers, 2006.

Agosto, Denise E., Sandra Hughes-Hassell, and Catherine Gilmore-Clough. "The All-White World of Middle-School Genre Fiction: Surveying the Field for Multicultural Protagonists." *Children's Literature in Education* 34, 257–75 (December 2003).

Algarín, Miguel, and Miguel Piñero. *Nuyorican Poetry: An Anthology of Puerto Rican Words and Feelings*. New York: Morrow, 1975.

Aparicio, Frances R. "Writing Migrations: The Place(s) of U.S. Puerto Rican Literature." In *Beyond the Borders*, 151–66

Aparicio, Frances R., and Candida Jacquez. *Musical Migrations: Transnationalism and Cultural hybridity in Latino/a America*. New York: Palgrave, 2003.

Ashcroft, Bill, Gareth Griffiths, and Helen Tiffin. *The Empire Writes Back: Theory and Practice in Post-Colonial Literatures*. London: Routledge, 1989.

Austin, J. L. *How to Do Things with Words*. Cambridge: Harvard University Press, 1962.

Baez, Jillian. *In Search of Belonging: Latinas, Media, and Citizenship*. University of Illinois Press, 2019.

Banks, James A, and Cherry A. M. G. Banks. *Handbook of Research on Multicultural Education*. San Francisco: Jossey-Bass, 2001

Barradas, Efraín. *Partes De Un Todo: Ensayos Y Notas Sobre Literatura Puertorriqueña En Los Estados Unidos*. San Juan, PR: Editorial de la Universidad de Puerto Rico, 1998.

Barrie, J. M. *Peter Pan*. New York: Aladdin Classics, 2003.

Belpré, Pura, and M. C. Sanchez. "Bilingual Puppetry at the New York Public Library." Speech, n.d. Pura Belpré Papers, Centro de Estudios Puertorriqueños, Hunter College (hereafter cited as "Pura Belpré Papers").

Belpré, Pura, and M C. Sanchez. *Firefly Summer*. Houston: Pinata Books, 1996.

Belpré, Pura, and M. C. Sanchez. "Folklore del Niño Puertorriqueño." Speech, n.d. Pura Belpré Papers.

Belpré, Pura, and M. C. Sanchez. "Folklore of the Puerto Rican Child." Essay, n.d. Pura Belpré Papers.

Belpré, Pura, and M. C. Sanchez. "I Wished to Be Like Johnny Appleseed." N.d. Pura Belpré Papers.

Belpré, Pura, and M. C. Sanchez. Letter to Margaret Bedan, March 5, 1961. Pura Belpé Papers.

Belpré, Pura, and M. C. Sanchez. "New York Public Library and Folklore." Speech, n.d. Pura Belpré Papers.

Belpré, Pura, and M. C. Sanchez. *Perez and Martina: A Portorican Folk Tale*. New York: F. Warne, 1932.

Belpré, Pura, and M. C. Sanchez. "Remembranzas Tropicales / Tropical Memories." In *Your On! Seven Plays in Spanish and English*, ed. Lori Marie Carlson. New York: Morrow Junior Books, 1999.

Belpré, Pura, and M. C. Sanchez. "Reminiscences of Pura Belpré White." Oral History, 1976. Transcribed by Lillian Lopes. Columbia University in the City of New York, 1976.

Belpré, Pura, and M. C. Sanchez. *The Tiger and the Rabbit: And Other Tales*. Philadelphia: Lippincott, 1944.

Belpré, Pura, M. C. Sanchez, and Antonio Martorell. *The Rainbow-Colored Horse*. New York: F. Warne, 1978

Belpré, Pura, M. C. Sanchez, and Christine Price. *Once in Puerto Rico*. New York: F. Warne, 1973.

Belpré, Pura, M. C. Sanchez, and Symeon Shimin. *Santiago*. New York: F. Warne, 1969.

Benjamin, Walter, and Hannah Arendt. *Illuminations*. New York: Schocken Books, 1969.

Benjamin, Walter. and Hannah Arendt. "Old Forgotten Children's Books." In *Walter Benjamin: Selected Writings*, 406–13. Boston: Harvard University Press, 1996.

Benjamin, Walter, and Hannah Arendt. "The Storyteller: Reflections on the Work of Nikolai Leskov," 83–110.

Benjamin, Walter, and Hannah Arendt. "The Task of the Translator," 69–82.

Beverley, John. *Against Literature*. Minneapolis: University of Minnesota Press, 1993.

Bhaba, Homi. *The Location of Culture*. London: Routledge, 2004.

"Bienvenido Song." Perf. Emilio Delgado and Bob McGrath. *Sesame Street: 40 Years of Sunny Days*. Sesame Street Workshop, 2009.

"Big Bird Visits a Casita." Sesame Street.com. http://www.sesamestreet.org/video_player/-/pgpv/videoplayer/0/07ee9f76-1562-11dd-a62f-919b98326687/big_bird_visits_a_casita>.

Blake, William. *The Songs of Innocence and Experience*. Institute for Advance Technology in the Humanities, Library of Congress. The Blake Archive. www.blakearchive.org.

Bradford, Clare. *Unsettling Narratives: Postcolonial Readings of Children's Literature*. Waterloo: Wilfrid Laurier University Press, 2007.

Brown, Monica. Illus. Joe Cepeda. *Side by Side / Lado a Lado: The Story of Dolores Huerta and Cesar Chavez*. New York: Harper Collins, 2009.

Burnett, Hodgson Frances. Illus. Tasha Tudor. *The Secret Garden*. New York: Harper Classics, 1998.

Carpenter, Humphrey. *Secret Gardens: A Study of the Golden Age of Children's Literature*. Boston: Houghton Mifflin, 1985.

Carroll, Lewis, and John Tenniel. *Alice's Adventures in Wonderland*. New York: Books of Wonder, 1992.

Castañeda, Antonia. "Language and Other Lethal Weapons: Cultural Politics and the Rites of Children as Translators of Culture." In *Mapping Multiculturalism*, ed. Avery Gordon. Minneapolis: University of Minnesota Press, 1996.

Coats, Karen. "Keepin' It Plural: Children's Studies in the Academy." *Children's Literature Association Quarterly* 26, no. 3 (Fall 2001): 140–50.

Cofer, Judith O. *Call Me Maria*. New York: Scholastic Press, 2004.

Cofer, Judith O. *The Line of the Sun: A Novel*. Athens: University of Georgia Press, 1989.

Cofer, Judith O. *Woman in Front of the Sun: On Becoming a Writer*. Athens: University of Georgia Press, 2000.

Colón, Jesús. *A Puerto Rican in New York, and Other Sketches*. New York: Mainstream Publishers, 1961

Colón, Jesús, Edna Acosta-Belén, and Korrol V. Sánchez. *The Way It Was, and Other Writings*. Houston: Arte Publico Press, 1993.

"Colorín Colorado . . . with Making Books Sing." El Museo del Barrio, September 18, 2010. http://www.elmuseo.org/en/event/target-free-third-saturdays-september

Dain, Phyllis. *New York Public Library: A Universe of Knowledge*. New York: Scala, 2006.

Davila, Arlene. *Latinos Inc.: The Marketing and Making of a People*. Berkeley: University of California, 2012.

Delano, Jack and Irene. *En busca del Maestro Rafael Cordero/In Search of the Master Rafael Cordero*. Rio Piedras, Universidad De Puerto Rico, 1994.

De Jesus-Arevelo, Wanda. *Julia, Corazon de una Poeta*. Fundación Puertorriqueña de Las Humanidades, 2017.

Del Moral, Solsiree. *Negotiating Empire: The Cultural Politics of Schools in Puerto Rico, 1898<n>1952*. Madison: University of Wisconsin Press, 2013.

Duany, Jorge. *The Puerto Rican Nation on the Move: Identities on the Island & in the United States*. Chapel Hill: University of North Carolina Press, 2002.

Eddy, Jacalyn. *Bookwomen: Creating an Empire in Children's Book Publishing, 1919–1939*. Madison, WI: University of Wisconsin Press, 2006.

Elliot, Zetta. "Decolonizing the Imagination: Afro-Urban Magic and the Door of No Return." *Horn Book* (March 2010).

Fayonville, Carmen. "New Transnational Identities in Judith Ortíz-Cofer's Autobiographical Fiction." *MELUS* 26, no. 3 (Summer 2001): 129–58.

Fernandez, Juncos, Manuel. *Antologia puertoririqueña, prosa y verso para lectura escolar*. New York: Noble and Eldrige, 1907.

Ferré, Rosario. *El Medio Pollito*. Rio Piedras: Ediciones Huracanes, 1978.

Ferré, Rosario. *Language Duel / Duelo De Lenguaje*. New York: Vintage, 2002.

Ferré, Rosario. *Sonatinas*. Rio Piedras: Ediciones Huracanes, 1989.

Figueras, Consuelo. "Puerto Rican Children's Literature: On Establishing an Identity. *Bookbird* 38, no. 1 (2000): 23–27.

Fisch, Shalom M., and Rosemarie T. Truglio. *"G" is for Growing: Thirty Years of Research on Children and Sesame Street*. Mahwah, NJ: Erlbaum, 2001.

Flores, Juan. *The Diaspora Strikes Back: Caribeño Tales of Learning and Turning*. New York: Routledge, 2009.

Flores, Juan. *Divided Borders: Essays on Puerto Rican Identity*. Houston: Arte Público Press, 1993.

Flores, Juan. *From Bomba to Hip-Hop: Puerto Rican Culture and Latino Identity*. New York: Columbia University Press, 2000.

*Follow that Bird.* Dir. Ken Kwapis. Sonia Manzano, Carroll Spinney, Jim Henson. Warner Home Video, 1985.

*Greater America: The Latest Acquired Insular Possessions.* Boston: Perry Mason Company, 1900.

Gonzalez, Ann. *Resistance and Survival: Children's Narrative from Central America and the Caribbean.* Tucson: University of Arizona Press, 2009.

Gonzalez, Juan. *Harvest of Empire: A History of Latinos in America.* New York: Penguin, 2000.

González, Lucía M., and Lulu Delacre. *The Storyteller's Candle.* San Francisco, CA: Children's Book Press, 2008.

Gubar, Marah. *Artful Dodgers: Reconceiving the Golden Age of Children's Literature.* Oxford: Oxford University Press, 2009.

Haiman, Ada. *Tulipan, The Puerto Rican Giraffe.* Self-published, 2014.

Hernandez, Carmen. "Interview with Piri Thomas." In *Puerto Rican Voices in English.* New York: Praeger, 1997.

Hernandez, Carmen Dolores. *Puerto Rican Voices in English: Interviews with Writers.* Westport: Praeger, 1997.

Hernandez-Delgado, Julio L. "Pura Belpré, Storyteller, and Pioneer Puerto Rican Librarian." *Library Quarterly* 62, no. 4 (1992): 425–40.

Jiménez García, Marilisa. "Old Forgotton Children's Books at CUNY." Journal of the History of Childhood and Youth. 9 (1), 7–14. 2016.

Jiménez García, Marilisa. "Pura Belpré Lights the Storyteller's Candle: Reframing the Legacy of a Legend and What it Means for Fields of Latino/a and Children's Literature." Centro Journal. 26 (1). 110–47.

Jiménez García, Marilisa. "Teaching About Hurricane Maria Recovery." Caribbean Connections: Puerto Rico. Washington, DC: Teaching for Change, 2020.

Jiménez-Román, Miriam and Juan Flores. The AfroLatin@ Reader. Durham: Duke University Press, 2010.

Jiménez, Juan Ramón. *Versa y prosa para niños. Con prologo del poeta.* Mexico: Editorial Orion, 1957.

Jiménez, Juan Ramón. *Platero y yo.* Barcelona: Plaza y Janes, 1987.

Kaplan, Amy. *Cultures of United States Imperialism.* Durham: Duke University Press, 1993.

Lázaro, Georgina. *El flamboyan Amarillo.* New York: Lectorum, 2004.

Lázaro, Georgina, and Antonio Martorell. *¿Y Por Qué?* Editoral SM, 2017.

Lewis, C. S., and Pauline Baynes. *The Lion, the Witch, and the Wardrobe.* New York: Macmillan, 1988.

Lewis, Oscar. *La Vida: A Puerto Rican Family in the Culture of Poverty-San Juan and New York.* New York: Random House, 1966.

Lopez, Lillian, and Belpré, Pura. "Reminiscences of Two Turned-on Librarians." In *Puerto Rican perspectives*, ed. Edward Mapp. Metuchen, NJ: Scarecrow Press, 1974.

Lurie, Alison. *Don't Tell the Grown-Ups: Why Kids Love the Books They Do.* New York: Avon Books, 1991.

Malavet, Pedro A. *America's Colony: The Political and Cultural Conflict between the United States and Puerto Rico.* New York: New York University Press, 2004

Malzberg, Benjamin. *Mental Disease among the Puerto Rican Population in New York State, 1960–1961*. Albany, NY: Research Foundation of Mental Hygiene, 1961.

Mandel, Jennifer. "The Production of a Beloved Community: *Sesame Street*'s Answer to America's Inequalities." *Journal of American Culture* 29, no. 1 (2006): 3–13.

Manning, Jack. *Young Puerto Rico: Children of Puerto Rico at Work and at Play*. New York: Dodd, Mead, 1962.

Manzano, Sonia. "Oral History with Sonia Manzano." Archive of American Television. http://www.emmytvlegends.org/interviews/people/sonia-manzano.

Manzano, Sonia. *The Revolution of Evelyn Serrano*. Scholastic, 2014.

Manzano, Sonia., perf. *Sesame Street*. PBS. 1971–present.

Marichal-Lego, Tere. *Maria Chucema Techaba Su Choza*. Self-published, 2018.

Martin, Michelle. *Brown Gold: Milestones of African American Children's Literature*. New York: Routledge, 2004.

Matos-Rodriquez, Felix. "Their Islands and Our People: U.S. Writing About Puerto Rico–1898–1920." *Centro* 11, no. 1 (Fall 1999): 35–50.

McFadden, Dorothy Loa. *Growing Up in Puerto Rico*. New York: Silver Burnet Company, 1958.

McGuire, Edna. *Puerto Rico, Bridge to Freedom*. New York: Macmillan, 1963.

Mickenberg, Julia L. *Learning from the Left: Children's Literature, the Cold War, and Radical Politics in the United States*. Oxford: Oxford University Press, 2006.

Miranda, Lin-Manuel. *Hamilton: An American Musical*. New York: Atlantic Records, 2015.

Miranda-Rodriguez, Edgardo. *La Borinqueña*. Somos Arte, 2016.

Mohr, Eugene V. *The Nuyorican Experience: Literature of the Puerto Rican Minority*. Westport, CT: Greenwood Press, 1982.

Mohr, Nicholasa. *El Bronx Remembered*. New York: Harper Collins, 1975

Mohr, Nicholasa. *Felita*. New York: Puffin, 1979.

Mohr, Nicholasa. *Going Home*. New York: Dial Books for Young Readers, 1986.

Mohr, Nicholasa. *In My Own Words: Growing Up in the Sanctuary of My Imagination*. New York: Julian Messer, 1995.

Mohr, Nicholasa. "The Journey Toward a Common Ground: Struggle and Identity." *Americas Review* 18, no. 1 (Spring 1990): 81–85.

Mohr, Nicholasa. *Nilda*. New York: Harper and Row, 1973.

Mohr, Nicholasa. "Puerto Rican Writers on the Island, Puerto Rican Writers in the U.S.: A Separation Beyond Language." *Americas Review* 15, no. 2 (Summer 1987): 87–92.

Moreno, Marisel. *Family Matters: Puerto Rican Women on the Island and the Mainland*. Charlottesville: University of Virginia Press, 2008.

Morrow, Robert W. *Sesame Street and the Reform of Children's Television*. Baltimore: Johns Hopkins University Press, 2006.

Murphy, Tim. "How to Get to Sesame Street." *New York Magazine*, November 1, 2009. http://nymag.com/news/intelligencer/topic/61744/.

Nieto, Sonia. "A History of the Education of Puerto Rican Students in U.S. Mainland Schools: 'Losers,' 'Outsiders,' or 'Leaders.'" In *Handbook on Multicultural Education*, 388–410.

Nieto, Sonia. *Puerto Rican Students in U.S. Schools*. Mahwah, NJ: Lawrence Erlbaum Associates, 2000.

Nieto, Sonia. "We Have Stories to Tell: A Case Study of Puerto Ricans in Children's Book." In Violet J. Harris, *Teaching Multicultural Literature in Grades K-8*. Norwood, MA: Christopher-Gordon, 1992.

Nuñez, Victoria. "Remembering Pura Belpré's Early Career at the 135th Street New York Public Library." *Centro Journal* 21, no. 1 (Spring 2009): 53–77.

"NYPL Honors Pura Belpré." *School Library Journal* (January 1980).

Ocasio, Rafael. "The Infinite Variety of the Puerto Rican Reality: An Interview with Judith Ortíz-Cofer." *Callaloo* 17, no. 3 (Summer 1994): 730–42

Ocasio, Rafael. "Puerto Rican Literature in Georgia?: An Interview with Judith Ortíz-Cofer." *Kenyon Review* 14, no. 4 (Autumn 1992): 43–50.

O'Sullivan, Emer. *Comparative Children's Literature*. Abingdon, Oxfordshire: Routledge, 2005.

Pedreira, Antonio S. *Insularismo: Ensayos De Interpretación Puertorriqueña*. San Juan, PR: Biblioteca de Autores Puertorriqueños, 1957.

Penrose, Margaret. *The Motor Girls in Waters Blue or the Strange Cruise of the Tartar*. Cleveland: Goldsmiths, 1915.

Persichetti, Bob, and Peter Ramsey. *Spider-Man: Into the Spider-Verse*. Sony, 2018.

Phillips, Jerry, "The Mem Shahib, the Worthy, the Raj and His Minions: Some Reflections of the Class Politics in *The Secret Garden*." In *The Lion and the Unicorn* 17, no. 2. (December 1993. Reprinted in the Norton Critical Edition of *The Secret Garden*. New York: W. W. Norton Company, 2006.

Piñeiro de Rivera, F. *Un siglo de literatura infantil puertorriqueña / A Century of Puerto Rican children's literature*. Río Piedras, PR: Editorial de la Universidad de Puerto Rico, 1987.

Piñeiro de Rivera, F. Arthur A. *Schomburg: A Puerto Rican's Quest for his Black Heritage*. San Juan: Centro de Estudios Advancados de Puerto Rico y el Caribe, 1989.

Quintana, Alvina E. *Reading U.S. Latina Writers: Remapping American Literature*. New York: Palgrave Macmillan, 2003.

Rambeau, John, Nancy Rambeau, and Richard E. Gross. *Island Boy*. San Francisco: Field Educational Publications, 1969.

Rexach-Olivencia, Laura. illust. Maya Pagan. *Por Ahi Viene El Huracan*. San Juan: Editorial Destellos, 2018

Ricouer, Paul. "The Model of the Text: Meaningful Action Considered as a Text." *Social Research* 38, no. 3 (Autumn 1971): 529–62.

Rivera, Raquel Z. 2007. "Will the Real Puerto Rican Culture Please Stand Up?" In *None of the Above: Puerto Ricans in the Global Era*, ed. Frances Negrón-Muntaner, 217–31. New York: Palgrave.

Roche-Rico, Barbara. "Rituals of Survival": A Critical Assessment of the Fiction of Nicholasa Mohr." *Frontiers* 28, no. 3 (2007): 160–79.

Rodriguez, Sonia Alejandra. "Conocimiento Narratives: Creative Acts and Healing in Latinx Children's and Young Adult Literature." *Children's Literature* 47: 9–29.

Rosaldo, Renato, and William Flores. "Identity, Conflict, and the Evolving Latino Communities: Cultural Citizenship in San Jose, California." In *Latino Cultural Citizenship: Claiming Identity, Space, and Rights*, eds. William V. Flores and Rina Benmayor. Boston: Beacon Press, 1997.

Rosario-Perez, Vanessa. *Becoming Julia de Burgos: The Making of a Puerto Rican Icon.* Campaign-Urbana: Illinois Press, 2014.

Rose, Jacqueline. *The Case of Peter Pan, or the Impossibility of Children's Literature.* London: Macmillan, 1984.

Rutherford, Jonathan. "The Third Space: An Interview with Homi Bhabha." In *Identity: Community, Culture, Difference*, 207–21. London: Lawrence and Wishart.

Saguisag, Lara. *Incorrigibles and Innocents: Constructing Childhood and Citizenship in Progressive Era Comics.* New Brunswick: Rutgers University Press, 2019.

Sánchez, Korrol V. *From Colonia to Community: The History of Puerto Ricans in New York City, 1917–1948.* Westport, CT: Greenwood Press, 1983.

Sánchez-González, Lisa. *Boricua Literature: A Literary History of the Puerto Rican Diaspora.* New York: New York University Press, 2001.

*Sesame Street.* Public Broadcasting Service. Prod. Sesame Street Workshop. 1969–present:

"Bilingual Fruit Song." Episode 1646. Air date: March 1, 1982.

"Captain Vegetable Rhymes." http://www.sesamestreet.org/video_player/-/pgpv/video player/0/091c53d7-d2d5-4f4c-aa90-507833791020/.

"Exit." Episode 926. Air date: November 29, 1976.

"Firefly Song." Episode 4165. Air date: August 15, 2008.

"Lost Bird from Paraguay." Episode 3986. Air date: February 11, 2002.

"Luis and Krystal." Episode 536. Air date: November 19, 1973.

"Lulu and Maria." Episode 3920. Air date: January 5, 2001.

"Maria and David." Episode 406. Air date: November 27, 1972.

"Maria at the Window." Episode 666. Air date: November 4, 1974.

"Me." Episode 1032. Air date: April 26, 1977.

"No Matter What Your Language." Episode 3664. Air date: November 27, 1997.

"Opera Day." Episode 3901. Air date: March 13, 2000.

"Placido Falls for Maria." Air date: February 5, 1988.

"Sesame Street in Puerto Rico." Episode 1316. Air date: November 26, 1979.

"Something in the Air." Episode 4046. Air date year: 2003.

"Spanish Word of the Day: Flor." http://www.sesamestreet.org/video_player/-/pgpv/ videoplayer/0/71add8e7-1548-11dd-8ea8-a3d2ac25b65b.

"Spanish Word of the Day: Niño and Niña." Episode 4040. Air date: April 18, 2003.

"Salsa Party." Episode 3917. Air date: January 2, 2001.

"Tito Puente and Oscar." Episode 3075. Air date: February 12, 1993.

"Tito Puente and the Timbalon." Episode 3092. Air date: March 9, 1993.

"Vamos a Comer." Episode 4133. Air date: November 9, 2006.

"What Happens Next?" Episode 2407. Air date: January 26, 1988.

Sesame Street Workshop. *2009 Annual Report: Can You Tell Me How?* http://www.sesame workshop.org/inside/annualreport.

Sipes, Lawrence R. "Children's Response to Literature: Author, Text, Reader, Context." *Theory into Practice* 38, no. 3 (1999): 120–29.

Smith, Katharine C. *Children's Literature of the Harlem Renaissance. Blacks in the Diaspora.* Bloomington: Indiana University Press, 2004.

Sommer, Doris. *Bilingual Games: Some Literary Investigations.* New York: Palgrave Macmillan, 2003.

Steedman, Carolyn. *Strange Dislocations: Childhood and the Idea of Human Interiority, 1780–1930.* Cambridge, Mass: Harvard University Press, 1995.

Stratemeyer, Edward. *Young Hunters in Porto Rico.* Chicago: M. A. Donohue & Co., 1901.

Thomas, Ebony Elizabeth. *The Dark Fantastic: Race and the Imagination from* Harry Potter *to* The Hunger Games. New York: New York University Press, 2019.

Tor, Regina. *Getting to Know Puerto Rico.* New York: Coward-McCann, 1955.

Torres, Lourdes. "In the Contact Zone: Code-Switching Strategies by Latino/a Writers." *MELUS* 32, no 1 (Spring 2007): 76–96.

Torres-Padilla, José L., and Carmen H. Rivera. *Writing Off the Hyphen: New Critical Perspectives on the Literature of the Puerto Rican Diaspora.* Seattle: University of Washington Press, 2008.

Tyack, David B. *The One Best System: A History of American Urban Education.* Cambridge, MA: Harvard University Press, 1974.

Tyler, Anna Cogswell. *Twenty-four Unusual Tales for Boys and Girls.* New York: Harcourt Brace, 1921.

Vega, Bernardo, and Iglesias C. Andreu. *Memorias De Bernardo Vega: Contribución a La Historia De La Comunidad Puertorriqueña En Nueva York.* Río Piedras, PR: Ediciones Huracán, 1977.

Velasquez, Eric. *Grandma's Gift.* New York: Walker and Company, 2013.

Villasante, Carmen. *Historia y Antologia de Literatura Infantil Iberoamericana.* Doncel, 1966.

Wakefield, Dan. *Island in the City: The World of Spanish Harlem.* New York: Corinth Books, 1959.

Walker, Alice. *In Search of Our Mothers' Gardens: Womanist Prose.* San Diego: Harcourt Brace Jovanovich, 1984.

Watson, Helen Orr. Illus. Margie C. Nichols. *White Boots.* Boston: Houghton Mifflin, 1948.

Weatherford, Carole Boston, and Eric Velasquez. *Schomburg: The Man Who Built the Library.* Candlewick, 2017.

Wells, Elizabeth A. *West Side Story: Cultural Perspectives on an American Musical.* Lanham, MD: Scarecrow Press, 2011.

Zentella, Ana C. *Growing Up Bilingual: Puerto Rican Children in New York.* Malden, MA: Blackwell Publishers, 1997.

Zipes, Jack D. *Breaking the Magic Spell: Radical Theories of Folk and Fairy Tales.* New York: Routledge, 1992.

# INDEX

immigrants and migration, 9, 14, 16, 18–20, 23, 26–28, 32–33, 35, 39–41, 48–49, 51, 68, 70, 88, 91, 95–97, 103, 110, 117–20, 122–23, 127–28, 140, 144, 149, 151, 153–54, 156, 197–98, 205–7, 214; circular, 52, 66–67, 182, 206, 211; First Great Migration, 196, 208; neorican, 66; Second Great Migration, 63, 196, 208

*Inés*, 75, 85, 101, 105–7, 185, 187–88

*In Search of Belonging*, 22

Instituto de Cultura Puertorriqueña, 180

*Insularismo*, 60, 126

*In the Heights*, 197

*It's a Different World*, 147

"Ivaiahoca," 103

Jiménez, Juan Ramon, 61–63, 66, 182, 185

Jiménez-Roman, Miriam, 17, 71, 75

Johnson, Lyndon, 153, 173

Jones-Shafroth Act of 1917, 21, 35

Jordan, June, 111

*Juan Bobo (Simple John)*, 126

*Julia, Corazón de Un Poeta*, 212, 214

Juncos, Manual Fernandez, 5, 24, 52–62, 65, 69, 72, 79–82, 85, 118, 181–83

Kant, Immanuel, 213

Kaplan, Amy, 20–21

Keats, Ezra Jack, 25, 30–31, 48–50, 111, 154

Keleher, Julia, 3

*Kiddie Lit*, 10–11

King, Martin Luther, 173

kinship, 36–43, 47, 117, 150

Klein, Naomi, 177

*La Borinqueña*, 29, 105, 200–204, 215

"La Borinqueña" anthem, 53, 57, 200

"La Carta de Victor Hugo a los Alemanes," 57

La Casa Del Libro, 206

*La Casa de Maria Chucena*, 209

La Clara, 4

*La Edad de Oro / The Golden Age*, 18

"La Guagua Aérea/The Airbus," 66

Laidlow, 63

land seizure, 20, 23, 39, 48, 144, 187

language, 3, 19–20, 24–25, 27–28, 40, 42–43, 54–55, 58, 65, 92, 96, 99–100, 104, 109, 118, 121, 147–74, 181, 188, 190, 206; American Sign Language, 160, 164; bilingualism, 25, 27–28, 65, 77, 85, 147–61, 164, 167, 171–72, 174; English, 5, 7–8, 25, 28, 30, 44, 50, 54, 58, 72, 80, 86, 90, 95, 100, 116, 119, 122, 128, 139, 148–49, 151–52, 156, 159–60, 162, 167–73, 188, 206; French, 188; Spanish, 8, 23–25, 28, 42, 47, 49, 52, 58, 60, 72, 80, 85–86, 90, 95–96, 98, 100, 106, 116, 128, 137–39, 146–49, 151–52, 155–62, 167–74, 206

*La Pieneta Colorada*, 180

"La Raza Cósmica/The Cosmic Race," 17

Larrick, Nancy, 12

*Last Stop on Market Street*, 16

Latimer, Catherine Allen, 96

Latin America, 5, 9–10, 12, 18–19, 23, 41, 47–49, 52, 58, 60–62, 65–66, 73, 75, 92, 102, 206

*Latino Spin*, 22

*Latinos, Inc.*, 22

*La Vida: A Puerto Rican Family in the Culture of Poverty*, 49, 153

Lázaro-Leon, Georgina, 5–6, 10, 28, 107, 178–80, 182–95

Lebron, Lolita, 204

*Lectura Infantil*, 55, 58–59

Lecturum, 190

"Legend of the Royal Palm, The," 104

Lesser, Gerald S., 154

Lewis, C. S., 133

Lewis, Oscar, 49, 153

libraries and librarianship, 12, 16, 23, 26, 38, 72–74, 84, 87, 91, 94–99, 105, 108, 112, 172–73, 177, 183, 197, 207, 208

"Library Work with Bilingual Children," 84

Lincoln, Abraham, 57–58

literacy, 3, 5–6, 12, 14, 27, 29, 37, 44–45, 52–53, 61, 71–108, 147–48, 162–64, 172, 182, 197, 208, 211

literature: African heritage, 23, 111; Afro-Boricua, 29; Anglo, 111, 114; Caribbean,

# ABOUT THE AUTHOR

Dr. Marilisa Jiménez García is interdisciplinary scholar specializing in Latinx literature and culture. She is an assistant professor of English and Latinx Studies at Lehigh University. She has a PhD in English from the University of Florida, MA in English, and BS in Journalism from the University of Miami. She was born in Bayamon, Puerto Rico.

Marilisa's research on Latinx literature have appeared in *Latino Studies*, *CENTRO: A Journal of Puerto Rican Studies*, *The Lion and the Unicorn*, and *Children's Literature*. Her dissertation on Puerto Rican children's literature won the 2012 Puerto Rican Studies Association. She is also a Cultivating New Voices Among Scholars of Color Fellowship recipient from the National Council for Teachers of English (NCTE).

Marilisa seeks to create pathways in her research between the multiple fields of Latinx Studies, Puerto Rican Studies, children's and young adult literature, comparative literature, and education. Her work with Teaching for Change seeks to bring together research and practical tools for classroom teachers advocating for social and racial justice in the classroom. She has worked as a classroom volunteer in Miami and New York City public schools and with the Children's Defense Fund Freedom School's book selection committee.

CPSIA information can be obtained
at www.ICGtesting.com
Printed in the USA
BVHW031354200221
600656BV00003B/12